FLEET AGAINST JAPAN

FLEET
AGAINST
JAPAN

By

FLETCHER PRATT

With a Foreword by Admiral Nimitz

ILLUSTRATED

HARPER & BROTHERS PUBLISHERS

NEW YORK AND LONDON

4-6

FIRST EDITION

C-V

This book is respectfully dedicated to the man who, though personally present at none of the actions described, yet set his impress upon all of them:

FLEET ADMIRAL CHESTER W. NIMITZ

Acknowledgment

If acknowledgment were made individually to each of the officers and men who has done so much to help with this book the list would be very nearly as long as the book itself. To them all, thank you; and to Rear-Admiral H. B. Miller most especial thanks for having placed so many facilities at the disposal of the writer.

Acknowledgment is hereby made to *Harper's Magazine* and to *United States Naval Institute Proceedings* for permission to use some of the material in this book.

Foreword

This Foreword is written at a time when the citizens of our country are intensely interested in the parts played—the job done—by the various branches of our Armed Forces. It is a singular blessing of a democracy such as ours that the individual citizen need not depend solely upon official utterances and promulgations in order to make his own evaluation. The Armed Forces of the United States have, in peace and in war, always functioned as the agents of the people and never as the masters. It has been particularly true in this war that the citizen has fought and bled and emerged victorious as part of *his own* fighting establishment. Regardless of the present or future command organization of our military and naval services, it is to be hoped above all else that nothing will ever occur to change this basic relationship without which no democracy can exist as such. Because of this, it seems very appropriate that a civilian should express his own views in this book. It is in a sense a civilian report to all of you who have served, all of you who have made our victory possible by your work at home, all of you who have seen your nearest kin go off to fight the enemy.

While Mr. Pratt has of necessity singled out certain individual ships and men, certain specific battles and campaigns, it is my belief that the intelligent reader will see this book in its entirety as an account of a job done by countless numbers of men serving in many different times and places to achieve a single end—total Naval victory.

C. W. Nimitz
Fleet Admiral, U. S. Navy
Chief of Naval Operations

CONTENTS

CONTENTS

LIST OF ILLUSTRATIONS

These illustrations which are all from Leyte Gulf will be found as separate sections following pages 52 and 180.

I. THE BASE

FLEET AGAINST JAPAN

AT THE head of No. 1 dock, at Norfolk, neat Roman capitals carved into the stonework inform the beholder that it was built "under authority of John Adams, President of the United States." Beneath them the ashlar still runs straight and true. This is the place where once the U.S.S. *Constitution* lay, and an iron barn roof went forth to duel with a cheese box on a raft and to destroy the navies of the world in a single afternoon. But the gate machinery is modern, and destroyer-escorts enter there to have weld cracks in their plates repaired or sick screws submitted to the surgery of the propane torch.

Beyond the dock lie the piers from which the midnight sound of loudspeakers and the distant rumor of tramping feet announced to many a navy wife that the ships were moving, moving to Africa and the turning point of the war. Around dock and pier and their memories has grown up a city whose military population alone ranks it as the largest city in the state of Virginia. The directly attached civil population puts the Base among the first twenty cities of the country, and there is no civilian among the three discrete municipalities impinging on the naval establishment who has not some indirect relationship to it.

That relation has not always been a happy or even an honest one. In fact, the story of the Base, since the news from Pearl Harbor broke in on the broadcast of a pro football game, might be written as a tale of a sort of super town-and-gown row. But this would be inaccurate, for though the relations of the Base with the surrounding country bulk large, they are a side issue. The business of a base is to keep the fleet at sea and in the air, and the commandant is normally so fresh from a floating assignment that he is not likely to forget it.

At least not in wartime. When the flames of London leaped up, ominous beyond the Atlantic, and the President proclaimed a national emergency, the commandant was a man who already had had several years' experience in his job—Rear Admiral Manley Simons, short and rubicund, with a distinctly twinkling eye and a figure that seemed composed of a series of connected circles. Popularly known as "Tom Thumb," he could explode into testy remarks; the next moment he would be laughing. Nobody ever saw him grim or tired. Technically his command was not the Base alone, but a much wider entity—the district, which included not only the Base but all the naval activities in the adjacent hinterland to the extent of three and a half states, one of which has no contact with tidewater.

Out of this grew the complexity of his position. A base, in the appropriate tight sense of the term, is a place where a fleet touches its foot to land before springing off again into blue water; it is required to furnish nothing but food, ammunition and repairs to vessels of the fleet. But Admiral Simons' base at Norfolk had been in the remote past the outgrowth of a commercial shipbuilding establishment which had had a side line of repairs, so that from the beginning it had united these functions to the others. In addition, the fact that the back country is agriculturally poor made procurement a problem and required that the Base admiral's authority be extended over considerable territory. Again, the peculiar conditions of early enlistments (crews were dismissed at the end of a voyage) had made it necessary that the Base have on hand a reserve stock of seamen for ships that were to sail again; and so recruiting and training, within the district already touched for procurement purposes, had become another logical part of the commandant's functions. The defense of the place against sea attack and of the shipping in the immediate area early fell within his purview; as a function of the protection of shipping he acquired direction of a naval air station.

This was Admiral Simons' command as it stood when the Spits began to duel with Heinkels over East Anglia in 1940. It called on him to unite the functions of soldier, sailor, engineer, purchasing agent, educator, storekeeper; and there was firmly established for his office a tradition of ubiquity, looking toward future expansions. As the pressures of total war caused these functions to proliferate, new offices were set up, each in a separate watertight compartment with the admiral as co-ordinating head. It is impossible to tell the story of the Base in any other terms than those of these individual units—"activities," is the local technical term.

The system by which these activities were strung together was by no means as neat or efficient as this outline implies. They at once showed a tendency to overlap, and the existence of a central coordinating authority in the Navy Department at Washington, operating through almost entirely autonomous bureaus, complicated the task of the Base and its little admiral.

For example, the newly constituted Atlantic Fleet might report the impending arrival of a division of cruisers which would require, among other things, seven tons of spinach. There would be an order on hand from the Bureau of Aeronautics that the light cruiser *Richmond* was to take aboard a new type of scout plane for a tryout. Also there would be on hand a communication from the Bureau of Personnel ordering the *Richmond* to turn over three gunner's mates for new construction, and one from the Bureau of Ordnance that this ship was to be furnished with her new forty-millimeter guns, a matter of greatest emergency. The Admiral Atlantic wished all the ships to take on ammunition, and this specific ship needed a repair job on her port forward casemate. The Admiral Atlantic insisted that she go to sea again within three days.

Now imagine the officers at the Base trying to meet all these demands simultaneously. Spinach is a perishable not kept in stock. The procurement officer can get it all right, but moving in seven tons presents a problem, as the freight schedules are very tight because the Bureau of Yards and Docks is using every available car for construction materials on their way to one of the island bases leased from the British. The three gunner's mates requisitioned from the *Richmond* happen to be just those who deal with that ailing casemate, and the officer of their department is so new that the captain is not at all sure of his ability to superintend the repair job without experienced hands around. If the cruiser goes to the aviation pier for her new plane at the only hour when it will be clear, she will be unable to make the dock where the 40-millimeters are installed at any time when the workmen there are on the job, unless she can get away from the ammunition barge in two hours less than the best time ever recorded for such a performance. It is unthinkable that a ship needed for war should be detained in port. Which bureau's orders rule?

The peacetime arrangement was to make the decision in such cases at the level above the bureaus in Washington, or after all to delay the sailing of the ship till the bureaus could be satisfied. The half war before Pearl Harbor strained this administrative structure to the breaking point under pressures both from the Atlantic Fleet and the bureaus. The fleet could and often did send the ships hammering out to sea regardless, for the Admiral Atlantic was Ernest J. King, a man who did not accept documents in lieu of action. The bureaus sent experts down to inquire how the Base activities might be better organized.

Now the reports of these experts were returnable to Washington, that is to the bureaus who sent them out; and in the course of their reorganization the latter frequently felt called upon to breach the watertight bulkheads separating the various activities of the Base. At its simplest, the thing would work this way: a recommendation from the Bureau of Aeronautics for the construction of a new landing strip would be turned over to the Public Works Office of the Bureau of Yards and Docks, which would set up the strip.

In addition new activities were constantly being set up. A letter would announce to Admiral Simons the arrival within a week of three thousand student enlisted men for training; the Base would have to find barracks, instructors and classrooms for them. The situation was one to test to the full the American genius for improvisation and organization. But if there is anything surprising about the result it is how well the job was done. In the *cordon sanitaire* days of 1941, when the *Reuben James* was being torpedoed, British seamen referred enviously to our ships as "luxury liners"; and there is evidence that the U-boat commanders considered American convoys too opulently escorted to be worth attacking. That such things could be was the achievement of the American bases—and especially of the Base.

II

In the meanwhile some of the hen's eggs laid by the experts were hatching into ducks and even ostriches. A good case is the establishment of the Advanced Base Training Command. Captain Richard E. Webb came down to the Base, at about the time Guadalcanal was being cleared, with a staff of twenty expert packers to set up what was then called Base Service Unit. The job of this unit was to get things like special radio sets for advanced bases out of their manufacturer's cartons and into packings that would insure them against breaking under the treatment they were likely to receive when being landed on coral beaches under enemy fire. At the same time a need for specialist units to render base services at exactly such places as Guadalcanal was making itself felt, and the department began to organize such units at the Base. A single specialist unit might consist of, let us say, an officer and a dozen men—for whom Captain Webb and his gang were packing the equipment.

The procedure was to order the officer to the Base and the men to its receiving station (which is a kind of transients' hotel for the enlisted), where both waited till they received sailing orders on the same ship that carried their equipment. But all this equipment was new and pretty fancy. Complaints began to come back from the Pacific that these specialist units did not know their stuff too well, under conditions that brought men and officers together for the first time aboard the transport and united both with unfamiliar equipment on some remote Pacific island. So it was ordered that instead of doing indifferent duties while waiting for transportation, the specialist units should be given special training with their new equipment.

Now this order was inconsistent with a previous one requiring the new equipment to be packaged for instant movement on arrival, and Captain Webb pointed it out. Moreover his gang of expert packers had by this time trained the normal staff of the supply depot to considerable skill in their interesting but not especially complex art. So the packers were turned over to the supply command for keeps; and Webb was named head of a brand new activity—the training of specialists for service at advanced bases.

The system on which the Advanced Base Training Command operates is approximately that by which chemists build up the complex molecule of synthetic rubber from elemental atomic bricks; and like the atoms of chemistry, the atoms of Advanced Base Service are known by symbols. Let us say that all those charged with the maintenance of weapons are designated by the letter M, and an M-11 unit is one specifically charged with the maintenance of airplane torpedoes. Experience has shown that fourteen men with certain tools can keep the torpedoes of an air squadron efficient. Seven torpedo specialists are accordingly drafted from the fleet and sent to the Advanced Base

Training Command with seven boots fresh from the training camp. They constitute an "acorn"—Acorn 252 (M-11), officially so designated.

These fourteen men go into an intensive six-week training course, which embraces not only their specialty but also the full commando course of the Army, for those advanced bases are right up where the shooting is going on, and at Tarawa the aviation maintenance acorns were getting the field ready to receive planes while it was still under Jap fire.

While Acorn 252 (M-11) is still in training, Admiral Nimitz has decided to take the island of Wiggiwug. It is within 420 miles of Jap-held Trollop Shoal, from which the Japs draw important supplies of phosphates, an activity that would be much discouraged by a couple of squadrons of torpedo planes based on Wiggiwug. Two squadrons will mean two torpedo-maintenance acorns. So in preparation for the capture of Wiggiwug, Acorn 253 (M-11) is attached to Acorn 252.

To both of them are attached Acorns 341 and 343 (C-6), composed of specialists whose duty is the maintenance of the planes that will carry the torpedoes; Acorn 98 (A-2), radio technical specialists, including a Japanese interpreter; Acorn 441 (M-3), antiaircraft gunners with their pieces; Acorn 771 (G-5), cooks, bakers and water supply men—and whatever other units are desirable. At this stage the acorns have lost their identity; the larger unit in which they are merged is called a "cub" and is supplied with its own commander and an administrative staff. This Cub is an organization specially designed to make Wiggiwug into an American air base fifteen minutes after the Marines have hit the beach. In addition to their other training the responsible officers get special courses in the geography, geology, biology and strategy of the island.

If the place where they are going is very big or important (we may suspect that Kwajalein fell into this category) the Cubs are combined into a still larger unit called a "lion," with Cubs to service ships as well as Cubs to service planes. If there is a change in plans the Lions and Cubs can be broken down into their respective Acorns and reassigned. They are (importantly) all naval personnel; they can go aboard a ship at any time and render the same services there. The system has obvious resemblances to the Einheit method of the German Army, but it has been carried much farther; and it is one of the basic reasons why no long pause for reorganization has been necessary after each forward step in the Navy's career of conquest through the islands.

Thus the Base had entered the business of furnishing personnel, not on the limited replacement scale implied by the existence of its receiving station, but as an office of the first instance. At the same time it was required to revolutionize its methods of handling materiel, on a scale that can be realized by the single statistic that when Rear Admiral Slarrow, the supply officer, reached the place in June, 1941, his activity has one thousand employees, whereas three years later it had six thousand, working at vastly increased efficiency.

Captain Webb's expert packers had something to do with this; so did the radical change in methods of handling food, with its emphasis on deep refrigeration. But the leading influence was Slarrow himself, a man whose eye lights up at the mention of personnel questions and who approaches them with a flexibility of mind astonishing to anyone who thinks of the Navy as a somewhat stodgy organization. In his gigantic office-warehouse (second only in size to the Montgomery Ward monster in Chicago) there is a wired radio circuit, hooked up to its own broadcasting studio. At ten-thirty in the morning everyone knocks off work and listens to a ten-minute musical program; while people are having lunch in the co-op cafeteria (price twenty-five cents) there is more music, news and comments on the news; and from three o'clock on, when energy begins to decline, there is a whole series of musical programs. (Incidentally, they built a battleship to music over at the Base navy yard, riveters pounding while a band blared "The Stars and Stripes Forever," and Slarrow had something to do with that too.) The workers go home at night in transportation provided by the Navy, to houses which in most cases the Navy has been instrumental in building for them.

Paternalism, you say? No, this is not paternalism but necessity, and Slarrow's preoccupation with the personnel problem grew out of that necessity. The draft began hitting him early and in the most sensitive spot, his stevedoring setup. Offhand one would class stevedoring as a job that can be done by any husky who can lift 150 pounds deadweight, but this is not true. Most navy loading is done by machinery these days, a good deal of special packing (Captain Webb's job) is involved, and at the very crisis a brand-new angle was added by the discovery of the palatized load.

This consists in tying a given unit of a ship's load—let's say the ammunition supply for a company of Marines for one week of action —to a platform of rough boards and mounting it on a pair of heavy wooden skids. One swing of a crane carries it to a ship's hold, another picks it out at destination, and by attaching a jeep or bull-dozer to what has effectively become a vehicle, the unit can be snaked up some beach of Eniwetok or Sicily in minimum time. The system was perhaps the major factor in such performances as getting a four-ship convoy into Guadalcanal at dawn and out by twilight, with the goods delivered before the Jap night bombers came.

But it demands a high degree of competence back at the Base, especially in supervision. Admiral Slarrow found that the draft was taking his competent men, in many cases putting them into khaki and sending them, with exactly the same sort of jobs, to an army embarkation point a few miles from the Base!

The draft difficulty was met by a little hell raising in Washington and some readjustment which eventually included the organization of navy labor battalions. This was another of the cases in which amphibious war was causing the functions of the land and sea services to converge. But the problem could be fully solved only by recruiting labor. The Base was necessarily located far from any great city, both to keep ship movements secret and to give vessels their earliest possible contact with land; and labor had to be sought in the back blocks. As several other base activities were simultaneously recruiting, the housing problem became acute at once.

The Base was located in the heart of an almost manorial polity, where a relatively few old families owned most of the real estate. They set their faces against the construction of temporary housing, which (they held) would turn into slums after the war. When a federal survey pronounced that four thousand more houses were needed in the district they countered with a survey of their own, which showed no housing shortage whatever. In the meantime Admiral Slarrow's expanding force was developing a terrific labor turnover as the boys from upcountry moved in, discovered they would have to pay sixty dollars a month rent, and moved right out again—without pausing to consider that even this figure was only approximately proportionate to the increase in their cash incomes since the days down on the farm when they had been giving five dollars a month for both rent and board.

The matter went up to Admiral Simons, who had a good deal of foxy grandpa in his make-up. He seized some occasion of public hullabaloo to make a speech in which he remarked that the federal survey had erred; the need was not for four thousand houses around the Base but for thirteen thousand; and the FHA would guarantee the builders against loss. Of course, as he had foreseen, the smart New York real-estate operators descended on the area. There were a lot of small-parcel sales and the recalcitrant first families woke up one morning to discover that several thousand buildings were actually under construction.

Some of the buildings had to be taken over by the Navy and operated as residences for the families of petty officers, though. The intended tenants from the hills couldn't get used to the complexities of life among hot and cold faucets, laundry chutes and indoor toilets.

III

That story is a fairly good example of navy make-do, and of the problems of any base as the connecting link between the sea service and the land that supports it. Across the bay at the navy yard the problems faced by Rear Admiral Felix Xerxes Gygax and his production officer, Captain William Thompson, were similarly concentrated around personnel, though in this case they took the somewhat different form of training and transportation. There was a long struggle to persuade the local transport company to buy more busses, solved only when the Base secured authority to take over the company if it felt in the mood, and itself worked out a co-operative arrangement by which little groups of workers could club together to buy their own busses or boats.

The general labor problem, however, was quite different from that normally met in war industries and could not be solved by using uniformed workers. The Navy has a deep-rooted conviction that the place for a first-class uniformed mechanic is aboard a warship at sea, and when it finds one in a shore establishment, tries to get him out of there as soon as possible. The navy yard at the Base is not merely a place where they build battleships (and lesser vessels) to music; it is also an overhaul port, the largest of its kind. A new ship is commissioned as a unit of the United States Navy, goes out on her shakedown cruise, and then returns to the yard to be made a mechanically efficient vessel. An old ship has received a bomb hit on No. 2 turret or torpedo at frame 74, or has merely been at sea for three years till all her working parts are worn down and the steam lines no longer hold steam; she too has to be repaired. All this business is overhaul. By the second year of the war the yard's assignments in this field had increased 73 per cent over December 7, 1941, while the yard's staff had increased by only 11 per cent.

The problem was not merely mathematical. Indeed during the early days of the war the Base had no trouble in recruiting whatever quantity of labor it wanted, with shipyard wages at their normal wartime level. The quality was something else. On overhaul every job is an individual artistic creation, the first of its kind; it demands not only intimate acquaintance with all the parts of a warship and their purpose, but also much skill in adaptation. The yard began to get its heavy load in 1940, and to train more men at once; but all through the first year of the war Captain Thompson was still operating with 25 per cent trainees in an establishment whose peculiar treasure was experience and whose boast was the number of families who had been yard employees unto the third generation.

In one direction this led to experiments like those of Admiral Slarrow in improving the general living conditions of the workers; another, to some extremely interesting discoveries in the field of industrial management. Quite early in the game the famous graveyard shift went out the window; Captain Thompson discovered he could get more production out of two nine-hour shifts than out of three of eight hours each. The key to this and to many questions besides was found in the matter of supervision—not at the management level, for as at all navy yards, the managing heads are officers of the Civil Engineering Corps—but down in the shops. The 73 per cent increase in overhaul work and a similar 72 per cent increase in new construction were achieved as soon as sufficient shop supervisors were trained to provide one for every twenty workers; but the yard never could find enough to supervise three shifts, and it would prefer to get the proportion of foremen down to one in sixteen workers.

The figure is particularly illuminating. It is exactly that which the armies of the world have discovered as the optimum for the smallest group controlled in action by a single man. The suggestion is that the keenest pressure of war is thrown on the minor leadership, as Julius Caesar once said in rather different words. Captain Thompson was willing enough to go to three shifts, but found that even at two he was operating against the law of diminishing returns on the supervisory problem.

What about using women? Back in 1940, when the heat came on, the yard began hiring and training them; it was one of the first heavy-industrial establishments to do so. By the date of Pearl Harbor it had 5,000, a somewhat higher proportion of them supervisors than their absolute numbers called for. In the second year of the war the figure was down to 3,500, with less than the due proportion in leadership positions, despite all pressures and a WMC survey of the district which showed 32,000 unattached and able-bodied women.

The Base was pouring too much money into the community in both navy and civilian payrolls, and women were getting too much of it by indirect methods to care to work for it. There is a little shop in Norfolk where old English silver used to be sold. At the height of the fierce fighting in Guadalcanal and Africa some worker's wife or sailor's sweetheart was observed in the place complaining that the handles on the beautiful oblong Georgian serving dish she had purchased the week before got too hot when she put it on the stove to make a beef stew in it.

IV

In other words, the silk-shirt era had returned—perhaps only in a localized area round the Base, where the constant release of sailors from long cruises with heavy payrolls made control peculiarly difficult, but with all the unpleasant entail of 1918. This was already apparent by the middle of 1942 and was responsible for one of the most remarkable activities of the Base—the Permanent Shore Patrol.

Normally when a warship reaches a liberty port, certain members of her crew are given night sticks and brassards reading SP and are detailed to keep the rest out of trouble. At the Base this didn't work; men were loath to arrest the comrades by whom they had so lately stood in battle and on the whole the seamen were more put upon than putting.

Admiral Simons found an energetic young small-town chief of police named Ingoldsby, had him commissioned, and set him to recruiting from local police departments (because these men would know the area best) a group for shore patrol work. In addition to their training as sailors they received special instruction in military law and in just where to draw the delicate line which separates the military cop, whose job is to make as few arrests as possible, from the civil policeman, whose record is determined largely by the number of his successful cases.

In fact, the key of Shore Patrol's operation was keeping the men fit for duty. Drunks constitute the greatest number of its cases (about a quarter of the total number of cases) but the least important part of its work; for with the coming of war Norfolk began to fill up with streetwalkers, cat houses, beer halls and the assorted clip joints normal to such a situation, with very little satisfaction to be had from the local authorities. Ingoldsby established an "investigation squad" of thirty men without the brassard. As soon as their reports showed a complaint to be justified he called on the proprietor of the place in question with a warning. If the latter persisted there was used against him the Navy's old infallible remedy—putting the place off limits, and stationing a couple of husky patrolmen at the door to keep any man in uniform from entering.

At one time an entire block was thus shut off for hiring prostitutes as waitresses. A couple of hotels went on the list after they had formed the interesting habit of renting rooms to sailors accompanied by girls and calling up the vice squad to raid the room fifteen minutes later. But the bulk of the cases are handled on hygienic grounds. Shore Patrol considers it none of the Navy's business how a sailor has his fun, provided he gets his money's worth and shows up in good shape at dockside the following morning. Thus an overflowing toilet at Sweetheart Dancehall or the fact that the hamburgers contain bad meat or the waiters are selling moonshine at $1.20 a drink will bring swift action; but Shore Patrol looks with some indifference on the plea that "victory girls" are using the place to make contacts with sailors.

None of their business. That falls within the purview of another Base activity, the Department of Welfare and Recreation, which set up its own big park within the base—forty-three acres with groves and a series of buildings. There are two outdoor swimming pools, a stadium with baseball and other athletic equipment for free, a roller-skating rink, a dance hall with bands and hostesses furnished by the USO, a prodigious beer bar and hot-dog stand, a poolroom, a bowling alley. When a ship comes into the Base a recreation officer boards her to find out what is desired in the way of organized fun—a dance? Girls and music will be provided. A "ship's party" with a ball game between C Division and the Black Gang? Equipment, beer and umpires will be at hand and a field held clear for the occasion. Announcement of the attractions of the park and how to get there go out over the ship's loudspeaker system.

But there is no urging; your American sailor is deeply suspicious of the official handout in any form, and the park didn't really begin to work till it was clear that visits were a matter of the individual's free choice. In fact, it was not in full operation till the summer of 1943 and by that time Admiral Simons was retired and Shore Patrol had a real crisis on its hands.

The new commandant was Vice Admiral Herbert F. Leary, the tall man with the craggy face who had seen the war firsthand as commander of the Southwest Pacific Fleet; he used to summon his flag secretary by calling his name through two closed doors. To him Lieutenant Commander Ingoldsby one day presented a case; the city of Norfolk had been fairly well cleaned up, but the same could not be said for the county that surrounded it for miles. A pretty foul prostitution industry had grown up in tourist camps and trailer camps so peripatetic that they were impossible to control. There was extensive bootlegging, with the usual concomitant of fights on the scale of small riots which kept Shore Patrol's prowl cars and ambulances on the trot. There had been six sluggings of sailors in a single night, one of them fatal. When Shore Patrol was lucky enough to find the perpetrators of these affairs they were held in jail for about three days and then released by a judge who was later found by a committee of the legislature to have paid for his office on a hundred-dollar-a-month installment plan.

"Are things like this every day?" asked the admiral.

"Yes sir."

"What do you propose?"

"The only thing I can think of is to put the entire county out of bounds."

"Then what are you waiting for? Make out the order."

The admiral signed it with as little flourish as a request for a hundred sacks of beans, and cut off from the community a high-purchasing-power group of nearly three times its own numbers. It was an economic death sentence; before noon of the next day the governor of the state was on the phone and there was presently a series of removals and legislative investigations—which Admiral Leary watched with a detached kind of interest.

V

For he was busy with the latest activity that had moved in on him—the Operational Training Command of the Atlantic Fleet. This was itself more or less an outgrowth of still another command which attached itself to the Base, the Atlantic Fleet Service Force of Vice Admiral William Sharp. "Service Force" is the lace-curtain name for what is more usually called the train—the oilers, repair ships, provision and ammunition carriers, seaplane tenders and et ceteras which follow a fleet into distant waters, and being parked at some convenient harbor there, give it a fairly close approximation of full base service. Military men must look a long way ahead and with gloomy eyes; in 1940, when Britain was fighting alone and it seemed not impossible that we soon would be, the Atlantic Fleet became an important entity. To its Service Force fell the job of preparing harbors all the way from Casco Bay to Fernandina as possible future bases of operations.

The destroyer-base deal gave us something better, but the new line of defense had to be built; and the task of assembling the materials, transporting them to the islands and getting the construction going quite naturally fell into the hands of the Atlantic Fleet Service Force, which not only had begun it for bases on our own soil, but was also able to use its own big floating workshops in places like Bermuda, Newfoundland and Iceland, where there were none on shore.

It was now 1941 and clearly Britain was not going down immediately. But the German subs were just as clearly coming our way; the Service Force by almost imperceptible stages changed from an organization supporting a battle line beyond the sea to a kind of general floating base for a variety of small craft on escort duty. This was lucky; when the U-boats did show up, on the heels of the Pearl Harbor attack, it became possible to shift the weight of the force rapidly, so that base service became as mobile as the anti-submarine craft themselves. For instance, if a sudden concentration of subs showed up off Hatteras, a destroyer tender, a couple of seaplane tenders, some tugs and repair ships could be rushed out to Bermuda, instantly converting that tourist paradise into a base well equipped for covering the Middle Atlantic approaches. If the Germans abandoned this hunting ground for the mouth of the St. Lawrence, the whole parade could instantly move to Newfoundland.

In the meantime also the shipyards were pouring forth the vessels of the two-ocean Navy. As soon as a new ship is commissioned she must be attached to some command. Since most of the yards are on the Atlantic the majority were obviously under that fleet during their shakedowns at least, and a good many of the smaller vessels were to stay there permanently. Servicing them was the province of the Atlantic Fleet Service Force; and as all the ships had to come into the Base for their overhauls following shakedowns, it was convenient to establish the headquarters of Service Force afloat in the Base harbor.

A Service Force is not exclusively concerned with ammunition and food; it also furnishes personnel when needed, and personnel began to be needed in quantity when the ships of the great destroyer-escort program came out. The only way to get experienced men was to take them from ships already afloat. The arrival of a ship for overhaul made an especially convenient time for this. Toward the end of 1942 so many key men were being taken from vessels just in from shakedown, for service on still newer ships, that some of the former might as well never have been shaken down at all. In February, 1943, Admiral King cut through all these difficulties by setting up at the

Base an entirely new activity—the Operational Training Command of Rear Admiral Leary.

Its function is to take a new ship from the builders and turn her over to an operating unit, ready to fight. Let's take the case of a new DE (destroyer-escort), in many ways the most typical. Her skipper is an experienced anti-submarine man, promoted out of another ship. He goes to the building yard at Port Newark after she is launched to supervise the fitting out of the ship. The exec probably is an old hand; he goes to the Base to meet the other officers and crew, something over two hundred of them. On the average 85 per cent have never seen water in anything bigger than a bathtub. The rest are technical specials—maybe a chief quartermaster from the *Helena* and a gunner's mate who was on the *Sodak* when she tore the Japs to pieces off Guadalcanal.

While the yard workers are finishing the ship the exec has to turn these men into a crew. They live in a barrack which bears the name of the ship, watches are set as they would be aboard, at the various classrooms they handle the equipment they will use; they become a team and the officers have a chance to observe that Schmidt will never do as a gunnery talker because his voice goes funny under excitement, or that little Joe Gasbatta has an unexpected talent for getting other men to work.

That is, the personal adjustments, the changes of assignment, are worked out ashore. When the ship is ready the crew goes aboard as a team, prepared to take to sea except for the single detail of becoming used to what it does to inexperienced stomachs. In prewar days a vessel of this size would have required six months for her shakedowns; now she does it in twenty-three days. Good job, too; one DE is credited with having knocked off a sub on her way from shakedown to overhaul.

VI

In October, 1943, Admiral Leary was translated to a higher sphere as commander of the whole Eastern Sea Frontier and Rear Admiral D. M. LeBreton came in to succeed him—a man as different from his predecessor as could be. Admiral LeBreton had seen destroyer service in the last war and done a great deal of attaché duty since;

he is one of the great line of American naval diplomats, smooth as glass, a natural administrator of whom it is said that he ran his eye over a vast report that it had taken his staff two days and a comptometer to prepare, and then said, "This figure's wrong," jabbing at one on page 2. It was.

It was a good time for such a man to come; W.M.C. and the services had begun their long quarrel over declining manpower and the Navy was being pressed to show that it had some need for the men on the payroll of the shore establishments. A circular went down to the district asking them how many men could be spared for sea service. With all the new ships it is possible that someone in Washington was chiefly wishful that the districts justify themselves by document, but if so they sent the wrong man to the Base. Admiral D. M. LeBreton took the circular at strict face value and since in any case he wanted to find out what was going on in his command, set out on a personal tour of inspection.

In the offices they still talk about that with an amazement slightly tinged by apprehension. The admiral was genial, smiling, polite, but he absorbed everything and showed a phenomenal ability to ask the awkward question. In the WAVEs headquarters he discovered that his Communications division (which handles all the messages coming and going by telephone, teletype and radio) had been almost entirely WAVE since the beginning of the corps, and Communications received a smile. But he also found that not a few officers of the other activities were southern gentlemen of the old school with the idea in the back of their heads that a girl could not both work and be a lady. To them went polite intimation that they might as well investigate the possibilities of replacing with WAVEs some of the personnel they were about to lose.

But chiefly the admiral's attention was directed to such activities as Operations and the inshore patrol. Both were and remain indispensable institutions. The former directs the movements of all ships within the purview of the Base and the district. If a vessel wants to get in a little antiaircraft firing practice, Operations makes the necessary arrangements. Inshore patrol is concerned with the protection of the passages and of the vessels using them. It is a command over a wonderful collection of marine oddities—net-layers, net-tenders, patrol boats from the size of dinghies up to that of cabin cruisers, tugs, minesweepers. During the rough days of the U-boat war off our coast, Inshore Patrol was in the front-line trenches—aye, and gave its blood, for the stouter sub commanders shot things out with the marine oddities and not infrequently sank them.

But with the coming of the blimps, PCs and DEs along the coast that was all dead and gone. Admiral LeBreton found the personnel of both Operations and Inshore Patrol roughly the same that it had been in the days when the subs were knocking off a ship a night, both in numbers and competence. As the old jobs slacked off new ones had been assigned, merely because the staff was there. Operations had become vividly concerned with the doings of a vast new center where armed guards from merchant ships were trained at the rate of seventy-two crews a month, and Inshore Patrol was much interested in the first experiments the Navy had made with all-Negro crews.

The admiral reported to Washington with a list of ten pages of officers' names and a whole small volume of enlisted men who could be sent to sea. Who would perform the functions they were doing? he was asked. No one; let the functions be abolished—for the Base and any base is necessarily a place of improvisations, impermanence and constant flux, as disorderly as war itself, whose only constant is keeping the ships at sea.

II. THE LEADERS

Battleship Admiral

DANIEL J. CALLAGHAN was born and brought up in the San Francisco of pre-earthquake days, a gracious, cosmopolitan, and rather bawdy city, somewhat continental in character. Such cities in Europe usually contain a stratum of families almost pietistic in their devoutness and their strict adherence not only to the observances but also to the moral code of the Church. These families are usually socially somewhat separated from the rest of the community; they gather round some particular church or similar institution and the home is of great importance to them.

It was so in the San Francisco of the nineties; and the Callaghan family were members of a group that pivoted around St. Ignatius' School, where young Dan got his early education. The difference was that in America and particularly in San Francisco an element of energy was added, quite foreign to the European experience, so that instead of living the cloistered existence of such a family in, say, Vienna or Dijon, the younger Callaghans got as actively into everything as so many monkeys. Young Dan was always down at the bay and frequently aboard the ship on which his uncle, the to-be admiral, James J. Raby, was then serving.

There were three other brothers; they must have brought home some rare tales from time to time. But the point is that they were early made to realize that the lush life around them belonged to another world. In their own lives, strict discipline was accompanied by a joyousness of outlook in which that exterior world had little part. The lesson was thoroughly learned; when young Dan Callaghan arrived at Annapolis in the summer of 1907, at seventeen, to make obeisance before the "God of 2.5," he had already seen more of life and was more mature than most men in the upper classes.

Physically also he attained maturity early. A portrait of him at the time (it is quite definitely a bad picture and may not be wholly representative) shows him as a young man with a lot of chin, eyebrows thin at the ends, and a serious, almost set expression around the small mouth. He was uncommonly large, both vertically and horizontally, for his age; a eupeptic man, whose abounding energy earned him the nickname of "Fire Engine," though he was occasionally called "Fat" and didn't like it because it was an injustice.

He might have been a tower of strength to the football team but early in the game hurt a leg so that baseball became his sport. In his fourth year at the Academy he made the varsity and his N; the student-official *Lucky Bag* describes him as "only a passably good first baseman" who, on being shifted to catcher, came into his own, with a powerful throwing arm that infallibly shot down base runners and a very considerable ability at steadying and soothing pitchers, who are always temperamental cattle. That the team lost nine out of sixteen games, including the all-important Army game, was hardly his fault. A study of the scores shows that Navy was held back all year by a lack of batting power in the outfield in spite of Callaghan's good work in getting low-score games out of contented pitchers.

The fact that he could do this was, indeed, symptomatic of his whole career at Annapolis. Other men unconsciously leaned on him, came to him for advice. It was not that he was a brilliant student; he was usually toward the upper fourth of his class but never near the top and it was remarked that his standing suffered by reason of the extensive letter writing he did. It was rather a straight matter of character; the problems on which his judgment was requested were nearly always ethical or closely approaching that category.

One of his classmates describes him as a "serious citizen" who never drank or smoked forbidden cigarettes or went in for practical jokes. One would receive the impression of aloofness if it were not also clear that he had all the Irish gift for politics, was always organizing something, showing up at every meeting and invariably making a speech serious in tone and convincing as to content, forever being elected to a committee to do something and frankly enjoying the opportunity this gave him to be in contact with other people.

That is, he was a notably friendly man, and one who is described as being extremely good company, a lively conversationalist in the serious style, luminous rather than witty. The rather odd thing is that no one can recall any brilliant or trenchant remark that he made, though the human memory keeps this type of recollection better than any other. His success as a speaker seems to have rested on the accent of sincerity he lent to ideas and ideals that might be considered commonplace. He behaved like a man who thought it was fun to keep the Ten Commandments.

His officers thought well of him and made him lieutenant of the first company. When he was graduated in 1911 (incidentally, in the same class as Admiral Norman Scott and General Lewis H. Brereton) his *Lucky Bag* sketch had this much to say:

"Dan came to the Academy a quiet, steady fellow, and leaves it just as quiet but steadier. One of the very few men who have not changed their good habits and who have not acquired bad ones. He is a rare combination of straightforwardness, dignity, and generosity that makes him one of the most respected and admired men in the Brigade. His claims to be a Red Mike have suffered sadly during the last two years."

The last sentence is cryptic, but the point to note is that the sketches in this publication were very frank and by no means always flattering.

II

In those days the young officers from the Academy were graduated with the rank of "passed midshipmen" which has since disappeared from the service. They were asked (as they still are) to express their preference for type of duty. Those who knew Dan Callaghan at the time say that he had already made up his mind to specialize in ordnance—it was one of the few personal matters he could be persuaded to talk about. He applied for a heavy ship. And so he regarded it as a favor to draw the armored cruiser *California*, then operating on the West coast, as his first duty assignment.

The exhilaration lasted till he got aboard and probably for a little while afterward. The ship was comparatively new; big, roomy, comfortable, without the hammocks and cramped decks of the older ships he had known during the midshipmen's cruises. She was a paradise for an officer studying ordnance, for like all the pre-dreadnaught vessels of her class she mounted no less than four distinct types of guns, and to his great joy Callaghan received command of a turret containing a pair of 8-inch guns, the heaviest pieces aboard.

There was a distinct prospect of early active service with its chance of adventure and promotion, for China had just exploded into the Sun Yat-sen revolution and our government, with a lively remembrance of how Chinese revolutions had turned out in the past and no foreknowledge that this one would be different, had already ordered the *California* out to Pearl Harbor to stand by for trouble.

Three of her sisters went with her. They made up the "Armored Cruiser Squadron," specifically so named, subject of a song by one of its officers of which the chorus runs:

Away, away, with sword and drum,
Here we come, full of rum,
Looking for someone to put on the bum—
The Armored Cruiser Squadron.

It was in every sense a hard-boiled and hard-drinking Navy in those days. The Armored Cruiser Squadron, from the fact that it was always on detached duty, showing the flag in foreign ports where whoopee was official and obligatory, was the most hilarious in the fleet, and Callaghan found he had picked himself out the most hilarious ship in the squadron. When she was not winning gunnery trophies— thanks to Callaghan and a battery officer named Bates—she was usually staging a heroic party.

The steerage mess, which is composed of the very junior officers, led the way. They were just out of Annapolis and now drinking was no longer a crime to them, but an evidence of manliness. Of course a good part of the special conditions on the *California* can be referred to the chance combination of personalities among the seven other passed midshipmen who had accompanied Callaghan on the detail. One, who became known as the "Unsturdy Oak," is described as having a conversation that never rose above the belt; he later had to be court-martialed and ejected from the service. Another was to commit suicide in a moment of alcoholic depression. But the *California* had her own special reason as well; it seems that the good people of the state were so proud of the cruiser that bore their name that they undertook to provide her officers with all the home-grown wine and brandy they could drink.

To be sure it was considered slightly beneath one's dignity to accept this official hospitality. But along toward the end of a pay period one after another of the young officers would call a boy and, with a somewhat conspiratorial air, send him down to the wine locker for a bottle of free booze.

All but Daniel J. Callaghan. When a bottle was broached, even a bottle of Scotch after a pay day, he refused with a good-humored tolerance that carried no sting and went on with the conversation; when the Unsturdy Oak embarked on one of his bawdy stories, Callaghan quietly slipped out to go lie in his bunk and read a book on ordnance.

Sun Yat-sen was achieving his revolutionary objectives without any more damage to Americans than might reasonably be expected in such a situation, but it was decided to send the Armored Cruiser Squadron across the Pacific anyway on a practice and training cruise. They made a couple of stops at the South China ports and with the coming of hot weather went up to Tsingtao, then in German hands, where the question of Callaghan versus John Barleycorn came to a head.

The Graf Spee's squadron was in the port, the same that was later sunk off the Falklands. There was visiting, one ship to another and back; and the German imperial Navy being what it was, the visits were a series of binges. It finally occurred to the *California's* exec that the demands of politeness would be satisfied with something less than having all his officers roll under the table every night, a process which was beginning to have its effect on some of them; also that he had a resource in that steerage from which echoes occasionally reached the higher echelons of command. He detailed three of the young men to uphold the honor of the ship in all future bouts with the beer mugs. One was the Unsturdy Oak, one was the suicidal alcoholic, and the third was Dan Callaghan. On the grounds that he had religious scruples against drinking Callaghan refused.

It was not the type of order whose rejection would be held punishable disobedience by a court martial. But an officer of executive rank can, and not infrequently does, make things extremely unpleasant for a junior who thus establishes himself as a disobliging fellow. Nothing of the kind happened with Dan Callaghan; all the refusal brought him was additional respect, and the Armored Cruiser Squadron sailed back to San Francisco, where home again was celebrated by the steerage with a masked visit to one of the hottest spots on the Barbary Coast. Callaghan stayed aboard as junior duty officer.

III

It was during this period that Congress passed the law automatically commissioning graduates of the Academy as ensigns, which advanced those who held the passed midshipman rank to ensign without examination. It is characteristic not so much of the future admiral himself as of what others thought of him that this was considered a break for him, since the examination at this grade was the toughest on the list and it was doubted whether he would make it. He was by now a well-qualified junior watch officer and the record of his turret had been brilliant, but this was felt to be because he got along so well with the men that they worked their heads off for him, whereas the examiners would want to know how he stood on differential calculus. The Navy had not yet taken its scientific training as a matter of course and started looking for leadership.

It had, however, been doing something about the physical condition of its officers ever since the days of the first Roosevelt. There was still on the books a fiat from that advocate of the strenuous life that every officer should walk thirty miles in three days at least once a month. The ship acquired a new skipper about this time—that McNulty who later adopted some Russian refugees and married one of them—and as one of the means of tightening up on the tough boys in the steerage he enforced the exercise rule. Officers were observed trotting unhappily around the quarterdeck mile after mile, with pedometers strapped to their legs.

At this juncture the ship was sent down to lie off the depressing palm-fringed coasts of western Nicaragua as part of the Wilson occupation. Ensign Dan Callaghan formed part of the landing party that went ashore with the Marines under their major (another not unknown to future fame—Smedley D. Butler), and with them participated in the shoot-and-run affair dignified by the name of the Battle of Coyotepe Hill. It was unimportant to everyone but the Nicaraguan who got knocked off and to Dan Callaghan.

To the latter it meant an opportunity to cover his thirty miles without that depressing round of the decks. He began doing his turn on the beach and was presently imitated by a few of the other officers. It was still a melancholy business plowing through the soft sand, so he organized a couple of baseball teams, sometimes playing with the pedometer on his leg to get his thirty miles into the official records.

Today they would call him athletic officer and an important cog in the ship's morale machinery, but in 1913 it was all new. The men loved it and Callaghan found out something fairly important about gaining their co-operation.

Then Mexico blew up. Madero upset the old tyranny of Porfirio Diaz; Huerta turned traitor on Madero and shot him; and the armored cruiser *California* went up to Guaymas on the Gulf of California to watch the West coast. There was much anti-Americanism among the Mexicans there. One Saturday afternoon a liberty party from the ship got soused in Guaymas. The shore patrolmen tried to arrest them; the chief of police in the town, a Huertista, cut himself in on the row and shot two of the patrolmen dead.

The excitement caused by this news was intense; everyone believed, in accordance with the George Barr McCutcheon tradition of the age, that the police chief's forty-five had fired the first shots of a war. Nevertheless Callaghan walked up to the captain and with the proper salute asked permission to go ashore for mass in the morning. No one else who was present at the interview now survives; all we know is that the permission was given and that Ensign Callaghan went to church next morning in an intensely hostile city, alone and unarmed. He continued to go to the same church every Sunday till the ship was ordered back to San Francisco and he was detached.

It is the navy custom to shift its young officers to a different ship and type of duty after two years, the idea being to produce a man who has no special technical prejudices by the time he reaches the upper ranks of command. Ensign Dan Callaghan, already beginning to specialize in ordnance, was thus assigned to the destroyer *Truxtun* as engineer officer.

But it is also the custom to alternate tours of sea duty with jobs on one of the shore establishments to give administrative experience. There is a certain amount of mystery in why this was not done in Callaghan's case. The probable explanation is that in those days nearly all the fleet was in the Atlantic and the available shore jobs were on the East coast. Callaghan had a very particular reason for wishing to keep San Francisco as his home post—to wit, that a considerable proportion of the letters he so indefatigably wrote were directed to a certain Mary Tormey, a singularly beautiful girl belonging to the same social group from which he had sprung. When the *California* put into her home port this long-range courtship had culminated in marriage. The *Truxtun* would give him more sea duty; but the destroyers of that day were more often in harbor than abroad on the bounding main, for which their construction did not suit them.

So Mrs. Mary Callaghan continued to live with her widowed mother while Ensign Dan's married life consisted of a series of visits from the destroyer base at San Pedro. There is a description of him from this period as "serious—much too serious—his smiles were rare. With his ship secured at the [Mare Island] navy yard for overhaul, it seemed that he could have gone home a great deal more than he did, yet he maintained an inflexible commuter's schedule which got him up very early in the morning and home very late at night."

IV

The seriousness no doubt dates at least partly from his experience in the roaring steerage of the *California* (he was to change later when he discovered that all officers in the Navy were not like that); but partly also it was due to the *Truxtun* herself. She was one of a class since made famous in fiction as *Delilah*, 420-tonners optimistically described as seagoing by their builders, coal burners with a whaleback bow forward that was supposed to make them seaworthy but only succeeded in making them cramped. There were sixty-one men and three officers, who lived a rugged life in rooms the size of a Chic Sale special placed dead aft over the screws "so that it was like sleeping in a coffee grinder."

This did not matter to Callaghan; at sea he never got any sleep anyway. The organization meant that all three officers had to stand bridge watches, and when he came off one of these it was back to the engine room to toil with machinery that had been built in 1901, had seen hard service, and was now thoroughly obsolete. As it turned out there was more sea duty than he had anticipated; no sooner had the destroyer been fitted out than she was ordered down to the Mexican coast, where the pot was still boiling.

There were no interior passageways through the ship. One had to get from one compartment to another by scrambling perilously across the deck and down a hatch, so that the food was always cold by the time it had been carried from the galley under the bridge to the wardroom aft. This did not matter much either, for the little destroyer rolled and pitched so furiously that it was impossible to keep a cooking vessel of any kind on the stove at sea and all the officers took their meals standing on the bridge in the form of corned beef or onion sandwiches with coffee on the side. There was no radio and the only light was provided by a five-kilowatt generator; and in cold weather the water that was perpetually coming down the hatches formed a film of ice across the deck of Callaghan's cabin from which his shoes stood up like islands.

"The bunkers in those ships," says one who served in them, "were in the narrow space between the skin of the ship and the boiler-room bulkheads and were divided themselves into small compartments by several athwartship bulkheads. The coal we usually got was very fine, almost powdered, and frequently wet. . . . This meant that a man had to go into each individual bunker through a deck hatch, carrying a candle and armed with a slicebar to strike the coal down. Between the smallness of the compartment, the powdered coal dust filling the air, the motion of the vessel, and the heat of the atmosphere it came near killing anyone who was not very tough. I never went into one myself . . ."

Dan Callaghan did, especially when the going was particularly rough—not as a devotee of the ancient chestnut about ordering his men to do nothing he would himself avoid, but because he considered himself the man best able to handle a difficult job and he wanted it over with. The men adored him, though he was the very antithesis of the usual destroyer officer, who was a rather dashing and raffish fellow always in some scrape.

Close relations between officers and crew were not unusual in those old destroyers, which had neither chaplain nor doctor. The men would bring up problems—"Well, you see, sir, I'm having a little trouble with my wife," or "Sir, there's a big ranch right next to that farm I own at Sausalito and . . ." With Callaghan this was intensified; in spite of his youth he acquired the name of "Uncle Dan" and in return for their respect he gave the men a degree of confidence unusual even for that service, where the men were all veterans and discipline was practically unnecessary.

That was what caught up with him. The *Truxtun*, with three of her sisters, had returned to the States early in 1915 to prepare for a cruise to Alaska. As she was tuning up for the trip the starboard condenser began to behave badly. Callaghan opened it up, found some of the condenser ferrules were corroded, and replaced them. The occurrence was not unusual and a spare supply of these small brass devices was carried aboard, but as they seemed to be going a little faster than normal, Callaghan drew on the nearest destroyer tender for forty-eight more, all she could give him. When he got to the yard, which was in May, he requisitioned another seven hundred in anticipation of the long cruise.

He was frantically overworked at the time and a good deal worried. His wife had a baby coming and was having none too easy a time of it; his younger brother had just graduated from St. Ignatius, was getting ready for his entrance examinations, and needed help and advice. Seniority had made Uncle Dan executive of the ship as well as her engineer officer.

In June the condenser balked again; forty or fifty more ferrules were replaced. In the early weeks of July, with everything ready for the big cruise and the ship running up the coast, it went irreparably wrong; the *Truxtun* had to signal inability to make the trip and go into dockyard to have the whole condenser replaced. In the Navy some person is always responsible. The board of investigation (which is a kind of maritime grand jury) found that the *Truxtun* condenser ferrules had shown a high rate of corrosion; that she was a freak ship, built by a Baltimore yard, slightly different from the rest of her class in the pitch and threading of her condenser ferrules; that the seven hundred ferrules taken in at the dockyard would not fit. In the judgment of someone topside, the failure to requisition ferrules sooner and to inspect meticulously for accuracy those that he did get constituted dereliction of duty on the part of Lieutenant (j.g.) Daniel J. Callaghan. He was relieved of his duties and ordered before a general court-martial, which had power to dismiss him from the service for such an offense.

There was a nine days' wonder in fleet wardrooms over the irony of the most conscientious man in the service being brought up on such a charge, but the wheels of the law ground inexorably toward the court-martial in August. Then it came out that the condenser plate had developed a case of galloping consumption for some electrolytic reason that not even the scientists could explain; no amount of ferrule replacement would have done any good. As for the seven hundred that did not fit, they had been received aboard by one of Uncle Dan's fireroom staff, a semi-illiterate (not uncommon in the Navy in those days) ignorant of the uses of a pitch gauge, who had pronounced them satisfactory in order to save his beloved chief the trouble. Callaghan received a verdict of full acquittal, the highest form of exoneration he could get from the court.

He had discovered with Thiers that *quand on est au gaillard, l'humanité se compose de lâches, de menteurs, et de paresseux.* The character was now complete; all the rest is in how it worked out. But when the twenty-five-year-old lieutenant went home after the court-martial it was noted by those who had not seen him for several months that his hair had become prematurely gray.

V

The clock turns to November, 1916, with Woodrow Wilson just elected for keeping us out of war and most people in the services doubting whether he would be able to keep it up. Lieutenant Dan Callaghan, having finished his tour of duty in destroyers by working up to the command of the *Truxtun,* was ordered up to Bremerton as engineer officer for the recommissioning of the old protected cruiser *New Orleans.*

She was one of the famous line of Elswick cruisers, and there were none better in the world—when they were built. This one had been built exactly twenty years before for the Brazilian government, had been bought by our Navy for use in the Spanish War, and then had retired to peace at the end of an anchor chain because nobody loved her.

The reason for this was that both British construction and Brazilian ownership had left their marks. To the former she owed her small size, about that of a modern heavy destroyer; a wardroom which would not hold more than four officers at a time, where the spirit locker was the largest piece of furniture; and officers' quarters in the traditional British position, dead aft over the screws where vibration could not possibly be missed. To the Brazilian ownership she was indebted for small bunkers and for valves, gauges, and working parts marked in Portuguese.

The service of U.S.S. *New Orleans* was one of hilarious low comedy. Her petty officers were Old Navy; her crew were mainly young reservists from Oregon and Washington, the very best of material. Their ship was a wandering curiosity shop and they were determined to have a good time. Those who saw Dan Callaghan during this service remember him as the life of the party, always joking, laughing, or eagerly discussing baseball. Whenever he could, he got ashore and played himself; when he could not, he trotted around the engine room, caroling a merry stave as he lifted a 175-pound valve into place; for as on the *Truxtun*, he often did things like that himself as the quickest way of getting them done. His life had smoothed out, with a fine son and mother both doing well. The younger brother was coming through at Annapolis; he himself was in line for promotion and the exec's billet on the ship. He had a number of friendships made in the wardroom, including one with a young navy doctor which was to last the rest of his life and play an important part in his career—Ross McIntire.

Not that they had an easy time aboard the *New Orleans*. When she reached the Atlantic the United States was at war and she went at once into the most nerveracking service in the world—convoy, mostly from Staten Island ports toward the Mediterranean. Because of her age and lack of speed she always drew the very slowest convoys—the concrete-hulled monstrosities and all the other knicknacks, six- and eight-knot ships that sometimes showed a minus figure for the day's run against the wind. Near the coast of Europe the convoys would be met by British destroyers and the *New Orleans* would turn back, which meant that she had to make double the Atlantic voyage every trip. This was more than her fuel capacity would permit. They built pens of light boards around her main hatch and piled them high with coal in bags, then shoveled loose coal in among the bags.

Of course this covered the whole ship with coal dust when the wind blew, and when it blew really hard the loose coal would start flying, then the bags and the pens that held them, so that approximately every third trip she had to put in at the Azores to coal ship for the return voyage. Nobody seemed to mind; in fact the only thing they did mind was that they never got a shot at a German sub or surface raider, out of all that weary voyaging. The only excitement came when they met a big disabled British liner off the north of Scotland in a gale. It fell to Callaghan to make arrangements for taking her in tow; she was five times the size of the little cruiser, and his captain reported afterward that he did not think any other engineer in the Navy could have made it, but Uncle Dan did. That gave him his step and executive rank; and late in 1918 his tour of duty on the *New Orleans* ran out.

VI

If he were to progress much farther in the Navy it was essential that he take a whirl at shore duty. He was probably not very delighted with the idea, but he conscientiously took up the assignment, which was at the Bureau of Navigation in Washington; and Mary Callaghan came East to join him.

Nobody who knew him will say very much about the two years he spent in that office, and their silence probably covers the fact that he was unhappy. He had now been at sea for seven years, the most formative of his life as to tastes and habits. Once the paper work was out of the way, everything had been free and easy with Uncle Dan. Now he was suddenly in a world of boundless protocol and red tape and questions of personality; and perhaps, too, it was a little difficult getting used to having women around all the time instead of for a week-end once in three months.

He played the game without flinching. People who visited his house of an evening, both in the Washington days and later, are unanimous in saying what a fine time they had with this good companion who mixed cocktails for all the guests, taking none himself, passed out cigars and cigarettes which he himself did not smoke, and served excellent dinners when he would have gladly done with a Bermuda onion sandwich.

He played the game at the office too, listening to endless requests for this duty or that, balancing, persuading. For the Bureau of Navigation had nothing to do with navigation. It was the personnel office of the Navy (which has since received a title in accordance with its duties) where assignments to duty were made and refused. To it came officers presenting kicks about being assigned to the staff of the governor of Guam, ten million miles from nowhere; or requesting duty aboard the *Birmingham*, because old friend Joe Gish was her exec—with all the surreptitious pressures that go with such a situation.

In normal times this would be bad enough for a friendly man like Callaghan, who hated refusing to do things for other people. But 1919 and 1920 were the particularly bad years, with demobilization, ships laid up, staffs pared down, and the department inventing all sorts of rules to persuade officers to leave a service that had room for only half of them, no matter how good their war records. Callaghan stuck to it for the full two years, giving no sign that he was doing anything but enjoying himself; but there is every reason to believe he was glad when it was over and he could go to sea again as assistant fire control officer of the new battleship *Idaho*.

The date was October, 1920. It is capital, marking a prime transition period, both in the history of Daniel Callaghan and of the Navy. The Washington treaties were just over the hill, the fleet was shifting to the Pacific to take on a character wholly new. Callaghan was now settled in his profession and in his specialization, his dislike of the East and his liking for service afloat. In the course of the next decade and a half he followed the line of duty normal to an officer of his background—short tours ashore on the Board of Inspection and Survey and with the naval R.O.T.C.; longer tours afloat on the battleships *Colorado*, *Mississippi*, *Pennsylvania*, and finally *California*, on the last of which he worked up to gunnery officer on the staff of the commander, United States Fleet, who was Admiral Leigh.

Callaghan now moved constantly from ship to ship, arranging gunnery problems and supervising drills. He was convinced that skill with guns, especially the big guns of battleships, would be the ultimately determining factor in any war, regardless of the surface eddies in the stream of naval thought that threw into prominence now the torpedo, now the airplane. About the smaller pieces he was less sure, particularly those in the antiaircraft category. It was only human for captains to put the best men in the big gun turrets, where they could run up scores that looked well on the ship's record and on their own. Perhaps some different system of scoring competitions—or perhaps a different type of antiaircraft gun . . .

Dan Callaghan had, in fact, become one of those people who form the fundamental policies of the Navy. Under its own peculiar system this policy making is not done directly and by orders, but through the exchange of ideas in wardroom conversations, leading up to a tactful suggestion offered to that lonely man, the admiral, who has learned that even a junior lieutenant may produce the key item that causes a whole program to succeed. There is too much executive detail for the admiral to consider, there are too many questions with an instant yes or no, for him to do much fumbling with ideas. That is the function of his juniors, especially the staff officers.

The system is peculiar to navies and, in its fullest development, to the American Navy. It is one of the reasons why that service operates more as a unit than most military organizations. "We do all our fighting behind closed doors and then get behind the line that wins out," one of its officers has said. The wardroom conversations are also the reason why it is rarely possible to assign any development to an individual, or to say what an individual has done. He is an influence which can hardly be described by anything more than a signpost indicating directions.

Dan Callaghan's influence was in the direction of more guns. We have a picture of him exerting that influence in the wardroom of his second ship *California*, chewing continuously on hard candies and drinking coffee as he talked (and he used to upset his stomach and to straighten out he chewed peppermint drops, which of course made matters worse, to the amusement of others). When, at the end of a day spent in exercises at sea, the young officers had hurried ashore to cocktails and dinner, he would go down to the wardroom with his box of candy, send for a cup of coffee, and talk. If the conversation turned away from gunnery or sport (he had added football to his range of interest since his son had turned out to be a crack player for St. Ignatius) he was a little apt to lose interest after a while and go off to his cabin to work. In the morning he would be up early, serious about his business—"stolid in his temperament, not a bit of Irish flash about him," one friend puts it. At sea he would have a handball board rigged on the quarterdeck with a cage over it and play by the hour, usually with the young athletes fresh from the

Academy, since no one anywhere near his own age could stand
against him.

VII

Under normal peacetime conditions less than one Naval Academy
graduate in a hundred attains the rank that permits him to hoist an
admiral's flag. An indispensable preliminary of this is that the candi-
date shall have commanded a large ship with satisfaction, since ideas
and the ability to lead a large organization do not always go together,
as Mahan demonstrated in his personal career. An almost indispensable preliminary of captaincy is that the man shall have been executive
officer of some big ship. Commander Callaghan was already marked
as a possible future admiral but his service in the higher ranks had
been almost exclusively staff; so in 1936 the Bureau of Navigation
gave him a chance to fill out his experience by naming him exec
of the heavy cruiser *Portland*.

He did a rather remarkable job. Under the peace establishment
the efficiency of a ship is determined by the results of various competitions—gunnery, engineering, etc.—against other vessels of her
class. The competitions are scored by a system so elaborate that it
often takes an Einstein to find out who won. In the good old American
spirit of competition the execs of the ships concerned used to sit up
half the night finding ways to cut corners on the rules—such as
slipping a little ethyl into the gasoline.

This is immoral. It is also a form of immorality which the Navy
can and does regard with considerable tolerance, since the ultimate
objective is to prepare ships for war, in which few holds are barred.
If a fighter pilot with ethyl in his gas can catch up with and shoot
down a Jap bomber, it is not the rules of war that will suffer, but
the enemy.

It was both the strength and the weakness of Commander Callaghan of U.S.S. *Portland* that he refused to have anything to do with
this legitimate cheating, so productive of new ideas. Whatever the
background, it was still cheating to him. He held strictly to the
rules as they were writ and kept his men to them, too; but the execs
of the other heavy cruisers, scouting force, speedily discovered that
if they wanted to stand number one in the fleet they would have to
beat the *Portland*. Throughout the year or more while he was her

exec she continued to rank first or second in every class of competition.

The performance so thoroughly settled the question of his executive ability that he was returned to staff as operations officer of the scouting force to wait for seniority to bring him into the range of captain's rank and his command. At this point chance and friendship took a hand.

The office of naval aide to the President was about to fall vacant by expiration of term of duty and Roosevelt consulted his personal friend and physician, Ross McIntire, about a new man for the job. In most administrations it is a position chiefly concerned with looking ornamental in full dress at public functions and standing behind the President to whisper at strategic moments that cruisers do not carry 16-inch guns. But McIntire knew that this President stood in no need of primary instruction and wanted a genuine seagoing sailor, whom he would use for rather different purposes. He recommended his old friend of the *New Orleans*, Dan Callaghan, with whom he had kept up a desultory correspondence. Roosevelt remembered Callaghan as one of the men he had seen and liked around the Bureau of Navigation back in 1919. And so Dan Callaghan found himself naval aide to the President—the commission signed in green ink on St. Patrick's Day as a compliment to an Irishman.

It was the beginning of what can only be described as a collaboration, in which Callaghan became more than ever an influence on our whole naval policy. The thirty-first President worked all his aides hard, but none harder than the naval man, in whose department he had an abiding interest. Captain Callaghan was continually being called on for some report, running down through all the bureaus to assemble every bit of information available on the subject and collating it in a form which enabled Roosevelt to make one of his famous snap judgments.

It was a job which found Uncle Dan at his most effective; after a few tries the President learned he could be trusted and let him work in his own way. From the beginning he possessed the complete confidence of the officers in the bureaus, who knew him as the man from the fleet, with the blue-water point of view. This favorable impression was increased by the incidental fact that Callaghan did not go in at all for "social stuff." His family remained in the West; he lived on the yacht *Potomac*, attended functions only when it was a duty, and when he talked, talked baseball or international politics, never a word about his job or his boss. The congenital cynics of the White House press brigade thought the world of him; he played everything straight off the chest.

Under the circumstances a good deal depended on how he presented any given question for Presidential action. People familiar with the situation are inclined to believe that he had rather more than a finger in the general increase of antiaircraft armament throughout the fleet, that was pushed so hard after the German dive-bombers showed what they could do to ships in the fighting off Norway. Especially he seems to have been interested in the introduction of the 40-millimeter Bofors, which was to prove the number-one weapon against close-in planes. At the time the 40-millimeter Bofors lacked a good fire-control mechanism; the sights on the first British-made examples that came over here were a definitely bad feature; so were the percussion fuses on the ammunition. It took a good deal of penetration on the part of both Callaghan and the President to perceive that the weapon had possibilities for development.

The details are not precisely important; the important fact is that Captain Callaghan had become one of what the believers in victory through airpower somewhat derisively called "battleship admirals." He thought that the arbitrament of battle at sea still lay with the gun and the ships that could carry it; and that such a ship was less than she should be unless she could furnish her own air cover.

VIII

In the spring of 1941 the heavy cruiser *San Francisco* needed a new skipper and Callaghan was in line for the appointment that would mean his admiral's stars. The President released him from his aide's appointment several weeks early to seize the opportunity.

With this ship, the first he had commanded since the old *Truxtun*, Captain Callaghan plunged into the void that surrounds the wartime movements of a vessel not actually in combat. The *San Francisco* was not in Pearl Harbor at the time of the attack; she is not mentioned in Admiral King's report as among the vessels present during

the Gilbert-Marshall raid, the bombing of Tokyo, or the Battle of
the Coral Sea; and by the latter date, indeed, orders were already
under way detaching Uncle Dan from his ship for more staff duty
with the rank of rear admiral.

It came about this way: Vice Admiral Robert L. Ghormley had
been recalled from his post as naval attaché in London to head the
recently formed Southwest Pacific Command. He asked the Bureau
of Personnel to recommend a chief of staff; he had no preference.
They knew Ghormley there at the bureau—a man who did a lot of
thinking on broad strategic lines, very accurate in his estimates of
situations and means, somewhat remote from those around him. To
form one of those duets of intellect and character which have always
achieved the most spectacular results in war (Hindenburg and
Ludendorff, Grant and Sherman) he would need a chief of staff
with good control of morale, driving energy, and offensive spirit.

"How would Dan Callaghan do?"

"Delighted; just the man I would have chosen if I had the pick
of the entire Navy," said Ghormley and went down to Nouméa,
where Callaghan joined him in June, just after Midway had been
fought and it had become clear that we possessed the means for an
offensive—provided we kept it small, both as to commitments and
as to area.

That was the genesis of the Guadalcanal campaign, which was to
prove so unlimited in commitment and area. As chief of staff, Dan
Callaghan had to fill in the details of the vice admiral's plan. It was
making bricks without straw. Ships had to be borrowed from the
little Australian fleet to furnish escort and gunnery cover for the
original landing. Marines had to be taken from garrison duty among
the islands. There was a shortage of working space, of equipment
items, and above all of officers to handle the thousand and one
details of staff work. When the four cruisers went down in the
Battle of Savo Island, their surviving officers were eagerly kidnaped
and plunked down at desks to handle some of the work over which
Callaghan had been sitting up so late that he grew red-eyed and
unable to play his usual game of deck tennis.

Savo, of course, changed everything in more than one way. "The
loss of the four cruisers left us inferior in strength for several months"
—during which the officers of the South Pacific Command made

even-money bets that they would shortly become another exiled government. The shifts and devices and desperate battles by which this was prevented have been told; there is no need to repeat or to comment on them here. When help did come streaming down from the north, it came with a new admiral, Bull Halsey, with his own chief of staff. Callaghan was out of a job.

But immediately he was in another. For Halsey wanted precisely a battleship admiral, a gunnery specialist strong on offensive spirit, to lead his cruiser division, and he thought Callaghan was that man. So Uncle Dan's flag went up on the *San Francisco*, his old ship.

Early in November he took her into the troubled waters of Iron-bottom Bay off Guadalcanal, covering a big convoy with other ships in company—a grouping whose strangely mixed units betray the shifts to which we were put to maintain our hold on the bloody island. There was another heavy cruiser, the *Portland*, with 8-inch guns; a light cruiser, the *Helena*, with 6-inch; a pair of antiaircraft cruisers, *Atlanta* and *Juneau*, with 5-inch; and eight destroyers belonging to three different classes.

The story of that November 12 has been told many times—how as the convoy lay unloading the Japs came over Florida Island with thirty-two torpedo bombers—how the fleet formed circle and while the Grummans from Henderson Field jumped the bombers from above, the 5-inch and 40-millimeter struck at them from below—and how only a single Jap soared away up the Slot with smoke pouring from his engines and a Wildcat riding him down. It was only the first gust of the whirlwind; that afternoon word ran in that the enemy were coming down to Guadal with the big parade—battleships in action for the first time in this war, with cruisers, destroyers, and numerous transports behind.

We also had battleships in the South Pacific but they could not possibly get there in time. If the Japanese closed into the beach the heavy shells of their battleships would certainly knock out the Henderson Field planes as lighter ships had once so nearly done before. The transports would come in with their thirty thousand Jap troops; there would be no way to prevent their landing; the slender force of Marines ashore, still barely sufficient to hold the line we had gained in August, would be submerged by numbers; and the island for which so much blood and treasure had been spent would become another and worse Bataan.

"Engage the enemy," were the orders to Callaghan, whose strength was perhaps a quarter of the forces now rushing down on him.

The Japanese (perhaps consciously echoing Mr. Hitler's remark about "military idiots") complain that it is difficult to fight Americans because we have no true sense of strategy. We fight, they say, at outrageous times and places under conditions no sane military man would accept. The kind of action they would have attempted off Guadalcanal under such conditions is fairly clear. There were a handful of PT boats with their torpedoes over at Tulagi; Callaghan's destroyers had approximately eighty torpedo tubes among them and his two antiaircraft cruisers mounted six apiece. In that black night the low-slung vessels could hide under the loom of the land; they could rush in as the enemy approached and with luck and good aim could slip enough torpedoes into the ribs of his big ships to discourage him, making their getaway with the help of speed and dark. The heavy cruisers could lie at a distance off Cape Esperance or the mouth of Lengo Channel and fire into the mess from long range.

This was the convention. This was what an officer with a proper sense of (Japanese) strategy was supposed to do. The proof of it is that the Japanese admiral disposed his fleet with great skill to beat off exactly such an attack. We do not know, nor shall we ever know, whether Callaghan considered this form of action. If the idea occurred to him or was presented by one of his staff, he could hardly do anything but reject it without a second thought. It was one of those trick solutions he had so consistently avoided when executive of the *Portland*. Quite aside from the physical morality of ordering other men into a desperate adventure where he could not lead—it was his province to be the leader and his flagship carried no torpedoes—there was an element of intellectual dishonesty in such a failure to use the main weapon of the United States Navy, in whose employment he had specialized. It would have involved a denial at the intimate moment of crisis of the faith he had always held.

Thus character—morality—by any name it is still the same—at the crisis of Dan Callaghan's life became the paramount issue. No more than St. Paul did he believe in faith without works. He would fight with the gun, yes, but one might as well do this thing intelligently. At any normal range the 14-inch shells of Japanese battleships would go through and through the sides of our lightly plated ships, while the 8-inch that were the heaviest we carried would merely produce some beautiful and rather appalling fireworks on their heavy plates. To achieve any result that would make a difference in the fate of Guadalcanal, it was necessary to get in so close that all shells would strike with the maximum velocity at which they left the muzzle, and no armor would be of any service. In an action under such conditions all chances would favor the lighter gun, which can be served more rapidly and is mounted on a platform a trifle harder to hit. Moreover such a combat would have the not inconsiderable advantage that Callaghan expected and would be prepared for it, while the Japs would not be.

After the transports and supply ships had been seen clear of the area, the *San Francisco* turned her prow westward again and led the little fleet back to the shores of Guadal. At one-thirty the *Helena's* TBS spoke to say the enemy were coming. Dan Callaghan turned once to close the range beyond a chance of missing, shouted: "Commence firing; give 'em hell, boys!" and the guns went off.

All that he had been, all that he was were concentrated in that moment; and in it a pair of 14-inch from the Jap battleship hit the bridge and killed everyone on it. Seventeen minutes later the enemy were beaten and on the run, with half a dozen ships down, and Guadalcanal was saved.

Nimitz and His Men

LIEUTENANT LA MARR was called from a late Sunday bath for immediate conference at the Navy Department, no hint as to subject, and was not a little put out as the car rolled through silent streets under the slate-gray skies of December. There were Marines at the door and unusual activity—for Sunday—in the corridors. La Marr learned that the news was war through a chance meeting with an acquaintance and hurried to the secretary's office, where there was already a desultory conversation going on among Secretary Knox,

Assistant Secretary Forrestal, Undersecretary Bard, and his own chief, Rear Admiral Nimitz of the Bureau of Navigation.

Admiral Stark came in a few moments later with his own flag secretary. "Good morning, how do you do," and the conference opened. The Secretary disqualified himself from expressing opinions except as moderator; Admiral Stark seemed to need more time to think things through. Both Bard and Forrestal thought there was much to be done but appeared hampered by lacking both information about what was happening out at Honolulu (where the machine guns were still hammering) and the intimate acquaintance with navy men and customs that was in possession of the two admirals. When the discussion came down to a specific point it was usually Nimitz' suggestion that was adopted.

His presence in the group was technically a solecism. He was only one of the bureau chiefs (there are seven) and a rather junior admiral. If there was to be a bureau head at the conference, why not (for instance) the man from Aeronautics? Why not the chief of the War Plans or the Ship Movements Division, or the head of the General Board, the elder statesmen of the Navy . . . Because it was in no sense a gathering of elder statesmen, debating with careful balance a line of policy, but a council of war. The keynote—whom can we trust? Nimitz of Bunav, which in spite of its name was the office charged with handling personnel and their assignments, would presumably know that; and he was also heir apparent to the command of the Pacific fleet.

A fleet commander in any navy holds office on much the same terms as a heavyweight champion. It is neither punishment nor fear that he will repeat his mistake that causes him to be removed when he is once knocked out. Confidence has been lost, and with it full control of the medium. When Husband E. Kimmel was appointed Cincpac there was a good deal of kitchen gossip to the effect that he had been brought in to succeed the careful, precise, defensive-minded Admiral Richardson primarily because he could introduce into the fleet a spirit of initiative: train it for attack, America's obvious strategy in a Pacific war. In those black hours when the last bombs were still falling on Pearl Harbor it was not evident from Washington how much damage had been done; but it was evident that neither in spirit nor in mechanical equipment did we any longer possess the means for an offensive.

Automatically the second name on the list was brought up—the list that had been prepared of desirable successors when Admiral Richardson reached retirement age. The name was that of Chester W. Nimitz; when he had heard at the time that his name was on the list, he had asked that it be taken right off again. Admiral Kimmel was his friend and he did not wish to compete; moreover he was very junior, even farther down on the list than Kimmel, who had been jumped up some forty-five numbers to the command. An American military officer who overleaps so many of his superiors in peacetime is bound to have a whole Sargasso Sea of ill-feeling dragging at his keel.

But in war no officer has any right to regard personal feelings, his own or another's. When Nimitz was notified that he would take over the Pacific Fleet, he made one request that instead it should be turned over to Admiral Pye, Kimmel's second; and that being refused, asked for his orders without further debate.

Discussions and arrangements had taken several days, with Admiral King, called in from the Atlantic command, participating. Nimitz had not only been operating in the domains of high strategy but also had been carrying on the suddenly complicated work of his own bureau. He had hardly slept at all and had eaten next to nothing. Just before he stepped on the train that was to take him to San Francisco a surgeon beckoned Lieutenant La Marr aside and told him that he was to be head keeper—to see that the admiral got some sleep and food during the trip, for he would be unlikely to get much later.

That trip was made under circumstances out of a picaresque novel. The admiral and lieutenant shared a stateroom; Nimitz was "Mr. Wainwright," with instructions to recognize no one; and in fact he did freeze his face up and highhat an old acquaintance from the academic world when the latter hailed him in a corridor. It seemed a wise precaution at the time. Whom could we trust? A freighter had been torpedoed between San Francisco and Pearl Harbor and PBYs were going down all over what had become a sea of mystery.

La Marr had been with his chief for over a year but on that trip found a Nimitz he had never met before. Around the Washington offices under the lax discipline of peace the admiral was known as a good deal of a sundowner, in whose presence four-stripe captains trembled; a man who demanded the last degree of official form and attention to detail. Now he became suddenly human, laughed, told jokes, made bad puns, was humanly bored by inaction, and to relieve his boredom taught the flag lieutenant to play cribbage. The first full report of the Pearl Harbor damage was in the latter's brief case and La Marr had been instructed to keep it from Nimitz as long as possible. With his mind on this the lieutenant was a rotten pupil; before they reached Chicago Nimitz told him he would never be a cribbage player and switched to a whole series of new varieties of solitaire, constructed by himself to illustrate the mathematics of permutation. It occurred to the lieutenant to wonder who was soothing whom.

At Chicago there was a wait between trains, employed in taking a long walk through streets littered with dirty ice and getting a haircut for the admiral. In the process La Marr let slip a remark that led his chief to inquire about the existence of that complete Pearl Harbor damage report. From this point on the character of the journey changed. The admiral took complete command and set up a routine which began as the afternoon train on the Santa Fe pulled out. Nimitz would have a couple of stiff cocktails, a big dinner, then compose himself for the evening with a section of the report, clucking gently as he read, murmuring from time to time, "It could have happened to anyone"; and so to bed at a late hour.

Not a word about what ought to be done or what he intended to do, and mornings devoted to card tricks or solitaire with the conversation instantly becoming trivial if the subject of the war leaked in. At the coast La Marr turned back to help clean up the work at the bureau; the admiral went on by plane to Pearl Harbor. Those who saw his meeting with Kimmel on the hill at Makalapa Drive described the latter as trying to draw him toward the building, while Nimitz hung back, looking and looking and looking to take in every detail of the wrecks along the shore. The story perhaps marks the difference between the two men.

II

Many of the more determinative institutions of the Navy lie outside the scope of official regulations. Among these is (or was, before the war) the "admiral's team." By the time an officer reached flag rank he had been in contact with a fairly good cross section of the juniors in the service and had established bonds of mutual liking and confidence with a certain number of them. It was natural that in making up staff or fleet assignments he should ask for men that he knew and liked. It was equally natural that the Bureau of Navigation should give him these men in whom he had confidence; that he should try to see his young men rapidly promoted; and that the effort of every young officer should be to attach himself as soon as possible to the team of an admiral who seemed marked for high command.

Nimitz himself had belonged to such a team—the team of Admiral S. S. Robison, on whose staff he had served during nearly all the last war, when Robison was commander of subs in the Atlantic and had not yet been translated to eminence as commander of the United States Fleet. On Nimitz' side the admiration remains almost unbounded: "I think Admiral Robison would do it so" is one of his ways of announcing a decision.

When the men of Pearl Harbor filed into the conference room on December 31 to meet their new chief they brought with them not only the black depression of that disaster but the knowledge that they had joined the wrong team. It seemed altogether likely that Kimmel was going back to face a court-martial. The best they could expect was that they would be called to give evidence, meanwhile taking some paper-work job near the scene of the trial and unimportant enough to give them plenty of free time for attending its sessions— following which they would have to endure the long struggle upward of leaderless men. The Nimitz team was due to move in.

It is not certain how many of them knew Admiral Nimitz except by name, as head of Bunav, which controlled their destinies. They found him sitting behind his desk, very straight, impassive (he has been called both tall and small but this is because he is rather short in the barrel and so wide in the shoulders that his apparent height depends upon the point of view), judicial, no jokes or trivia. He told them that in his opinion the standard of any group of American naval personnel was high; that he had urged the appointment of Admiral Pye in Kimmel's room and had been overruled; that he wanted the present Pacific Fleet staff to stay and work with him, without a single change.

That moment has been described as the true crisis of Pearl Harbor, the victory following the defeat which made all the rest possible. It was also the first of what became daily conferences in the dun-colored building on Makalapa Drive, with all the ranking officers at Pearl Harbor present and the admiral in the chair.

There is no use pretending that these gatherings were all devoted to sweetness and light, especially in the beginning when the news was universally bad. It was inevitable that the air officers—Halsey, Forrest Sherman (who had written that refutation of the independent air force idea which is still basic in all discussions of the subject), Aubrey Fitch, and the other Sherman, Captain Fred of the *Lexington* —it was inevitable that these officers should have a predominant place in the discussions; they led the only effective striking force the Navy then possessed. They were not a little resentful over the first piece of news that had met Nimitz on his arrival—that the carrier task force for the relief of Wake had been recalled because a Jap fleet in some strength had appeared off the island to prepare a landing. None of them, particularly Halsey, could be described as mealy-mouthed at any time. On the other hand there were the "battleship admirals," who would have been something more than human if they had not, to a degree unadmitted even to themselves, felt thrown into the background by the air forces. Pye and Theobald at least of this group were little more given to polite understatement than Halsey; and they were honestly convinced that sending cruiser-carrier forces into waters where they could encounter enemy battleships might result in a disaster that would lose our last resource and the war. The *Scharnhorst* and *Gneisenau* had sunk the carrier *Glorious* and her escort off Norway; the only successful carrier strikes of the war to date were Pearl Harbor and Taranto, where the victims did not know there were carriers within a thousand miles until the planes reached their target.

The strategic questions which they debated were, of course, settled a little later at Coral Sea, when our carrier groups were trapped back against Australia by the Japanese Fleet rounding the Solomons, and the Jap battleships fled from the contest; but the important point here is Nimitz' solution of the personal question. At some date early in those discussions the violence of the argument reminded him of a story. He told it, and was rewarded by seeing faces relax into laughter and the conversation, when it was resumed, go forward on the basis of an effort to find common ground. Whether the later development of storytelling into a regular Nimitz technique resulted from conscious imitation of Abraham Lincoln or not, no one but the admiral himself can say; but he did develop it out of an excellent memory, an ability to read rapidly, and a literary skill which permits him to furbish up many an item dredging from an old volume to fit a new case.

The preparations for the Saipan operation, for example, produced a few verbal fireworks between army and navy commanders and an expression of opinion that they never could agree. "This all reminds me," said Nimitz, "of the first amphibian operation—conducted by Noah. When they were unloading from the Ark he saw a pair of cats come out followed by six kittens. 'What's this?' he asked. 'Ha ha,' said the tabby cat, 'and all the time you thought we were fighting.'"

(*En passant*, the admiral's sense of humor is particularly well developed. When the submarine *Darter* sent a dispatch asking permission to cruise outside her assigned area into another where she thought she might find more "meat," Nimitz dictated a reply: "Yes my darling *Darter*; shoot your fish at the Japanese, but duck their patrols like you orter." The staff thought it too undignified to send.)

III

The sundowner and hard taskmaster was in fact becoming the leader and co-ordinator—the president in the old sense of that word. But this was a change in the service, not in the admiral. Chester Nimitz had always been a man who preferred oil to blasting powder, a good-natured and friendly man who thought of the convenience of other people. The story of the sailor who called has become a classic of the Pacific. An ordinary enlisted man, he had made a bet with his shipmates that when their vessel reached Honolulu he would pay his respects to the admiral. Nimitz not only received him and talked man to man, but called out a photographer and had his picture taken with the sailor so the latter could prove he had won his bet. There is also the fact that when the admiral leaves his office for an evening conference, press of business never keeps him from inquiring whether his marine orderly has had chow and dismissing him to go get it if he has not.

It was the service that had changed—from the routine performance of peace where men required to be jacked up, to the point where they would shout and pound the table in support of an opinion on such a matter as whether light cruisers ought to lie in the line with the heavies. While they shouted and pounded, Nimitz listened carefully, telling one of his stories when the dispute began to generate more heat than light, anxious above every other thing to familiarize himself with the thought patterns of these men around him in the conference room, to discover where the line of ability lay.

There is a navy custom which requires the commander of a ship or group to call on the ranking admiral when he enters harbor. It had sloped off at Pearl, and it was generally assumed that the custom would be discarded altogether on the coming of war, along with such matters as wearing dress swords. Instead Nimitz extended it, making the call practically obligatory and setting aside the hour from eleven in the morning for such receptions. His actual technique in handling them did not spring full-blown into being, but as it worked out the visitor would be introduced, hand shaken, "Glad to have you with us," and asked to sit down.

Then he would immediately be faced with the most embarrassing possible question. "What are you doing about quinine?" was demanded of a new medical supply officer. And when Captain Cassady of the carrier *Saratoga* reported in after the raid on Surabaya, "Why didn't you send the planes back the second day?"

The answers were filed away in a memory that is capacious without being phenomenal. It was, however, less the answers themselves than their character, the way in which they were made, that the brain behind the pair of gray eyes was interested in observing. The admiral of the Pacific was looking for men who are at their best in meeting a particular type of difficulty, and his memory for behavior patterns really is phenomenal. This is one of the reasons behind a feature of the Pacific war that has not failed to strike professional observers—the frequent changes of command, not only in the higher ranks of admiralty, but even down among task groups, divisions and individual ships. It is not a matter of giving each one his turn, but the developed Nimitz method of picking a commander according to the task to be performed and letting the man work out his own destiny.

This should not be taken to imply that Nimitz is a mere psychological executive, translating the major strategic plans worked out by Admiral King into terms of administration afloat—that he has no strategy of his own. From the first hours of the war Washington played hands off with regard to everything but the broadest outlines of naval policy. Both King and Nimitz have heartily agreed with the criticism leveled at the British Admiralty during the last war, when it tried to conduct the tactics of the Battle of Jutland from its offices in Whitehall; and moreover the distance from Washington to Pearl Harbor is so great that radio is the only means of communication adequate for speed, with the chances of interception and betrayal that method involves.

Almost as soon as Nimitz had finished his historic conference with the Pearl Harbor staff, therefore, the institution of another series of conferences began—with Admiral King on the Pacific coast, both naval chiefs flying to the meeting place. Such journeys are the only occasion when Cincpac takes to the air. He came up through the submarine service himself, does not particularly enjoy flying, and always returns exhausted from these trips.

But that may be as much the result of the conferences as of the journey, for Admiral King has an insatiable appetite for facts and figures and there are not many more tiring occupations than conducting such a conference at the absolute peak of mental alertness for several hours on end.

IV

It was at one of the earliest of these conferences that the Marshall-Gilbert raids at the end of January, 1942, were decided upon, as a practical experiment to shed some light on the then debatable question of whether cruiser-carrier forces could take care of themselves on a long-range oceanic move. It is significant that the commander chosen was Halsey—not for seniority alone (seniority can always be avoided by one device or another) but because Nimitz had already remarked him as a fighting leader who would slug on through if he found himself faced by unexpected odds. Aside from the later raid on Tokyo, this was the only occasion when there was any opportunity for a Nimitz or an American grand strategy during the first seven months

The first bombs of the great battle; *Nagato* under attack from our carrier planes on the morning of October 24.

The Surigao Strait group; a pair of Japanese battleships maneuver under attack on the morning of October 24.

In Sibuyan Sea; *Musashi* of the main Japanese battle force takes a torpedo; she sank not long afterward.

Flier's eye view of a Jap battlewagon; *Yamato* under attack with a bomb hit forward; some of her antiaircraft guns amidships are already out of action.

The Japanese attack; a bomb scores a near miss off one of our big carriers while a 40 mm. crew watches from another.

Princeton hit; the light carrier badly on fire as a destroyer closes in to give assistance.

The attack on Sherman's group; a Jap plane burns on the water as the light carrier *San Jacinto* heels over in a maneuver to avoid enemy bombers.

Princeton burns; a destroyer comes alongside to take off survivors on the afternoon of the first day of the battle.

A moment before the explosion; *Birmingham* pulls alongside *Princeton* to assist her just before the explosion that finished the carrier and nearly wrecked the cruiser.

Princeton burns; from the deck of a big carrier men watch the efforts to get the flames under control.

Under attack; the Jap flight-deck battleship *Ise* steaming through a torrent of bomb splashes, and already afire.

Last of the major Jap carriers; *Zuikaku* afire and already in bad shape on the morning of October 25.

The jeeps under attack; one of the escort carriers makes smoke as the Japanese battle fleet comes into range.

Salvo; these are the multicolored splashes from the shells of a Japanese battleship close aboard an escort carrier, all close, but no cigar.

Almost got her; a perfect straddle from a Jap battleship around the escort carrier *White Plains* as planes take off from another escort carrier in the foreground.

Gambier Bay gets it; the unfortunate escort carrier in the middle of a salvo fired by a Jap battleship (in circle). A little later the American ship was hit and went down.

of the war. All the rest was defensive fighting conforming to the moves of the enemy.

On a slightly lower level of strategic thinking a novelty was introduced into naval war by the employment of the carriers in individual, widely separated task groups, with the planes achieving concentration only over their targets. The method was so consistent throughout the early campaigns, and under different commanders, that it seems only reasonable to attribute the determining decision to Nimitz. It has more than technical importance: when the Japs came up to Midway they had all their carriers in a tight group in accordance with the old principle of concentrating for battles, and they lost them all, while only one of the more widely spread American carriers was attacked.

After Midway it became possible to think in terms of the strategic offensive. Until the memoirs are written we shall not know whose proposal it was to go into the Solomons, but the final decision on a project of such envergure would rest with Admiral King rather than Admiral Nimitz. What Nimitz did do was to ask that Vice Admiral Robert L. Ghormley be brought in to head the area and the operation.

A good deal can be said about that big, bald, alternately smiling and sulphurous officer, regarded in the upper ranks of the service as the lineal successor of Sims and Plunkett, as one of the most intelligent men ever to wear the blue and gold. A strategist primarily, if one understands by strategy the art of distributing forces in a wide area so that the result of any contact with the enemy can hardly be other than favorable. It is true that Nimitz had already discovered one strategist of a high order in Raymond Spruance, the victor of Midway; but the Cincpac had felt the need of a first-class strategist on his own staff at Pearl Harbor and after the Battle of Midway brought Spruance in to head that staff.

Moreover the amphibian command for the Solomons expedition was to be in the hands of Richmond Kelly Turner, who bore a reputation for cold, ruthless efficiency. Spruance was out of the same box, and Nimitz may well have wished to achieve a combination of commanders who would not be all of a pattern which tends to have an adverse effect on general morale when it is too much emphasized.

Finally, Ghormley had made a special study of the geography and oceanography of the Solomons area.

So Ghormley took command of our first offensive. And on its second night there was demonstrated the military truism that the best strategy can be vitiated by tactics—when the Jap torpedo-carriers came down the Slot to sink four heavy cruisers and cripple a fifth, the whole heart of the expedition.

On the morning the landings were to be made in the Solomons, Admiral Nimitz had stepped outside the door of his office to the pistol range that had been set up against the steep side hill on which it stands; and, as was his custom, worked off the nervous tension by banging away at the target with the .22 he uses for such occasions. The first good news was brought to him there; he knocked off and went back to work. When the story of Savo Island reached him, it was observed that the admiral stayed on the range for a long time, his face set, pouring the small bullets into the target as rapidly as he could shoot before going indoors to dictate new orders.

One of them obviously would have to be for the relief of Ghormley. He had been nearly seven hundred miles from the scene of the disaster and could hardly be held directly responsible for it, but the thing had happened under his command and the moral effect would inevitably be somewhat the same as in the case of Kimmel and Pearl Harbor. Moreover the campaign in the Solomons was now no longer one in which strategy was particularly useful. It had suddenly become a question of straight dogged defense against superior forces till help could come; and Nimitz, to whom the secret of the imminent invasion of Africa had been confided, knew that help could not be sent soon. There was only one logical commander for the job—Halsey.

Halsey had been ill at the time of Midway and was still not a thoroughly well man. It took some time to make arrangements for the change, for Halsey to familiarize himself with the problem. It was mid-October before he was fully in control, and a thrill of hope and delight ran through every nerve in the fleet at the announcement, falling so fortunately with the cruiser action off Cape Esperance, when the debt of Savo Island was paid and overpaid. The two-and-a-half-month interval was probably the blackest period of the war for Admiral Nimitz back at Pearl Harbor: the second crisis he had had to meet, with the Marines barely clinging to Guadalcanal, the

Navy under fire for concealing losses, and some of the command and staff appointments in doubt.

No one noticed any change in the admiral's outward demeanor at this period. In fact, if anything he became more human, more considerate of his subordinates, and developed to new levels the invincible Texanism which is one of his more engaging minor traits. It is to this date that the story of the photographed sailor is usually referred. At the same time a cactus plot was added to the garden behind his living quarters, and one of the staff caught the admiral teaching his steward how to make Texas cactus jelly. In the field of public business Admiral Ghormley was brought in to become head of the Fourteenth Naval District (Honolulu) where his good strategic brain would be available at headquarters, and was summoned to the conferences there, which were now made part of the daily routine.

Strategic plans normally have to be made about eight months before the guns begin to shoot. It takes that long to assemble the supplies, "fleet in" the ships, conduct the rehearsals. By January, 1943, it was evident that the Japs had given up Guadalcanal for dead and were now only concerned with sealing it off by a ring of island fortresses so that it would be of no offensive use to us. At home Forrestal's shipbuilding program was a success; at least three of the new heavy carriers were afloat with several of the lighter type; the new cruisers and battleships could be counted on. The mechanical means for developing an American offensive strategy were thus reasonably well assured. But what line was it to take?

If it seems to us obvious that the correct direction was up the line of the Solomons, this is at least partly because it was the line successfully taken. The attack on Guadalcanal had been defensive in its implications—it was designed to secure the Australian lifeline against the thrust that remained undelivered only because the Japs were a bare week late in getting Henderson Field ready for use. That line was now secure; and the classical doctrine of American strategy (as revealed by every prewar discussion with the exception of a few heretical items that assumed our fleet would be operating from Singapore) was for a central Pacific offensive. A central Pacific offensive had the obvious advantage of offering a prospect of bringing the major Japanese fleet to battle—something for which the Japs had had a considerable reluctance ever since Midway.

Nimitz plumped for the Solomons line, with the long, slow, costly campaign of beachheads, air battles by day, and destroyer fights by night that it subtended. He had not told his reasons, but in the light of subsequent events there is not the slightest doubt but that he made the correct decision. Our forces had neither the numerical superiority nor the training adequate to conduct a sustained offensive in the central Pacific, and anything less than a sustained drive would have produced more Guadalcanals, with a long struggle to hold each small step gained. Moreover a strong central Pacific offensive, without the groups of carriers that battered down the Japanese land-based planes operating from atolls adjacent to any island under attack, would play into the hands of the Japanese defensive system. Carriers in numbers sufficient really to seal off an island against outside air help were not available before the fall of 1943, when Tarawa was taken with the operation covered by carrier raids against the supporting fields in the Marshalls.

It is possible that some of the thinking laid at Nimitz' door really belongs at that of Admiral King, though the latter has continually tended to confine his function to criticism (in the sense of revision and approval) of proposals put forward from Cincpac. It is certain that a good deal of the planning, particularly on the technical side, came from the new officer brought in to head the staff in the spring of 1943. This was "Sock" McMorris, Charles H. He had come up rapidly; had been only a captain in charge of the *San Francisco* during the Cape Esperance battle, then had got his stars and the appointment to command the Aleutian patrol force, at the head of which he had conducted the little-regarded but truly decisive action off the Komandorskie Islands.

McMorris' memory is prodigious, particularly where figures—tons, dates, distances—are concerned; and in a few of those brief conversations during the courtesy calls Nimitz found him possessed of a remarkable ability of seeing his way through a tangled web of such figures to an over-all evaluation of a position. This was the man Nimitz needed to head his staff in the complex type of war now opening.

It involved finding another place for Spruance; and that place was at sea, as the head of Task Force 58, which conquered the Marianas and fought the first battle of the Philippine Sea. A flood of light is thrown on Nimitz and his methods, on the daily conferences and official calls, on his work as a "specialist in human reactions," by a comment made at this time by one of the officers at headquarters. "Yes, the admiral thinks it's all right to send Raymond out now. He's got him to the point where they think and talk just alike."

It is also noteworthy that during the period of the first Philippine sea battle, when the question still hung in the balance of what would happen when the great Japanese air attack came roaring in, and whether the Marines would be able to maintain themselves at Nafutan Point without the immediate support of the ships, Nimitz went outside his office as usual to relieve his nervousness by shooting on the pistol range. But this time it was a challenge match with one of the junior officers. He fired slowly, laughing and kidding his companion whenever the latter drew a pair of Maggie's drawers. Spruance was in command of the ships.

V

The process that had begun on the bleak last day of 1941 was by this time practically complete. The fleet was rebuilt. The mechanical and statistical advance of the U. S. Navy during the war has been noticed fairly often, with accompanying graphs. What has generally escaped attention is that there has been a moral and technical advance of no less importance since the days when an officer looking over the news from Pearl Harbor could remark, "This would never have happened to the Atlantic Fleet," and an Argentine paper could say that "The British Navy is skillful, the German thorough, and the American—photogenic." For this development in the Pacific Fleet Chester W. Nimitz must receive the credit, as he would have to bear the blame if it had not taken place.

This is by no means to suggest that he remained the prime mover unmoved. He has changed a good deal, in spite of having one of those quietly dominating Teutonic personalities which is perhaps best illustrated by an anecdote from his high school days, when he insisted to his teacher that four of the answers in the back of the arithmetic book were wrong. (They were.)

The change is partly physical. The fleet surgeon, with whom he and Admiral McMorris share living quarters, is inclined to frown on the stiff game of tennis Nimitz likes to play, and his exercise mainly consists of a long walk before a seven-thirty breakfast. The exception is when a very private conference with a single individual is toward; it is normally held on the horseshoe court at Makalapa Drive, well clear of anything that might shadow eavesdroppers. The admiral has to watch a waistline that tends to grow under the admiring ministrations of his Filipino cook, an ardent but not very successful amateur taxidermist who keeps the place full of bird skins.

There are changes in outlook as well, of course. Navy men generally are positive, self-assured, given to vigorous snap judgments—the natural product of an existence cloistered round by orders and regulations as sharply definite as stone walls, allowing exactly so much liberty of action. It is possible that the Nimitz of Bunav differed from this pattern, but the evidence is not satisfactory. The Nimitz of Pearl Harbor certainly departs from the norm in the direction of flexibility and an effort to understand causes—which is to say that constant contact with the best minds of the Navy has left him less sure of things than are his juniors.

And for that matter, contact with the best minds of the enemy across the tips of the engaged swords. It is the admiral's habit, as it is the habit of every good military man, to try to anticipate the enemy's move by imagining himself in their position and, with the aid of information about their observed movements, figuring out what he would do. The process paid rich dividends in the Coral Sea battle (as a mere matter of strategy, the policy of sending so large a proportion of our then slender sea strength so far from base was exceeding bold, no matter what information Nimitz had); and at Midway (where the move through the central Pacific might well have been the feint and that toward Alaska the main attack).

But after the decisive November battles off Guadalcanal, noncomprehension began to set in. "I don't know exactly what I'd do in their situation, but I wouldn't do that," Nimitz confessed frankly. For something like eight months the campaign in the upper Solomons was a gigantic game of bluff in which the Japanese again and again failed to strike with their superior forces. The admiral had established a moral superiority over them.

To an outside observer it would look as though the only thing he did not understand was that he *had* achieved this superiority; that he could not believe any naval men would so abandon themselves to the substitution of stratagem for strategy all along the line. But the result was that Nimitz began an effort to get at the Japanese thought process. He reads a good deal before going to bed, very rapidly, absorbing a book a night with ease. Now his reading was directed toward everything he could lay his hands on about the Japanese, from Lafcadio Hearn to *Off Port Arthur on a Destroyer*. With the aid of Admiral McMorris, whose abilities make him peculiarly useful in a case like this, some remarkable conclusions were reached.

One of these was that the Japanese commanders on the firing line, by the very conditions under which their state has so nearly achieved the totalitarian ideal, were required to report success in any mission they undertook; and that their own upper ranks of command were required to believe these reports even when they contradicted rational reasoning. Out of these conclusions grew the special movements of strategy that led from Saipan to the second battle of the Philippine Sea, with its disaster to an entire navy for the only time in this war. But that is another story.

III. THE SHIPS

Fighting Machine

THERE was a race between the New York and Philadelphia navy yards over their respective new battleships and New York won it in 1941 with their *North Carolina,* so she became the name ship of the class, drawing all the photographers and big shots aboard for the trials and hullabaloo. The *Washington* went into commission in a comparatively businesslike manner. She was under a businesslike captain, Howard H. J. Benson, who had put in quite a bit of time in administrative posts and at the Academy. Her people settled down quietly to learn about each other and their ship.

As one of the first two new battleships built in twenty years she was, of course, a prize assignment of the service. Officers and crew alike were conscious of having been hand-picked for ability. They were Old Navy right down to the water tenders and radio strikers, so they knew what to expect. No surprise to them that the skipper should turn out to be a sundowner who held white-glove inspections every Saturday, put a man on report for wearing his hat on the back of his head, and made the engine room staff change from dungarees to undress blues before going to chow. That was the price one could expect to pay for belonging to the proudest ship in the service. And the exec, W. P. O. Clark, was all right—a big, husky guy with no nonsense about him, who allowed any common sailor to approach him on deck when there was something on the latter's mind. In a good many ships, especially the larger ones, a chit from a division officer is required before a petition can be presented.

They had a measure on Clark's competence early, the first time the ship tried to take in planes. There was a seaway on; the aviator did not like the look of things and kept giving her the gun again just before he was due to come in, while the ship rolled through the waves, switching her tail back and forth like a burlesque queen in the effort to make a lee for him. Clark seized a megaphone (no loud hailers for him!), ran aft to the catapults, and with three shouted orders had the

63

plane aboard. The incident gave the crew an idea he would take them a long way. When they had got back to Norfolk and the *North Carolina* came in to join them for a shakedown run to the southern drill grounds, the *Washington's* band came out on deck and played "Here Comes the Showboat" at her, and Commander Clark grinned.

The crew approached that period of test in any case with a spirit of fine disdain for the exterior world and its thoughts. While the *Washington* was lying in Philadelphia, fitting for sea, the British *Resolution* had come in for repair—an old ship that had seen two wars, with an old, competent crew. They were invited over to see the *Washington's* movies and to sample her excellent food (she already bore the name of a good chow ship) ; and the American sailors decided at a series of unofficial meetings that since the British did not draw high pay they should be treated to beer in the local bars whenever there was liberty.

This effort at fraternization was a signal failure. The times were out of joint; Greece had just gone down and Crete been taken from the air with frightful losses to the British Navy, Rommel had driven Wavell back to Egypt, England stood alone against Europe in arms, and Englishmen had an enraged consciousness that they were fighting our battle while we hung back. "Nice ship you have here but what are you going to do with her?" they asked airily, or snickered over the white-glove inspections so foreign to their own customs. There were incidents—brawls and the intervention of the shore patrol—and it was reported that one of His Majesty's jollies was returned to his ship in a state of alcoholic insensibility with "God Bless America" tattooed on his chest after an evening devoted to expressing exactly the opposite sentiment.

That had the merit of humor, but most of it was not humorous— black eyes and pants pulled off and the *Washington* going out for her practices in a mood of by God, we'll show 'em.

The engineering department, necessarily the first to get organized aboard a new ship, had already shown them at the time of the trials. The ship reached a speed well above the designed maximum (how much above is still a state secret after four years) from the new super-heated boilers. Commander Strothers (who had succeeded the much-beloved Commander Murphy) had that department; he was an Academy man who had left the service but had come back in for the emergency, and was much liked by his staff for his habit of letting them alone except in connection with their work. Now it became the turn of Communications and Gunnery; and of all departments in the ship the latter had the most to do, not merely because a battleship lives or dies by its gunnery, but also because everything was new.

The nine 16-inch guns that formed the ship's main battery were a new pattern, with a heavier shell than a 16-inch had fired before, higher elevation, and a host of annexed problems; for if the gun goes higher at the muzzle, it must descend lower into the bowels of the turret at the breech, with awkward angles for loading. The secondary batteries were the famous Navy 5-inch .38, probably the best anti-aircraft gun in the world, but they had never before been used in twin turrets or in such concentration, which offered many chances for mixup in the fire control. The light AA guns were .50-caliber machine guns scattered around the deck and four quads of the Navy's new 1.1, still in the experimental stage.

The boss of this equipment was Commander Harvey Walsh, one of the key personalities aboard. The gun crews thought he was the next thing to the Archangel Gabriel; he was easy to approach and he always had a word for them or an hour for their problems. He impressed other officers as rather cold and aloof at the time, but this may merely have been because he was particularly busy and not at all happy about the solution the ship presented to the problem of antiaircraft gunnery.

He did not agree with the opinion then current about air attack—expressed in the most authoritative of all naval publications—that aircraft could accomplish nothing more against heavy ships than to slow them up for a subsequent action with the guns; and quite early in the drill period he became convined that the 1.1 was a dud. It had too many jams; he was lucky when he could keep one barrel firing out of a quadruple mount, and he was sure that this was not the fault of his maintenance men, the gunners' mates, because he had spent enough time with them to know they were neither incompetent nor lying down on the job. His solution of the problem was to make the 5-inch guns so efficient that attacking planes would never get in; and in Captain Joe Platt, officer of the Marines who manned the starboard 5-inch battery, he was lucky enough to find a man who shared his ideas.

II

So the *Washington* finished her shakedowns with a "Well done" from the admiral; came back to Norfolk and settled down for the normal period of yard overhaul, the period in which all the mechanical gadgets that have failed to work well are repaired or replaced. Seventy-two-hour liberties were granted.

Norfolk is the world's worst liberty port, not excepting the spic places in the Caribbean. Except for those who had beat it out of town to see relatives in Virginia or North Carolina, the *Washingtons* were wandering rather disconsolately around Norfolk in a tight little group when a man in a green suit came up and told them the Japs were attacking Pearl Harbor. That was good for a laugh; they were wondering what Orson Welles would think of next when a siren began to blow somewhere and then augmented shore patrols came through the streets, calling liberty men back to the ships in harbor. It is significant of the state *Washington* had already reached that none of these parties came from her. Commander Clark had contented himself with sending a sheaf of telegrams to the men at a distance, perfectly satisfied that the rest would come aboard under their own power. He was not disappointed.

That night the ship moved out into the stream and at dawn went to general quarters. All the planes on the airfield were suddenly warmed up for an early take-off and it made a terrific racket. It was thought, not improbably, a German air raid, and fighting ammunition was gotten up into the ready boxes. A few days later the United States battleship *Washington* steamed out to sea and into the war.

Not into the shooting part of the war just yet. It normally takes six months of shakedown to make a battleship an effective fighting unit, and the fact that the process cannot be hurried is proved by the performance of inexperienced ships in action, like the British *Tiger* at Dogger Bank in 1915. Moreover, there was some question about what to do with the *Washington* and *North Carolina* now that we had them. The task force idea of mixed squadrons with a pair of such big bruisers at their core was being talked about but had not yet been tried. Everybody was still thinking in terms of the old-fashioned battle line with long queues of ships pounding each other. These new ships did not fit into any battle line we could compose; their great speed and the enormous range of their guns would be wasted working with our older ships. Of course, a real emergency . . .

But by February it was clear there would be no immediate emergency call for battleships from the Pacific. The Japs were fanning out below the equator, and in the Marshalls our cruiser-carrier forces had given so good an account of themselves that battleship stiffening was unnecessary. On the other hand there was a real emergency in the North Atlantic, where the Germans had their huge *Tirpitz* among the Norwegian fjords, backed by a pair of pocket battleships and the same number of heavy cruisers, with *Scharnhorst* and *Gneisenau* (that had lately run the Channel) soon to come. Given the German propensity for using such ships as heavy raiders, it was important to cover the Murmansk convoy routes with vessels that could both run fast and hit hard. The *Washington* was ordered to Scapa Flow as flag of a United States squadron under Admiral Giffen, "Alkali Ike, the toughest cowboy that ever rode a bucking warship."

She also had a new exec, Commander Arthur Ayrault, moved up from navigator, a smallish blond man, who did not immediately affect the general organization. This organization had proceeded with considerable smoothness under Clark's leadership to an era of good feeling of a kind rarely seen on a warship and difficult to define in precise terms. One of her petty officers put it: "You never saw a requisition aboard that ship. If you wanted a wiring job done, for instance, you called the electricians and they'd get the parts from the storeroom and if there had to be any paper work they'd all fix it up later."

The method is rare, not aboard warships alone. Part of this integration was undoubtedly due to the fact that the crew felt themselves a unit against an inimical cosmos. There was nothing to do ashore at Scapa but drink warm beer at the canteen and nobody could get used to it. (The Marines were an exception; they hobnobbed with their opposite numbers in the British service and worked out an exchange of cigarettes against tots of issue rum.) A little of the legacy of Philadelphia was still hanging around. When British sailors came aboard they were a little apt to talk about luxury liners and to be answered with remarks about cleaning ship; nor could our allies understand how any naval officer who respected his cloth could go fishing on equal terms with enlisted men, as a couple of *Washington* lieutenant commanders did up in Iceland.

The point about all this is that it was not allowed to become a mere contribution to interallied bad feeling, but was used by both Captain Benson and Walsh of the gunnery department to promote the efficiency of the fighting instrument. A battleship, they never tired of pointing out both directly and in the ship's paper *Wash Rag,* answers all remarks with her artillery; there is no other reply. The climax came on one of the Iceland runs, during maneuvers with the Home Fleet. A plane came down the line towing a sleeve target. The British battleships in turn fired at it in a perfect passion of flame; our people were astonished at the speed with which their Bofors 40s would put out shell. The sleeve target reached the *Washington* and Commander Walsh's 5-inch: "We just put five bursts ahead of the target like we always would, then five astern of it and then shot it down. The British stood there with their mouths open and after that they would believe anything of us."

So they fired their guns and chased the shy *Tirpitz* through the freezing mists that left no one comfortable aboard but the engine room staff. The ship's press got out certificates for all hands to prove they had crossed the Arctic Circle; there were submarine alarms night and morning with general quarters; once out ahead there was a collision in the fog, a frightful noise that made men below think the ship had been torpedoed, and the next minute sailors were drifting by through the icy water, clinging to furniture and gratings. There was a rush to the sides; some began to yell insults, thinking a German sub had been run down and this was her crew, but others had sense enough to note that the uniforms were British and to throw life-saving equipment. Captain Benson took a dim view of the occurrence; the *Wash Rag* next day pointed out that there had been confusion unbefitting an American warship, and scuttlebutt began to spread that the ship was being ordered home.

It was true. As she slid down through the mists argument blazed up around the decks as to whether she was a lucky ship or not. A happy ship, yes, but she was named *Washington*; and that name, though more frequently borne than any other in the history of the U. S. Navy, had never been taken into action by any ship since Benedict Arnold's galley went down on Lake Champlain in the Revolution, and that one was not properly a naval vessel at all, being manned by soldiers. Often a bridesmaid, never a bride, was the record of the warships *Washington*; and the crew of this one had thus far shared the experience, hearing the vast echoes of Midway only through the radio from halfway round the world.

One blowing March night they had indeed worked up to full speed off the Norway coast with the loudspeakers announcing, "We will probably meet *Tirpitz* at 0400"; but at 0300 speed slacked off and the word went through the ship that the British admiral in charge was turning back, since the course they were on would bring them into range of land-based bombers with the dawn. Scuttlebutt had it that Alkali Ike Giffen requested permission to push on with the *Washington* alone, but they wouldn't let him, and that was bad luck. In opposition to it there was only the remark made by the oldest chief aboard when she went into commission—he could tell by the way her flag broke out she was going to be a lucky ship.

III

Sailors are permitted within certain limits to swap jobs with others of similar rate; a second-class storekeeper ashore may change places with one on a destroyer. When the *Washington* came in to have her light antiaircraft armament revised, Captain Benson observed with perfectly justified satisfaction that he was bombarded with applications from men on the shore establishment who wanted to exchange into his ship, and that there were no takers. There were naturally some changes aboard, however; the new guns meant new men, which produced some difficulty in the living spaces and line-ups at the gedunk stand; and Benson himself was shifted to make room for Captain Glenn Davis.

Captain Davis was putting to sea after two and a half years in the Bureau of Ordnance. It is a type of change frequently made in the Navy: officers coming out from desks where they have absorbed the latest strategic doctrine to take over a ship that has already become a going concern and acquired the general tactical doctrine that develops so rapidly in war experience. For the crew the change required major readjustments of attitude. They discovered that instead of the stiff, rather formal and Old Navy Benson, they had a skipper who took a vivid interest in them as personalities, poked into the mess spaces and tasted the contents of kettles, abolished the rule about wearing blues topside, was particularly generous with leave and liberty.

This in turn reacted into the exec's department. Ayrault had generally been forced to struggle against an entirely deceptive appearance of frailty and for this reason he probably drew the lines a little tighter than he otherwise would have. Under the easygoing Davis this check-reining produced some conflicts of personality which came to a head in the case of Steamer Stimpson's beard. Ayrault had conducted a purge on beards aboard the ship greatly encouraged by Admiral Giffen, who had all the normal westerner's dislike of facial hair. (The growing of beards had in fact been spreading toward the fantastic on the cruise north.) Stimpson was a turret captain, very efficient. He had a honey of a beard, a chest-protector; when Ayrault made him cut it off he got himself photographed first and persuaded the ship's service store to sell the pictures at a dime apiece to anyone who wanted a souvenir of what a real navy man looked like. Ayrault stopped the sale; Stimpson bought the entire stock and distributed them to all hands for free. Thus Stimpson scored a point, but the ship scored a point too, for it was felt that a desirable immunity to exterior influence had been demonstrated.

The matter has more importance than is apparent at a glance. This was the summer of '42; and Commander Walsh had still a lot of work to do on those new guns before they could be considered efficient. We were being told, that summer, that the route to victory lay through the skies and a good many of us were believing it; Pearl Harbor and the *Prince of Wales* had demonstrated the uselessness of battleships. When such a doctrine runs through the heads of the service you get a change in strategic plan; but when it reaches the men in the ranks what you get is military paralysis. In the Leyte campaign Japanese aviators got to flipping over on their backs and bailing out before anyone fired at them; and everyone remembers what happened to the Italian Navy when it became convinced its efforts were useless.

The admiral who came aboard did not believe it was all up with battleships either. They had had admirals aboard before—booming Alkali Ike and for a time the strange, severe, reserved Wilcox, who liked to slip away from his marine guard and stand all alone at night in the light lock of the navigation bridge, meditating in solitude some problem of his own. But both these belonged to conventional types; behaved according to fashions established for admirals. Willis Augustus Lee was a new specimen; smallish, always with a good morning for the bridge gang, not thinking it beneath his dignity to tell them jokes or to listen to theirs. At sea he would pace back and forth whistling to himself while Captain Davis placidly munched a cud of gum, or lie on the lounge in his cabin, reading from a pile of paper-backed novels with gaudy covers. When business was toward he was most often found in Plot or CIC (Combat Intelligence Center). For gunnery was his passion; he did not at all agree with the procedure of certain captains who tend to put their less good men in the turrets, where their defects will be covered by the movements of a co-ordinated mass, saving those with keen mechanical aptitude for departments like Communications, which will make the ship look good in competitions.

Admiral Lee was the only man who could draw the aloof Walsh out of his retirements; and with the admiral leading there developed aboard a kind of conversational circle—subject, gunnery—somewhat as a group of young intellectual professors at a university might assemble daily to examine in fascinating detail the technique of fiction or the theory of the engineering state. If they did not meet, Lee would pop out of his cabin and drag them in; he was always doing it.

Walsh was a leader in that circle and so was his assistant, Lieutenant Commander Ed Hooper, prodigiously dynamic, explosive and sometimes peppery, forever in a hurry to get somewhere, who approached gunnery problems from a standpoint of exalted analytical mathematics. After a shoot Hooper would work on graphs, formulae, and functions far into the night. His conversation was so loaded with the calculi and Abelian equations that sometimes Walsh and Captain Davis would begin to look slightly helpless and Lieutenant Commander Roy Thompson of Lee's staff, who was enough of an algorist to understand and make clear what was going on, would smile and translate into practical terms.

When the conversation reached these grounds two others came in strongly—Joe Platt of the Marines and Lieutenant Commander Henry Seeley, the air defense man. Big, blond, imperturbable, Academy, but with his feet thoroughly on the ground, Seeley was one of those archetypical naval officers of whom it has been said that if you want somebody to build a bridge or feed a hundred thousand people, you could not do better; if you want someone to discuss the idea of free will, you could not do worse. He was as nearly as possible the antithesis of both Walsh, the specialist in human relations, and Hooper, with his fine theoretical brain. But the three meshed together as perfectly as a system of well-ordered gears—under the presidency of Admiral Lee with his small smile and his belief that it was the province of young men to produce ideas, of the leaders to collate, to criticize, and to employ them. "He was a man who never went by the book but rather checked up on it to see if it was right"; he was always ordering gunnery practices under odd conditions, turrets firing with relief crews or other freakishness that might occur in the emergency of battle.

IV

This was the battleship *Washington* when she went through the Canal, with a false name painted under her stern for the benefit of any spies that might be peeking, and down into the South Pacific where it was too hot to play baseball ashore. At the end of October, 1942, Ayrault was promoted out of the ship and Commander Walsh moved into his slot as exec amid general pleasure. The news of the Battle of Santa Cruz floated in, with its proof that a modern battleship was so far from helpless under air attack that she could take care of companions as well as herself; and there was rejoicing in the gunnery group that met in the admiral's sitting room. Halsey was in command, the Japs were pressing close, there was every prospect of action; and at the base they gazed with envious curiosity at the battleship *South Dakota*, with the white star of a Jap bomb hit on her No. 2 turret, and her bandaged captain.

All that Halsey had, to meet the greatest of all the Jap thrusts for the recovery of Guadalcanal, was those two battleships and the carrier *Enterprise*, with an assortment of cruisers and destroyers. The enemy preparations began to reach the assembly stage at the beginning of November. There was a supply problem on Guadalcanal, where the fighting had been intense and promised to be more so; and all plans had the proviso that *Enterprise* could not again be used in close action (as at Santa Cruz), for she was our last carrier. Admiral Richmond Kelly Turner was in over-all charge of the operation of supplying the land forces on the bloody island; all else hinged on that issue. He planned that the light ships should take the convoys in, and he beat the Japs to the punch by getting the first shipment to Guadal on November 11, when there was a violent air battle.

On the twelfth the big American convoy arrived at Guadal, with Rear Admiral Dan Callaghan and his cruisers. Thirty-two Jap torpedo planes tried a surprise attack on it in the afternoon and were all shot down. But at the same time our scouts picked up the news that a heavy Jap force was moving down from Rabaul. It is not clear whether our fliers got an accurate count on the Jap ships; but our intent was that Callaghan should fight a damaging delaying night action, while *Enterprise,* lying well out to the south with her guardian battleships, should strike at the cripples in the morning with all the force of her air groups.

That night Callaghan saved Guadalcanal in a fight against a Japanese force that was four times his strength and was headed by battleships; but he was killed and his cruiser squadron was wrecked past the possibility of any immediate action. On the *Washington* they heard about it and made bitter comment over using their own iron colossus as an antiaircraft cruiser. But *Enterprise* did get her planes off with the day, and they helped the Henderson Field fliers mightily in sending down the Jap battleship that Callaghan had hurt.

Enterprise and her escort turned south again in the afternoon to keep beyond range of shore-based Jap bombers. During that night the Japs made fallacy of our original plan by coming down with an entirely fresh force to give Guadalcanal the worst shelling it had ever received. Meanwhile our scouts over the Shortland Islands must have been reporting that a group of enemy transports had been assembled under cover of still another force of Jap battleships. The enemy had lost a squadron to Callaghan; very well, he would put in another, accept whatever damage was necessary, but get that island.

So in spite of the danger of rocks, shoals, and torpedoes among the narrow passages, our battleships would have to be put in by night; they were all we had left to meet the new Jap thrust. On the thirteenth, then, *Washington* and *South Dakota* dropped *Enterprise* astern and started the run up to Guadal.

Captain Davis called a conference of gunnery officers to say they were going in, remarking that the safety of the ship was in the hands of the 5-inch battery men, who alone could keep at a distance the fast Japanese destroyers which used their torpedoes so well. It became clear the *Washington* could not reach the Slot—the passage through the islands—in time for that night's show; and with the day, the day of the fourteenth, the radio began to carry the whoops of the Henderson Field fliers as they fell on the Jap transports in their slaughtering eight-hour attack. News of it spread along the decks; as the ship eased up to the offing of Guadalcanal for a night run in, the best opinion aboard held that the enemy would turn back and that this would be a bombardment mission.

But the enemy did not turn back. They were there, on the theory that if even the remnants of this force of theirs broke through they would be enough to win the island. They had their own air scouts; they must have seen the wreck of Callaghan's squadron moving out, minus *Atlanta* and *Juneau*: *San Francisco* all a mess, *Portland* limping from a torpedo hole, hardly any destroyers. They knew, within the terms of wartime information, that we had nothing on the surface with which to oppose their attack. Just after midnight they came down around both flanks of Savo Island, destroyers and leaders in the van, behind them the battleships and the leavings of the transport convoy.

Washington and *South Dakota* had just circled that island, with four of our destroyers out ahead. Up on the bridge of the *Washington* nothing could be seen; down in her magazines the battle circuit spoke—5-inch permission to load, 16-inch load with armor-piercers—and a thrill went through those narrow steel rooms, for the only way of unloading a naval gun is via its muzzle. "Whooee" shouted one of the Negro powder-passers, and turned a handspring.

"Five-inch commence firing," said a voice from the bridge, and out blazed the battery: HIT, HIT, HIT on the first of three Jap flotilla leaders up against the Savo shore, followed by a deeper shock from the *South Dakota* as she opened with her big guns and murdered another Jap flotilla leader in a matter of seconds.

The hit ships flared and went out like flash bulbs. Before their image had died from the eye, a whole group of Jap destroyers with cruisers in the van rushed out from behind the island—six to ten together—for a torpedo attack on our battleships. "You could see the splashes from their cruisers walk up on our destroyers and then one of them [the destroyers] get hit and fall apart," says a man who was forward on the *Washington*. (The lost ship would be the *Walke*.) Another man in the starboard positions saw the flash and felt the shock as Captain Joe Platt's guns lashed out and three of the Jap ships began to burn. Marvelous shooting, incredible shooting!—but the Japs had launched their torpedoes, which came boiling through the water all round the *Washington* as she bucked, twisted, changed speed and direction to avoid them.

Out on the fantail they saw the wreck of the *Walke* come drifting past and dragged a heavy life raft across the deck to throw it over. It struck the water just as the *Washington's* big guns let go with a shock that shook the ship so hard that the men below thought she had been hit, and all the *Walke's* survivors shouted from the water. "There wasn't a single call for help; they were all yelling 'Give it to them!'" one of the fantail men remembers; for all those shells from the *Washington* had gone into a Jap battleship, and she was burning monstrously as the *Washington* poured twelve complete salvos into her, every one a hit. Her return fire went over our ship, "making," said one of the men who heard it, "a sound just like a big train climbing a grade on a snowy night, puff, puff, puff."

"We've got her!" shouted someone over the battle circuit, and down in the magazines the Negro powder men were chanting "You pass it out and we'll pass it up!" as the enemy battleship turned majestically on her side to sink in a red glare of flame. "Fire on the lights, fire on the lights," Commander Walsh was pleading, and they saw he had noticed what everyone else had missed: that from the Jap line a couple of searchlight beams had picked out *South Dakota* and she was being hit. The *Washington's* 16s and 5-inch fired together; the lights went out; there was another change of course— and *Washington* was suddenly alone in a dark ocean, not *South Dakota* nor the Japs nor any other ship near her.

The battle had lasted less than half an hour. The ship did not have a man injured nor a scratch on her paint.

V

The story of a battleship is like that of a love affair, reaching its dazzling honeymoon climax in those few moments of action to which all her own history and a whole lifetime of effort on the part of her officers have been merely the prelude. The postlude is not unlike that of other honeymoons. Details that escape attention at the moment are lovingly recalled and enlarged upon:

"There were twenty-seven of those torpedoes out there."

"Aw, nuts! If there'd been that many one would have hit us."

"We went from twelve knots to flank speed and back down again in five minutes. You know the skipper must be just about the best ship-handler in the world; I don't know yet how he kept us from getting hit with all that stuff flying around."

"Did you see big Tollman? He said he was out on the bridge when the 5-inch went off and he remembered that personnel should shift to protected positions in action, so he went into the con; then the 16-inch went off and he shifted to the wardroom, and then the Jap shells started to come over and he shifted right on down below the armored deck."

There are also the reminders that the world has not been made perfect which crop out after other honeymoons. The first lieutenant beefed about that life raft. He would have to explain its loss to the Bureau of Supplies and Accounts. And when the ship got down to Nouméa, there was the *South Dakota*, pretty much battered around the upper works and already being publicized as "Battleship X." That did not sit too well; the *Washington*'s felt that they had done most of the work and received none of the credit, while the *Sodak* men considered that they had taken all the beating, they were the only ones up to their necks in the fight, and the *Washington* was claiming too much to rank with them. There were some arguments and maybe a few bloody noses; the place was hot and sticky. The New Caledonians, whether natives or colonial French, were not very friendly.

Commander Walsh did his best to relieve the boredom that settled down over the ship like a blanket in the reaction from battle to another regime of training, by organizing as many as three recreation parties a day with beer and a ball game on the beach. A good many of the crew got liberty and conducted their private recreation programs, largely on the lines of trying to get something to drink. A number of the local laundresses were doing a little bootlegging on the side, their staple being cheap Australian champagne, which had to be drunk warm and from the bottle. It was not an exhilarating beverage under any circumstances, and it did not help very much to relieve the tedium. The majority of the men were glad enough when the ship's patrol runs carried her over to the New Hebrides, where at least one could go hunting for wild hogs, bush chickens, and the small gray doves that were so hard to hit.

Patrol, training; training, patrol. *South Dakota* went home for her repairs, and another of the new battleships replaced her, and it was gradually borne in upon the command that the battle off Guadalcanal had been decisive; the Japs would not again be drawn into a position where they would have to shoot it out with our battleships. Alkali Ike Giffen came down to take a cruiser command and was cheered when he visited the ship, which made him blush; the move to the upper Solomons began, and light craft entered their period of nightmare slugging in the close waters of the Slot where *Washington* could take no part; and in April she went up to Pearl Harbor to get some new 20-millimeter guns.

Also to get a new captain. The beloved Davis had received his admiral's stars. He was replaced by Captain James B. Maher, known as "Silent Jim" in the fleet from his habit of never speaking in anything less than a full-gale roar. Maher had been skipper of the antiaircraft cruiser *San Juan*, which shot down so many Jap planes that her bridge looked like a polka-dot dress with the rising sun flags painted all over it.

Not unnaturally Maher thought that although his new command was a marvel with the big guns it would be possible to improve her antiaircraft work; but when at practice he would suggest to Hooper (now gunnery officer) that Seeley up in AA plot do this or that, the former would remark, "Let's let him go ahead; I think he's on the right track." This demonstration of solidarity was astonishing; one does not usually contradict a captain's suggestions in the Navy. Still more unusual was the fact that man after man, drafted out to go back to the States as part of a nucleus crew for new construction, came up with a request to stay aboard, though the transfer meant a spot of leave. Captain Maher began to realize that he had drawn first prize; and on their side the men of the *Washington* "felt we had lost damn little when we got him as Davis' relief."

Maher led the ship through a long new series of exercises—necessary because the whole character of the war had changed after the foothold on Bougainville was won. We had now the means for the great central Pacific drive which began at Tarawa and Makin. The battleships, which had been the last line of defense, were to lead as the first wave of attack. Those aboard got an inkling of what this new war would be like when they came up to the rendezvous for the Gilberts operation and saw eleven carriers come over the sea rim. No one on the ship had ever seen more than three together and many had not seen even one in the whole period of their naval service. Three carriers detached themselves from the group and ran up with *Washington* and another battleship to cruise south of the Marshalls as a buffer against Jap efforts to interfere with the landings, whether this interference came by sea or air.

Actually the Jap counterattack came by air, just as the quick red tropic twilight was changing to the night of D-Day, with the radio bringing news of the trouble the Marines were having on Tarawa. A string of scout planes first, that dropped float flares to outline our fleet; then a long stream of torpedo-carrying Bettys, coming in as though shot out of a hose, low down to the water, the most difficult position to hit. Our air patrol was under the leadership of Butch O'Hare, who had trained them in a novel tactic of his own. His men fell on the Bettys; the sky along the horizon was briefly streaked with flame and tracer; the destroyers' guns barked out at the edge of the formation; and then there were only three of the Japanese planes left, scudding in low from different angles toward the battleship against the black background of the sky.

The *Washington's* guns fired so rapidly that aboard one of the carriers they thought she had been hit and was burning; but it was not the *Washington* that burned, it was one of the torpedo planes collapsing in a pyramid of flame that lit up the sea for miles, while of the other two nothing again was ever seen. "Well done," signaled the carrier admiral; on the *Washington* they went wild, popping out of doors and cheering "just like somebody had hit a home run in a ball park. It was lucky the Japs didn't have anything to follow up that attack with; we were all too busy congratulating ourselves to pay any attention to them."

That set the key of the campaign. For the next eleven nights running there was a Jap torpedo attack at twilight, always the same— the rising of dark, the air battle on the rim, the swift rush of Japs in threes or fours, a crash of fire from the battleship, and one or two Bettys burning on the water. It would be about the seventh night, after the men had had their supper, that Commander Walsh looked down the deck and remarked pridefully, "Guess we won't have to sound general quarters tonight, Captain"; and Maher, following his glance, saw that all over the ship every man was in position without orders, some having a final cigarette before the orders to douse lights, some oiling their pieces or checking the ready boxes.

Suppose we leave them and their ship there, preparing for battle in supreme confidence of themselves and their instrument, knowing that no carrier or other vessel under battleship protection was ever hit by bomb or torpedo. The *Washington* was to have other adventures, not a few—the great bombardment of Nauru, when the Japs were treated to a surprise breakfast of 16-inch shell; the attack on Kwajalein; the fighting in the Marianas, where all those enemy planes were shot down; the war in the islands to the west. But by now nothing in all this was new for her or her men. She had become an entity which would survive remarkably within its bounds of character through all changes of personnel; as much an entity as a club or a city. Almost alone among the ships of the Navy she has never had a nickname; she has had few courts-martial; she remains a ship where requisitions are seldom necessary. As one of her ex-officers put it: "Not a temperamental ship like the *Sodak*, with a lot of interesting characters, nor a madhouse like some others, but a quiet, businesslike fighting machine."

CA 25

FAHEY, the Burke and Debrett of the American Navy, describes her as "our earliest treaty cruiser," with a tonnage of 9100, 32.7 knot speed, ten 8-inch and eight 5-inch guns, but this is only about as much as a peerage gives on the life and personality of an individual. When her keel was laid at New York Ship's Camden Yard on June 9,

1927, she'd already been on the designing boards for over three years and authorized for more than a twelve-month. She and her sister *Pensacola* were the first warships to be built for the Navy since the Wilson fleet went down the drain at that Washington Conference which did so much to convince the Japs that they could and should build up to a successful Pacific war. About the time *Salt Lake City's* keel was laid the famous secret memo told Jap naval officers that they would thenceforth consider themselves at war with the United States and the cruisers laid down at Kure that year were the first of the cheats, with tonnages only vaguely related to those reported to the other treaty signatories.

This country was still in the "era of beautiful nonsense" when we were never going to have any more wars, so when it was reported that the four new Jap cruisers were to mount twelve 8-inch guns there was all the time in the world to send our pair back to the mold loft and see whether American designers too could not get that many on the tonnage, the wise tradition of the American Navy since the days of the frigate *Constitution* being that our captains shall never be sent into an action out-gunned by the enemy. The designers could not make twelve guns on the ten thousand-ton limit. Indeed they had so much difficulty getting ten aboard that *Salt Lake City* was criticized in Congress as crowded, uncomfortable, all but un-stable.

This was not all, as her first crew found after the champagne and ceremonies were over and they got her out to sea. In the effort to save weight the upper decks had been carried aft only far enough to enclose No. 1 funnel, then picked up again some distance beyond around No. 2 stack, leaving a kind of well between, where the free-board was not much more than that of a destroyer. When she got into a swell waves washed through this, pretty effectively isolated the two sections of the ship; and what was a good deal worse for the feelings of the crew, the arrangement gave her a curious broken-down look that caused inextinguishable laughter when she joined the fleet and brought her the name of *Swayback Maru.*

Still a ship; a new ship, the first in seven years, very beautiful floating down the Delaware in her dress of white paint, where her likeness was taken to be published in the Navy's official magazine over the caption At Last! (Japan already had ten of those heavy cruisers afloat and two more ready for the launch.) She ran her trials, fired her guns and Captain F. L. Oliver settled down to find out what he had.

He found he had a good deal of an experimental job. A wet ship, as has been noted; one whose peculiar turret arrangement with three guns over two made problems for the gunnery officer (it is almost impossible to synchronize the firing of the two types of turret); one that was not capable of holding speed with the light cruisers, and one which steered badly. Later in the game, when the new heavies of the *Northampton* class came out and *Salt Lake* was formed into a division with her sister and *Chester* of the new type, both the others hated having a position behind her in a column at maneuvers. She was always sheering out or performing some other unpredictable antic.

By the time the *Astorias* joined the fleet, the pride of the Navy and the best heavy cruisers built anywhere till the treaty restrictions came off, *Salt Lake* was definitely rated as belonging to the second string. Not a good gunnery ship, at the bottom of the fleet in it by 1939; always standing somewhere around ninth and tenth among the heavy cruisers in engineering performance and a step or two higher in Communications. What really held her from higher consideration in the eyes of the admirals, however, was the fact that while she had been gracefully growing old they had learned a good deal more about heavy cruisers and their place in the fleet. In the light of experience the *Slick City* (as her crew called her) belonged to the earliest type of Washington Treaty freaks. Every naval nation possessed one or two; they were called the "paper-clads" for their almost complete lack of armor. It was predicted freely that the first time they got hit by anything heavier than a rifle bullet the crew would find themselves swimming.

Not that it mattered. In '41, which is when the story really opens with Captain Ellis M. Zacharias taking command at the Mare Island Navy Yard, where she had been undergoing a refit, the cruiser *Salt Lake City* was only two years from "replacement age" under the terms of the treaty. Nobody really expected her to be replaced with Europe ablaze and the Japs executing their double shuffle around the Pacific—she was a dowager, destined for duties that took account of her age and infirmities. In the latest face-lifting operation the tripod mast aft had come down to make room for a heavy antiaircraft tower which gave her more than ever a swayback appearance; in an earlier one they had given her some extra 5-inch and taken away her torpedo tubes. She had acquired the silver service presented by the state to the old battleship *Utah* when the latter was converted into a target vessel, and kept it in a glass case in the wardroom where the leg of the foremast went through, much admired and never used. She had also acquired a whole set of little traditions and objects peculiar to herself, like the special steel ladder under turret No. 3, put there because the turret officer fell through the hatch one night off Waikiki and broke his behind.

II

Captain Zacharias took command and began to shake the old lady out of her settled ways. He was a tall man, so broad in the shoulders as to look somewhat out of proportion; very ambitious and talkative, good-looking; had lived long in Japan and was expert in the language. He had spoken over the radio there and the station got letters praising the singular purity of his diction, written under the impression that he was a local literary man. As usual there had been a good many changes among the crew during the period in dock, experienced petty officers drawn off as nucleus men for the new destroyer construction and replaced (since the national emergency had been proclaimed) with reserves.

The latter amounted to some 25 per cent of the total complement and the skipper was perfectly aware that in so old a ship with many men aboard since first commissioning, the natural tendency was to give these "feather merchants" the works pretty heavily. He addressed all hands by loudspeaker while Golden Gate still loomed astern. A quarter of the crew were reserves (he said); they might not like it but must remember that the time was surely coming when the reserves would be 90 per cent. It was required of every man not only to perform his duties but to train others to perform them and train himself to teach still others. They were all amateurs together.

The speech was pretty well received, gaining impetus as the voyage went on. It was a four-month trip and for Old Navy men conditioned to easy conditions of peace a hard one—all the way down to Rabaul and Torres Strait, familiarizing themselves with the region and covering the movement of a Dutch ship whose most important cargo was a number of pilots to join the Flying Tigers in China. It was summer and below the equator abominably hot in the ship's never very adequate living spaces, rendered more crowded still by the men who had been added to handle the extra antiaircraft equipment.

The exec, Commander Noble, developed a heavy case of asthma and could not sleep, becoming in spite of himself bad-tempered and capricious. He would order a thing done, forget what he had ordered and then make the fur fly. Provisions ran down to monotony; the ship was continually on Condition III, which none of them had known before except for brief periods during maneuvers—all in all a fairly tough plate of beans to chew. But the new men took it all as a part of the naval life where they had expected hardship, the old ones were ashamed to be behind them, and there was no question about Skipper Zach's heart being in the right place. He would much rather say, "Don't do it again" than stop a man's liberty when he came to mast and was always prowling about below, figuring out how something might be done better. Especially in the engine spaces, where notable improvements were being achieved under Engineer Officer Kobey. When *Salt Lake* reached Long Beach in October the results of the general engineering competition were totted up, it was discovered she had jumped from ninth place to first among the heavy cruisers of the fleet and was entitled to wear on her stack the greatly coveted E for efficiency.

She did not sport the decoration long. Hardly had leave parties shoved off when news came through that Hideki Tojo was premier of Japan. There were some people caught napping by that event and by what followed it, but Ellis Zacharias knew enough about people over there to be aware that it signified the Japanese militarists had thrown their caps over the windmill. He interpreted in the strictest sense the alert that presently came through from the department. All leaves were canceled (some *Salt Lake* men had to fly back from the East coast at their own expense), liberties were restricted to fifty miles from dockside and the ship, though technically having a recreation period, was placed on twelve hours' notice for sailing. It is perhaps significant that there was comparatively little grousing. "The old man knows too damn much about those yellow bastards," was an effective silentiary.

Back at Pearl the first mission was to join *Northampton* and *Chester* in escorting the carrier *Enterprise* under the flag of Rear

Admiral Halsey out to Wake Island, whither she was taking a dozen fighter planes for the marine garrison. The international situation was tense and Halsey fully agreed with Zacharias. Wartime cruising watches were set aboard all the ships and orders issued to fire on any submarine sighted; aboard *Salt Lake* they brought up live ammunition and stacked it in the ready boxes beside the 5-inch and 1.1s. The older men took these preparations with a grain of salt; they had been through these alarms and excursions before and when the radio down in the engine spaces blared "Attack on Pearl Harbor—this is no drill!" one dollar would have brought you a dozen that it wasn't true.

Then the calls began to go out for nurses and blood donors and somebody called down from topside to say that *Enterprise* was flying planes with war loads of bombs and torpedoes. The incredulity did not really melt till the following morning when Halsey led his ships into Pearl with all hands not on duty at the rail looking things over. The first thing visible was *Nevada* with the hole in her bows, then *California* and *West Virginia* tilted over at their disastrous angles and still burning with only half of *Arizona*. On some ships when that sight was seen the reaction varied from anger to tears; aboard the old *Salt Lake* where they knew everything, there was only astonishment and dismay. "What a mess," remarked a young water tender to a chief standing beside him. "Sort of takes the wind out of your sails, don't it?"

"Well, you can put the wind right back in because this is the business. This is where we start work."

III

That afternoon the cruiser began to take aboard survivors of the attack to build her crew up for wartime strength. They had all volunteered for duty but many had no clothes or official papers, some were burned or nervously shocked, and had to be put to bed immediately. The tales they told did nothing to lighten the general feeling that this new war was pretty well fouled up. Fortunately the chief was perfectly right about their going to work. They sailed at dawn with Halsey's *Enterprise* task group to an area north and east of Oahu, partly to guard against any repetition of the December 7 attack, but chiefly to clear out the Japanese submarines which had been operating in that region and had already sunk one ship there. We know now that the group was so omnipresent and that it so severly bumped around the subs on which it got contact that the Japanese Admiralty called off the whole operation, but they did not know it in the task force at the time and the general feeling about the war going sour was not lightened by the fact that many of the volunteers had to be put ashore and sent to the hospital when the ship got back to Pearl.

They were replaced by boots and the ship got a new exec (Noble had been hospitalized on the return from the trip south) in Commander E. E. Stone, who had held the same appointment aboard *California*. He proved just the man to pull the crew together after their megrims and the rather lax discipline into which they had fallen under the easy Zacharias. Strict, yes; Commander Stone made it clear at once that the existence of the war relieved no one from the necessity of keeping regulations, but rather increased the obligation as the key to battle efficiency. But he was approachable; you could walk right up to him on the quarterdeck and he would consider your problem with reason and good sense. There was a signalman first class, for instance, who wanted his chief's cap with the extra pay and privileges, but the quota on chief signalmen was full.

"You've done some quartermaster duties," said Stone, looking at the man's Q card. "Do you suppose you could pass for chief quartermaster with a little studying? If you make the examination, I'll rate you up right away, but you'll have to do a lot of work on navigation in order to make out if you get transferred to another ship."

He did pass, was rated and grateful. In fact most of the crew came to feel they owed a personal debt to Commander Stone, who took a particular amount of trouble over chow during the next cruise, the long voyage down to Samoa with the first convoy of troops to that place. *Salt Lake* had always had the reputation of being a bad chow ship, even in the days of Kitts, the brilliant exec who preceded Noble and had helped bring her from the bottom to near the top of the fleet in gunnery standing. But Stone cured that; he was always bringing the stewards up sharp when they didn't do things right. Was also one of the first men in the fleet to take up the problem of fatigue, which later received so much attention; arranged his plan of the day so there would be at least one period when no ship's activity was toward but the normal sea watches, calling that the Siesta—"and boy, we siestaed."

Any ship, but a warship particularly, develops a personality of her own which is imparted to all but the most resistant characters aboard and some reason is usually found for transferring them elsewhere. There was the carrier *Franklin,* famous for as fine a collection of rip-roaring old-time seamen as ever drove a shore patrol nuts; the submarine *Seawolf,* where it is reputed that no one ever spoke above a whisper; The *Bremerton,* cruiser, loaded with men so mechanically minded they were said to spend their spare time regulating each others' watches. The important thing about the old *Swayback Maru,* drifting down the latitudes to Samoa, was that under the influence of Captain Zach, Commander Stone and Kobey the engineering officer, she was achieving a new personality, quite different from the "grow-old-along-with-me" with which she had watched the improved heavy cruisers shoving her into the background. Bob Casey the correspondent noted it when the loudspeaker declared that the captain had an important announcement to make.

It was so bad a loudspeaker as to have acquired the name of "Donald Duck" (that's what you get for serving aboard an old ship) but Captain Zach's voice came through clear as a bell. The day after tomorrow the ship was going to run in on Wotje in the Marshalls and bombard positions there—the first American offensive of the war. "We are likely to encounter some opposition. We prefer it that way. Nobody wants to bet on a sure thing."—And he went on to say he was satisfied their drill would show results. A day or two before, while they were refueling under way, lashed to a tanker, the ship refused suddenly to answer her helm and began swinging toward a crash. Back in the darkness of the steering compartment the watch was named Lorisco, seaman first class, who had once before been in such an accident and not knowing what to do had since taken the trouble to find out. This time he was aware of the steering failure and without orders made the correct switch-overs "—undoubtedly saving the ship from severe damage." Lorisco's name was being transmitted to the Department for recognition; Captain Zach thought all of them would do as well in action.

Casey compared it to Knute Rockne between halves; the man-to-man stuff without overemphasis that really gets 'em. There was a good deal of excitement and debate after the speech. What did the Japs have in there? Nobody knew, since Wotje had been held incommunicado for twenty years now and the logical assumption was that the opposition would be pretty terrific. Out to the west the enemy were moving down through the Shan States and their ships driving ours from Java Sea; they looked invincible.

But the actual performance on that Sunday the first of February was more in line with Captain Zach's bet on a sure thing. The cruiser steamed along through a bright smooth sea in the breaking dawn with the destroyer *Dunlap* attendant, trembling to the shock of her own artillery and when the return fire was nothing or next to it Captain Zach relaxed the rules about battle stations to permit as many men as possible to see what was going on. Down below Kobey became dissatisfied with the loudspeaker's account of shells striking, smoke ashore and *Dunlap's* execution of a miserable little minesweep that came out and tried to fight back with her 3.9-inch guns. He sent a water tender up to make a personal report; he arrived just in time to see in the coming light "like a worn and hazy movie the 8-inch guns blowing a mangy atoll to pieces" with a big freighter steaming in among the shell splashes and going down. Four similar ships went down; an oil tank went up in black smoke with streaks of red and the cruiser *Salt Lake City* swung off northeast to join her carrier just as a formation of Jap bombers, the only ones to leave the ground, came soaring over in a counterattack.

They were after *Enterprise* but so harried by our fighters that only one reached drop point and that one got caught in the fire of *Salt Lake's* 1.1s, burst out all over in bright flame, skidded across the deck of the carrier and vanished without a splash or a spot of oil. The 1.1 man who had done the business turned up a face of amazement—"he was there and now he's gone," and the first battle was over.

IV

Afterward there were a dozen singing parties all over the ship, but none in the skipper's cabin, where a conference of department heads was being held. The performance had achieved the results on which payoffs are made, but it had a distinct air of amateurism. The lookouts had been sloppy about identification, the bridge signalmen had given one of the ship's returning planes a cut at the wrong time so it cracked a wing against the vessel's side, and there was a bad job of snafu on deck when they tried to launch a boat for the aviator so the destroyer had to pick him up. There were no evil consequences from this inefficiency because the Japs themselves were so bad— obviously surprised, their gunnery nervous and—well, unlucky. With three distinct straddles on *Salt Lake* they got no hits. They would do better next time; so must we.

Thus Captain Zacharias to his young men, steaming up to Pearl Harbor. He knew he would be leaving the ship soon to use his knowledge of Japanese at ONI. So would Stone, who had made his fourth stripe and for whom the skipper had vainly tried to get the command. (The Department said he was too junior for so big a vessel, but less than two years later had him commanding a 45,000 ton battlewagon.) The reserves would come flooding in, now, far more ready than Old Navy men to take on the character of a partic- ular ship rather than that of the service as a whole. So much of the war Navy (and Zach's own future too) would depend upon the traditions and the methods picked up by those new men when they came aboard after the old leaders had moved on. Raids like the one in which they had just engaged and the adventure to Wake and Marcus in which they shared as soon as the task force had time to rearm and reprovision could be regarded as a kind of training oper- ation with live ammunition. This was probably more important than any results achieved either in the war of attrition or in keeping the enemy off balance and uncertain of our plans.

On the Wake-Marcus raids, in fact, it was still possible for one of the bridge signalmen to turn and say incredulously, "Why, they're shooting at *us*" when the tall waterspout from shore went up along- side, and at the former island the ship for the first time fired short fused 5-inch. But Correspondent Casey saw how much more rapidly than before the doors clanged to and men ran up the iron ladders when GQ was rung as *Salt Lake* went out again, north and west under Halsey's flag on a mission completely mysterious till far at sea one morning they woke to find themselves accompanied by the new carrier *Hornet*, her deck lined with twin-engined army planes none had ever seen on a ship before.

"Now hear this—" said the loudspeaker and the captain told them of the coming raid on Tokyo, the most spectacular and encouraging event of the early war. *Salt Lake* had more share in that operation than the casual part of a cruiser covering the carriers, thanks to one of the lookouts, the sharp-eyed young boot named Pace. The ship was well back in the middle of the formation when he spied on the horizon that vessel of the Jap deep-sea patrol, contact with which caused the premature launching of the strike. No one else saw the enemy; in fact when *Salt Lake* signaled over to *Enterprise* with the news they wouldn't believe it and the cruiser *Nashville* with a squadron of fighters was only sent out on routine check. Pace's discovery was fortunate indeed, for the Jap had just begun to get off his radio message. It was recorded and passed back to Pearl Harbor; the decoders said so much as went through made gibberish but one more half sentence and the Japs would have been warned of Doolittle's coming. Captain Zach called young Pace over and rated him up on the spot; then took the loudspeaker and told the crew what he had done.

It was almost the last thing he did do for the ship. The orders calling him in to Naval Intelligence were already on hand, only no relief had arrived when Halsey's task force sailed after two days in port, on a run that proved futile, down to Coral Sea. They were a day's steaming away when the *Lex* went down and the Jap carriers were so brutalized in the battle there and it was probably a good job for the enemy that he got away so fast. He would have had Halsey and the *Enterprise* on his neck in another sixteen hours. Now it was mid-May, *Salt Lake* had not been at a dock since before the war began, the main feed pump had lost its overspeed trip, and there were various other things wrong that could only be fixed at an anchorage. *Enterprise* turned north for her date with Tojo's armada among the mists and mysteries of Midway; *Salt Lake* was detached for Brisbane and the crew made liberty.

It was a good liberty. The Aussies had a lively sense of what Coral Sea meant to them and the old *Swayback Maru* was a friend who had visited there before the war. Men were picked up in the street and taken to lunch by perfect strangers, feeding to repletion on those enormous steaks that cover a platter. Zach's relief caught up with him there and Stone had already left before the Tokyo raid, relieved by Commander Grayson Carter, a big man with a red face who had something peculiar in the bone structure of his hips which made the seams of his trousers take a spiral as they ascended; it fascinated the men. The new skipper was Captain E. G. Small, with a face as hard as a Dresden china dog. "Boy, I'd hate to meet him up a dark alley," was the comment when he came aboard, and they quickly found he lived up to his looks as per the incident of the amateur leadsman.

He was learning to cast as the ship ran out one day and in the normal spirit of naval jest someone had instructed him that regardless of the result of his throw he must yell, "Fourteen fathoms and no bottom!" every thirty seconds loud enough to be heard on the bridge. At about the eleventh repetition there was a counter call of—"And fourteen days and no liberty for that stupid monkey." Made it stick, too.

Several of the department heads went as well and it was a different ship, with J. F. Brewer who had been first lieutenant, moving up to gunnery officer. He was Academy, class of '26, but had resigned after three years, and down to the emergency was labor contact man for a big coal firm in Jersey. Perhaps he didn't know as much about the technical details of his new specialty as some others, but he was an expert on the personnel side and the men couldn't do enough for him nor he for them, so that the momentum of Zach's careful training carried right on through.

We have an account that shows it from one of a group of ten new ensigns who joined Salt Lake during the Coral Sea cruises she made in company with the Australian squadron. They had been chasing the ship halfway round the world and caught up to her by riding out on a tanker, then over by breeches buoy, not the most pleasant proceeding in the world since the line dipped and a couple of them got their tails wet. They were V-7s and had brought the old-fashioned enormous sea chests, which were piled on the deck of the tanker to the amazement of the old Salt Lake men, who had seen nothing like that for a year and a half; came aboard damp and rather shamefaced, expecting to be ridiculed and resented by this eminently Old Navy ship, by reputation one of the tightest of all. "But we were taken right into the family. Everyone was anxious to help and there was an old enlisted man named Lambert who appointed himself my personal guardian. He had a laugh that would ring all through the ship."

V

The period of Coral Sea cruising would have been idyllic had not food run down so low; at one time they were even rationed on bread, one slice per man per meal and precious little to go with it but beans and rice. Now it came to an end; the move up to Guadalcanal was on and *Salt Lake* a part of it, more or less an orphan as she had to work with the newer, faster and stronger ships of the *Astoria* class—*San Francisco* and *Minneapolis, Astoria* herself, *Quincy* and *Vincennes*. The bee was definitely on Chief Kobey and his V-7s with the equatorial heat all but unbearable in the old ship's poorly ventilated engine spaces, but she was not found wanting in any formation and the crew began to learn that if Captain Small could be fierce enough with them, he could do as much in their interest. There drifted through the ship the story of the towering fury with which he had demanded fresh meat for his men the last time in at Espiritu; and there was no question but he was a ship-handler of the first order. "Never see *this* ship getting it that way" was the key of the discussion in the chiefs' quarters the day *Wasp* went down.

They were attached to a cruiser squadron now, Task Force 64 under Admiral Norman Scott; running patrols up from somewhere west of the New Hebrides to somewhere south of Guadalcanal; hopeful of action but not seeing much chance of it since the yellow bastards were so chary of engaging except under conditions that gave them ineluctable advantage. Everybody a little gloomy and frightened by the progress of the war, which was going badly, east and west. The Savo Island battle had been a dreadful blow; three of our best cruisers down and the Australian with no return. At Midway we showed the monkeys couldn't fly planes with us, but they had clearly won every surface action of the war, maybe they really had something too good for us. *Astoria* had been the prize gunnery ship of the fleet; what did we have that was better than she?

This point of attitude in the squadron and the Navy is important as Norman Scott moved up toward Guadal on the night of October 11 with the heavy cruiser *San Francisco*, two lights, *Boise* and *Helena*, four destroyers and *Salt Lake City* which matched none of the others in characteristics. The surface Navy was under an evil star and the cruiser divisions most particularly. They had been up

the night before on the report the enemy would run one of his Tokyo
expresses, but no Japs. Tonight was one of the hottest ever seen in
the Solomons, so hot men sweated right through their heavy kapok
life jackets and lay in exhaustion on the decks with the water of their
perspiration to a perceptible depth about them.

An evil star; as *Salt Lake*, last in line, made the turn past Cape
Esperance she swung around the catapult and shot off a plane, loaded
with flares for use in case the enemy came. It reached bridge level
when something went wrong, there was a violent explosion and with
the tail one mass of flame the machine dived to quenching in the
black water.

"Who was in it?"

"Tait and young McGowan."

Tait the aviator, one of the few who had done anything to keep
the wardroom from being a mortuary during those days of strain;
young McGowan the little blond mech, one of the best liked men in
the ship; and now their presence was betrayed the enemy would turn
back. At such moments men cling for support to something, and
there was none for the men of the *Salt Lake* in any surrounding
circumstance, only what they could gain from the memory of Captain
Zach's confidence before the battle in the Marshalls and their own
confidence in the hard-faced man on the bridge.

"My heart started going up and down just like a yodel," remembers
one of the deck gang but, "Well, who's going to be the first to get
a medal?" demanded Lambert in the engine room with his booming
laugh and one could feel the tension relax around. *San Francisco*
out ahead reached the end of her eastward course under Savo and
turned back west, the others turning in succession behind her. Then
at 2340 from *Helena*, the only ship equipped with modern radar, an
electric TBS:

"Here they come."

One of the destroyers switched on searchlights and white in the
blare was a Japanese heavy cruiser, one of the *Kokos*, pointed straight
at the center of the American line with her guns all trained out to
starboard ready to bombard the shore, the rest of their fleet behind
her in that perfect position of the stem of a crossed T where every
naval officer dreams of catching his opponent. "What a beautiful

ship!" someone on the bridge had time to cry just as all the guns in the fleet went off together.

"Then it was a nightmare." The Jap ships broke formation, plunging wildly in all directions to escape the deadly trap, their destroyers rushing to cover them with a torpedo attack. The night was streaked with long pennons of gun-flame and bars of smoke and *Salt Lake*, whose entire first salvo had gone into the leading Jap without the splash of a single miss, shifted to a big transport behind and put shells into her rapid fire till the screws at her stern caught a gleam of the fitful light as she plunged. The rush of a Jap destroyer was stopped by *Helena* and *Boise*. "She split open just like a melon" and the tall splash of the final salvo came up through the place where her stacks had been. *Salt Lake* caught another destroyer in her search-lights and smothered her in 5-inch. Another was burning and there was a shock beneath the tumult in our own line where the destroyer *Duncan* was torpedoed. Then *Boise* got it.

She was just ahead of *Salt Lake* in line, maybe three hundred yards distant which is nothing at those speeds, and the Jap heavy cruiser *Furutaka*, uncommonly well led that night, hit her with a salvo of 8-inch that penetrated her armor belt and sent up all three forward turrets in a horrible gust of flame. The American cruiser staggered out of line but *Furutaka* had a perfect gunnery solution and hit her again . . . not more than once. E. G. Small, giving his ship a little right rudder with revolutions for flank speed, hurled her right into that perfect gunnery solution between the Jap and the burning *Boise*. *Furutaka*'s first salvo burst across the *Salt Lake*'s upper decks; at least one shell of the second came through above the armor belt into the forward fireroom, killed one man, knocked a big blower all to bits, cut the exhaust steam line and set the oil in the bilges alight. There was no third Jap salvo; *Salt Lake*'s return caught her fairly at a range where her armor might have been so much cardboard. She broke in half and the halves went down, the lights went out.

Up on *Salt Lake*'s forward 5-inch position Koslowski the giant loader who could pick up a shell in one hand leaned over to slap a shoulder of his friend, little Acree the gun pointer, who had slumped forward tiredly with his head on the piece. "We fixed 'em that time, kid!" but kid slipped to the deck and they found that a shell fragment of that first exchange had taken out half his stomach without driving him from his place, faithful to death and the end of the battle.*

VI

They could not get the bilge fire out, fog nozzles and modern control methods being something only heard of at this time, so they finally had to seal off the compartment and let it be smothered by the escaping steam as the ship moved down to Espiritu alongside crippled *Boise*. The detail went over to help the repair parties aboard that "reluctant dragon" and got a little foretaste of how the fleet would look on the *Salt Lake* from now on. "Here's a *Salt Lake* man" the *Boise* sailors cried at chow time and shoved him up to the head of the line.

Best of all, the first people to meet them on the dock were Tait and young McGowan from the plane; they had made their rubber boat, paddled it to Guadal and then flown down. When the damaged fireroom was opened up it was discovered the beams were pretty well warped, so now there had to be a trip back to dock and everybody was hopeful that it would be to the States with leave. But the need for cruisers was too great, it was only to Pearl Harbor. The yard period was a long one since they gave her a general overhaul at the same time, replacing the 1.1s with the new 40 and 20 millimeter automatics and revising a good many of the internal features in favor of better damage-control arrangements.

The whole show was a bitter disappointment to the crew, two years from home, wanting leave and feeling they had earned it, the ship so uncomfortable to live on, filled with air lines, welders' torches and racket. Only 20 per cent did get leave and these for but sixteen days. Commander Worthington Bitler coming aboard as exec to replace Carter (who was being promoted) found discipline slackening, the ship dirty and morale at a fairly low ebb, nobody caring very much any more about the old *Slick City* tradition of taking new men into the family. The new decoration, Presidential citation, had just been announced. Bitler thought that getting one for the ship would straighten matters out and that she deserved it, the first American vessel since Santiago to sink an enemy in a gun duel and

---

* They named a destroyer escort for him, DE 356.

this in an action which raised the spirit of the whole service. But Captain Small was one of your cold New Englanders who do not believe in pressing such matters so the new exec had to try something else.

Of course they were raiding him at a terrific rate for experienced petty officers to form nucleus crews with all the new ships building, giving him boots instead to be shoved in at the bottom of the ladder and forcing the rating up of men he already had. Familiar navy procedure but seldom done at this speed or to this extent before and a good many of the new men coming out from the various specialist schools in the States were not well briefed on the elaborate new gear the ship was taking aboard. There had lately been established at Pearl Harbor itself another series of schools with instructors whose main qualification was combat experience. Bitler went right down the list, enrolling every man he could possibly spare from the ship for every course he could get them into—antiaircraft, fire-fighting, engineering, Diesels, torpedo, gas warfare—and sent them off to live and work up in the hills.

As for those still aboard . . . he had noted among the signs of slackening discipline a tendency to be late at GQ drills, which were a bore when the ship was in or near base. With Captain Small's cooperation a list was now posted on all the ships' bulletin boards of penalties to be automatically assessed for such tardiness: five minutes late, one hour extra duty; five-ten minutes late, two hours; second offense, two hours and so on.

About the time these devices were put into play the ship changed captains again; Small was getting his stars. The new man was Bertram D. Rodgers, a Pennsylvania Irishman, no relation to the famous naval family, which is Maryland. He had come up through the lighter-than-air service and like most men in that branch was very easy and friendly, affable in his manner. The skipper of a big cruiser is supposed to spend most of his time in the rather grim isolation of his own cabin, but with dockyard workmen crawling all over the place there generally seemed to be some racket or something going on around the cabin and Captain Rodgers was to be found down in the wardroom with his boys—a prodigious change from the days of both Small and Zacharias.

She was a new ship in other ways as well when she steamed out of

Pearl Harbor in early March, 60 per cent brand new as to crew and most of the rest so recently come to the service that they would have been counted boots back in 1940. "Not an Old Navy ship at all any more" mourned one man who had come aboard as a water tender and was now a machinist's mate, first, a little disgruntled by his own promotion. "In the Old Navy you got rated for savvy and you picked up doing things the Navy way for five years; now these guys just listen to somebody else for six weeks and then go get savvy out of a book. Study, study, study, what the hell kind of a Navy is this anyway?"

Or not all out of books. There was Lyle Ramsey, the F division officer, one of those mental mathematical marvels, who could memorize all the cards in three or four deals of bridge. He used to check the range finders in his head without benefit of instruments and on the way out went shaveless for three or four days with some idea of producing a beard. Bitler told him that the rule was the same for officers as for enlisted; aboard *Salt Lake City* there would be no interference with personal liberties, but beards were apt to make handling a gas mask difficult and anyone who wanted to support whiskers would also have to wear the mask three hours a day for familiarization purposes.

VII

The prow was turned north; they were bound for the Aleutians to relieve *Indianapolis* as the only heavy cruiser on station. If the engine room had suffered during the Solomons campaign, it was now the turn of the deck gang with the high swells of the North Pacific washing across the cruiser's waist and up into the 5-inch positions when she rolled. Those kapok life jackets would get wet right through by spray at slightly below freezing temperature, one would shiver uncontrollably and after a four-hour trick seem unable to get warm again. They talked of old days in the south and the hard fighting around Guadal and a singular character named Stober who had been in the head when a fragment of that Jap shell came through and dropped hot on his knee. He gave a yell and literally leaped right out of his pants, leaving them behind. The war was all changed now, the Japs were on the run and the new men, getting savvy out of books, tended to feel they could never quite unite with these others.

. . . Which shows how little they knew. Behind the curtain of those northern mists the twenty-five hundred Japs on Attu and the something like ten thousand on Kiska had called for reinforcement and supply. Their general thought he might even make a forward campaign against the American forces that were conducting a not very effective aerial siege of the two islands. Both sides had submarine scouts all over the place and the enemy knew that Admiral McMorris, commanding for us, had to hold the station only two of the twenty-three-year-old light cruisers, *Richmond* and *Detroit,* with a handful of destroyers. Now was the time to erect their Aleutian outpost into another Solomons complex.

They made up a convoy; two large and very fast supply ships with a transport. For escort there were provided eight destroyers, two of their three-funnel light cruisers and a pair of the big ten-gun heavies that were contemporaneous with *Salt Lake City*—one each from the *Atago* and *Nachi* classes. Their route was along the shadow of the Kuriles, well north past but beyond view of Kamchatka, to drop down toward Attu and Kiska from the northwest, keeping beyond range of our air scouts till night had fallen. Our people had some inkling that the Japs might try to reinforce. *Salt Lake* had hardly reported to Adak before she was moving out fast to the west under McMorris' flag with *Richmond* and the destroyers *Monaghan, Dale, Coghlan* and *Bailey* in company to search the only area planes could not readily cover, far up toward the Komandorskies. The morning of March 26 found them in a long patrol line abreast of and only just visible from each other under an overcast impenetrable at two thousand feet but with perfect visibility on the surface of the cold, slick, slaty waveless sea.

It was not yet eight when *Richmond*'s lookouts spied three sets of masts and then three more, the first set clearly transports or cargo, the second a light cruiser probably and two destroyers. "Concentrate on me" signaled McMorris from *Richmond* and stepped up speed—those old light cruisers could always go. But before they reached gun range of the turning enemy, down from the north and well to the eastward of our forces came the gross of the Japanese, and now they were between our ships and their home with double strength in numbers and something more than double in force. *Richmond* put out signals for a turn southwest, but before it could be made the *Atago* opened fire, a perfect straddle half over and half short on our flagship but the shells coming from so great a distance they fell perfectly vertical and there was no damage.

Salt Lake fired back. Short. Walked up the range and fired again —short but less so. Both Japs were shooting at her now and their gunnery was remarkably good, the salvos pitching close aboard, visible "like BB shot" as they came, with Captain Rodgers standing in the bridge wing, coolly estimating where the next load of death would pitch down and conning her away from the spot with flicks of the rudder too slight for the Japs to observe. "Do you know, sir, that stuff's dangerous," commented a Negro messenger seriously to Bitler, who had his helmet on backward, but nobody laughed. They were caught and they knew it.

But at the third salvo the care Commander Brewer had given his gunners and the genius of Ramsey the fire-control man paid off. There was only one splash but a great burst of black smoke at the base of the *Nachi*'s control tower through which tall pennants of flame licked round the whole structure. The Jap wove uncertain for a moment, her salvos missed a beat and *Salt Lake* was round the dangerous turn, running southwest on a course that permitted only the use of her after turrets. Then her fire control failed.

Ramsey phoned down about what switches to pull (he worked out that problem in his head too, which few others could have done) and they got the control back in for two salvos more. Then the ancient mechanism failed for keeps under the shock of the heavy long-range charges and the turrets had to go into local control. The advantage gained through gunnery was lost through accident—or not quite lost, for though the Japs might have cut corners, they were making no attempt to close into the American fire and as the *Nachi* squared away again on course there was a jerk and lack of co-ordination about the enemy movements that suggested something was wrong at the head.

Long after the men of the *Salt Lake City* learned that a Japanese admiral had died under their shells, but of that nothing now on the long southwestern run. It had gone for nearly an hour when *Salt Lake* scored again and heavily, a hit well aft on the enemy flagship that caused her to slow up. As she dropped back McMorris swung his whole force east and then north to get at the Jap light ships that had been hanging in that direction, like *Richmond*, outranged. There was a sharp flurry of action; *Salt Lake* hit one of the Jap three stackers as she turned away, one of their destroyers was hit and definitely dropped out of the battle. Then their *Nachi* got her damage under control and came cutting across the circle. For a time there was duel with all the guns on both sides working; then *Salt Lake* was hit and again hit the enemy in return.

The old *Swayback Maru* had taken two hits before this, one amidships that demolished a plane and caused a few casualties and one in the windlass room forward, but this hit now was serious. It came through well aft among the oil storage compartments and shaft alleys. All the men of Repair 2 jumped to their feet but Lieutenant Terrill back there, who had been all through it at Cape Esperance shouted "Everybody lie down!" and got them in hand till the damage could be investigated. It was bad enough; water rising rapidly in the bilges with heavy fuel oil that congealed to lumps when it hit the icy liquid or turned to blue vapor where it struck escaping steam. A party volunteered to look into the shaft alley. It was neck-deep in that mixture of water and oil-ice, but with hand pumps and bailing they got a man in, who reported that a big scoop had been taken right out of one of the shafts and nothing could be done about it.

Topside meanwhile the destroyer *Dale* had given the big cruiser smoke cover and she had made a slight turnaway which left an escape route open if she could ever get to take it. But it had also been discovered that the after turrets were running out of ammunition and Captain Rodgers called for volunteers to pass shells from the forward handling rooms. They formed a chain along the rolling deck, covered with its two-inch film of ice and oil, and many a heavy 8-inch slug was tossed in the water when a splash close aboard suggested that the next one might be a hit. The job was done, the ship was opening fire on the new course when that rising water below reached from fuel tank to fireroom.

There was a puff of steam from the funnels, a chief at the wing 5-inch looked over the side and cried "We're slowing up; my God, we're stopped." On the bridge the navigator took off his gloves, shook hands with Captain Rodgers and said gently, "Well sir, it's been nice knowing you," while the chief signalman pulled tight his life jacket, kicked off his shoes, then looked at the icy sea and remarking, "No, too cold" put them back on again. Farther aloft a man went out of his head and had to be knocked down with a wrench.

But the squadron was not done. Since they first sighted the enemy Captain Riggs of the destroyer division had been asking permission to attack. Now while *Dale* again wove a smoke cloud around the damaged cruiser, McMorris released them and they rushed at the Jap heavies. "We never expected to see them again" and sure enough before they had half covered the intervening distance down came a salvo that frightfully hit *Bailey* and another all round and into *Coghlan*. Riggs fired his fish while he still had them to fire and swiveled around, his lookouts noting accurately that one of the turrets on the *Nachi* was opened out with the guns spread V-fashion, and only one of her turrets firing.

They turned from that attack; and at the same moment the frantically laboring men in *Salt Lake*'s engine room got the feed lines cleared, came tearing out of the smoke ready for action again. "We're getting a little low on armor piercers," Commander Brewer remarked to the skipper. "Mix up some HC in each salvo" was the reply, and the first splashes of the rejoined battle came up partly blue for the armor piercers, with taller, thinner and white ones for the HC. The enemy cruisers kept right on round the turn they had made from our destroyers—from *Salt Lake* they could see one of them had a list—opened a furious AA barrage into the overcast and ran. "Request permission to pursue," signaled Riggs of the destroyers.

On the bridge of *Salt Lake* there was an amazed silence for a long five minutes. Then Captain Rodgers observed conversationally, "They must think the army bombers have come."

VIII

Now followed the reaction which is usually forgotten in thinking of a great, thrilling and, in this case, decisive battle. (Decisive since the Japs never again attempted to reinforce the Aleutians, it altered their whole strategy.) Everyone was glad to be alive, but tired past speaking, all nerves on edge and life hardly worth the trouble. "You never get over the strain of a five-hour battle like that," said one of the officers two years later when he was aboard another ship, looked upon there as a somewhat strange and lonely individual, always partly lost in a memory that those around him could not share.

Down in the engine compartments they were still exhaustedly fighting the tides and trying to get performance from machines that threatened to quit altogether when asked for more than ten knots. Fire control was getting its equipment in order—the Japs might come back—growling and cursing that they would have sunk both the enemy if the damn machines had worked the way they should. Signals was keeping an eye on *Bailey* which was near to foundering. The galley fires were not working; in the mess spaces the enlisted were making out as best they could with the leavings of yesterday's supper, and in the wardroom eight or ten wounded occupied most of the tables with exhausted mess boys passing cans of cold Vienna sausage and pieces of stale bread. Also the arguments were on.

If—and if—and if, but swinging to a substantial body of agreement that Captain Rodgers was the best skipper and the best ship-handler the Navy had ever seen and that we owe our lives to the guys in those goddam tin cans. About the latter at least something more could be done than merely cheer *Bailey* and *Coghlan* on their arrival at Dutch. Somehow a message sent just after the battle had been garbled in transmission and the base interpreted it to read that *Salt Lake* was returning with eight hundred casualties. All the nurses in Alaska were flown out, clear from Sitka and Fairbanks, to be waiting when the ship came in. With the blessing of the officers the crew of the *Salt Lake* dug down to buy all the beer in town with other drinks in proportion and threw a tremendous party and dance for the destroyer men. It lasted all day till seven in the evening with the destroyers and *Salt Lake* telling each other how wonderful they were; if anyone was sober it was his own fault and the shore patrol kept their hands in their pockets except when a man needed carrying.

On top of this came the glad news that the ship would repair her battle damage at San Francisco, which meant leave after three years from home for many of the men. Captain Rodgers, who was always careful to include some little personal message to the crew in the mimeographed PLAN OF THE DAY which is a ship's internal newspaper had let the crew know he was pretty well satisfied with their performance. He had a big GO TO HELL pennant made, one foot of length for each day the ship had been out of port, in the old tradition;

dressed ship and went through Golden Gate with everything flying, expecting to be greeted with bands and welcomings like *Boise* after Cape Esperance, where she had indeed put on far less a performance than that *Salt Lake* had now given on two occasions.

Nothing of the kind. They found the communiqué on the battle was one lousy little paragraph without even mentioning the name of the ship. Not only were there no parades, official or unofficial, but leaves were few in number and of short duration and duty at the dockyard heavy, with one watch on and one off. All hands felt disappointed and indignant at such treatment after their hard ordeal, and when *Salt Lake* sailed again there was a fairly heavy list of absentees. Moreover the cruise was back to the fog and cold of the Aleutians with Admiral Giffen's big fleet for the recapture of Attu and Kiska and tough duty since the watch schedules gave them another dose of four hours on and four off. There was also a shortage of heavy-duty sea clothing aboard though when the ship put into Dutch you could see all the base workers wrapped up in it, comfortable as Teddy bears.

The reaction was a series of petty infringements of regulation which would have made it difficult for Captain Zacharias to recognize his well-behaved ship. But Rodgers was unfailingly patient and amiable— came up to the wardroom for movies and sat talking over coffee afterward till the young division officers all began to feel their problems were little compared to his own. Bitler seconded him with an equally unfailing ingenuity. "Now look here," he would say to a man who the shore patrol had picked up in an establishment of low repute; "Don't you know they have all those places listed? They send me these reports about picking you up and I have to report back what action I have taken. If you want to work that sort of thing it's your business, but make friends with one of the yard workmen and get him to let you use his apartment. Next case."

Gradually she pulled herself together again, tightening up in preparation for the next action and once thought she was going to have it when a PBY reported masts sticking through a low surface fog. But it was a false alarm and so were other reports and the Aleutian campaign closed out and the cruiser *Salt Lake City* went down to the Gilberts on carrier guard and saw a big fire blazing in the distance that was the end of the *Liscombe Bay* and fired at planes and fired at the shore and the new cruisers began to come out so they dropped the old lady one step more down the scale as an escort for tankers. Ashore the men of the newer ships were inclined to kid the *Swayback Maru* about it, but the argument they got in return was "Well the *Salt Lake City* has killed more Japanese than any other ship in the war and she can still put out ten 8-inch shell every twelve seconds."

IV. THE CAMPAIGNS

The Aleutians

THE shortest route from the Orient to America runs under the shadow of the Aleutians. The Manila galleons used to pass there, bound for Darien with their loads of gold, and when southwest gales struck them, could see the tall pillars of rock veined with snow and smoking with fog. The islands contain some of the richest fishing grounds in the world, some of its worst weather and no trees whatever. The charts in use for parts of the chain at the outbreak of war still bore the notation "Made from the Russian survey of 1864"; and though the islands are all small the interiors of many had never been surveyed at all. Among them was fought the strange campaign by land and sea and air, a mixture of courage, brilliance, bungling, resource and lack of resources, divided command and unified purpose, all under the veil of a censorship that yielded nothing to those of Germany or China for restrictiveness and sheer stupidity.

A good case of the last is that throughout Alaska territory the people for nearly two years of war never got a magazine or a newspaper from which all reference to Alaska had not been carefully clipped; and that correspondents were not allowed to mention the presence of our troops and Amchitka and Adak till they had been there for six months, with Jap bombers coming over almost daily and telling the world about it all the time in radio broadcasts. A good case of the bungling was sending men specially trained in desert warfare to fight a campaign on Attu. A good case of the resource was the escape of Lieutenant Rodebaugh's PBY, and of the brilliance, the singular operations of the Blair Packing Company—but these are part of the main line of the story, and that story can only be built up against its own background.

That background begins with the fact that the group which held Alaska to be the key of the Pacific was founded by the two great heretics of American strategy—hunchback Homer Lea and stormy Billy Mitchell. It includes the other fact that the territory is a get-rich-quick country, whose inhabitants in legislature assembled have year after year refused to vote any taxes whatever on themselves, but who are extremely articulate about the laxness of the federal government in making improvements for them—that any land connection to Alaska must pass through a foreign country while the sea connection is in the hands of a monopoly with an extreme sensitivity to competition—that all such efforts to make the country self-sustaining in food as the Matanuska colony have failed dismally—that it had only one railroad, running from Anchorage up to Fairbanks.

The strategic effect of these conditions is to make Alaska in a military sense a chain of islands without the means of self-support, to be held and used only by a power having full control of the sea. The official theory of the power that had Alaska in 1941 ran strongly against its use as a field of military operations. This last is more important than it looks. It contributed heavily to the mental climate, the atmosphere in which decisions were made. It lay at the base of such arrangements as that which placed army forces throughout the area under General John L. Dewitt of the Western Defense Command, with his headquarters at the Presidio in San Francisco. This was not too serious at the operational level, a private agreement between Admiral Theobald of the Navy and the army commanders in the area placing the troops under naval command for moves; but it was no help at all in matters of morale, supply and censorship. Alaska was the only part of his command where there was any fighting and he was farther from it than he was from Chicago. The same intellectual climate was responsible for the report of the Hepburn Board in 1938—a board that wanted additional bases in the Caribbean and Wake and Guam armed to the teeth, so that no imputation of soft pedaling will lie:

> The weather conditions of Alaska are so changeable and so severe that . . . in spite of their favorable strategic location, the Board does not favor the Aleutian Islands as a site for the main Alaskan base . . . A location at Kodiak offers greater advantage for maintenance and operation . . . The Board has selected Sitka, Kodiak and Unalaska as offering the most favorable natural sites for air bases.

Sitka is back next to the continent, in the arms of Canada; Kodiak is well east and south of the Alaska capes; Unalaska is less than halfway along the Aleutian chain and the facilities recommended for that spot were to support one squadron of twelve patrol planes.

The war was to demonstrate that no factor really overrules the strategic—not weather nor living conditions nor lives.

II

The actual situation on the day of ill omen was this: at Sitka the antique liner *City of Baltimore* housed a thousand workers, who were making a good job last as long as possible while they set up facilities for two squadrons of seaplanes. At Kodiak the derelict *Yale* housed a similar party who had run the price of red eye up to $5.50 a quart in town; at Dutch Harbor (Unalaska) there was another gang on the old *Northwestern*. Kodiak had a hangar and one runway; there was a temporary pier, no revetments, the major portion of the artillery was lacking and there was almost no ammunition.

The Army was building air bases at Seward, Anchorage and Fairbanks, at the last of which there had been for some time an experimental station concerned with testing all types of equipment under conditions of extreme cold. The last activity had moved faster than anything else; they had a couple of B 17s up there and had learned a lot about keeping planes flyable under tough conditions. The Anchorage base had its runway with a single squadron of dowager B 18 bombers and a squadron of P 36 fighters that had been hot stuff eight years before. The schedule called for five thousand troops to be in the posts governing the airfields. In October, 1941, the War Department announced "new garrisons" at Seward, Kodiak and Dutch Harbor. They consisted actually of two below strength National Guard regiments.

These men constituted the Alaska Defense Command under General Simon Bolivar Buckner, named after his father, who surrendered Fort Donelson to Ulysses S. Grant. The ridiculous censorship came down hard on them and still harder on the base workers, who were also stirred no little by an order requiring the evacuation from the territory of all women unable to prove residence of many years' standing. Even private mail was censored; then and later most of the news the territory got of the war in Alaska came from Japanese radio broadcasts. Who was responsible for this is not clear. No one has ever admitted it. But it is clear who could have put a stop to this nonsense—that is, Major General John L. Dewitt, the same man who turned his thumbs down in an expressive gesture when the idea of building air bases out among the islands was suggested. A lot of the base workers quit, even when they had to take certificates prejudicial to future employment and the morale of the Alaska Defense Command began to go down as rumor chased rumor and the Japs crowed over the radio.

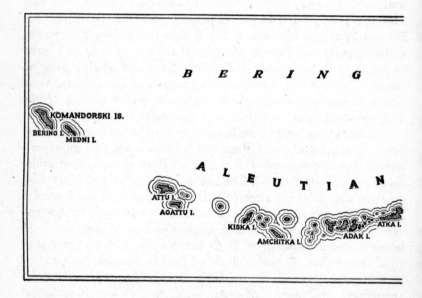

But they took no more vigorous action. We know the Japanese strategic concepts only by their effects, but it seems they planned a war in three main stages. Having eliminated the striking force of the United States fleet, the first stage was the seizure of an empire in Malaya and the East Indies, with their resources of materials and labor necessary to support the rather long war they expected to have to fight. The most immediate danger to this empire was from the south and southwest, the Anzac region. The second stage was to prevent a concentration of Anglo-Saxon forces in that region; it was to be cut off by the seizure of the Andamans and Burma in the west, with naval operations against any British forces approaching from that quarter. By the capture of the New Hebrides, New Caledonia and perhaps the Fijis and Samoa in the east the Anzac region would be fully cut off and its reduction would become a subsidiary operation.

The third phase was the attack on the American continent via the Alaska line foreseen by Homer Lea, while Midway and Hawaii were knocked out by a major expedition. The whole Alaska business could well afford to be left till late in the game, for the Japs could

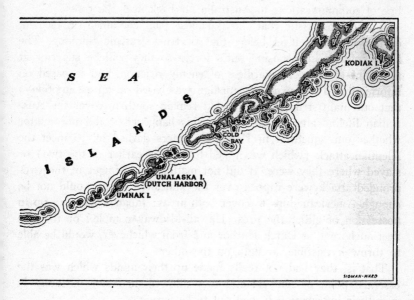

read English newspapers and well knew how far there was to go before even the modest recommendations of the Hepburn Board were translated into actual defenses.

The first stage of the Jap plan went through on schedule and perhaps even ahead of it. In the second the Japs were aided by the great good luck of eliminating piecemeal all the British naval forces that could be spared to attack the southwestern corner of their triangle of empire—first *Repulse* and *Prince of Wales,* then *Cornwali, Dorsetshire* and *Hermes,* both groups caught by overwhelming concentrations of aircraft before the British became fairly aware of the new tactics. In the meanwhile the Gilbert-Marshall raids, the air attacks on Wake and Tokyo, had demonstrated that the United States Navy was also awake to the uses of sea-borne power; and at Coral Sea in earliest May a part of the imperial program failed.

Why? Because the Pearl Harbor attack itself was a failure; it had not eliminated the American Navy's striking force, only transferred it from the gun to the airplane. In the Japanese view it therefore became necessary to proceed to the third phase without waiting for the completion of the second. Success would sever the American line of communications to Australia far back near the roots.

It is characteristic that this Japanese plan contained an element of trickery on a level below that of true strategic thinking. The latter consists in disposing one's forces so they will be superior at the point of contact regardless of enemy reaction, and is based on information. The Japanese campaign was based on an assumption— that our main striking force would remain south to cover the Australian lifeline after Coral Sea. If this happened it did not matter whether our squadron in Hawaiian waters dashed off to meet the Aleutian attack (which was timed to fall the earlier of the two) or stayed where they were. It did not matter if one finger of the two-pronged attack were rapped over the knuckles. There would not be enough American ships to cover both areas; Japan would end up in possession of either the great Hawaii-Midway complex or the fine fleet anchorage at Dutch Harbor and from whichever, would be able to throw irresistible strength on the other.

That is, they had not really made up their minds which was the essential point of contact; and they allowed no factor of safety in case their information turned out to be wrong.

III

A lot of it was wrong. The extent of their miscalculation, the overwhelming nature of the forces they faced has only gradually become clear. There was Spruance with the carrier striking force rushing toward Midway to give the Japanese Navy the worst defeat it ever had. There was a force of battleships rumbling toward an action which it never reached. Somewhere south of the Aleutians in the fog there was at least one American heavy cruiser and she would hardly be alone. But she was still well distant from Dutch

Harbor when a radioman thrust a sheet of flimsy into her skipper's hand on the morning of June 3, 1942.

. . . . It said: ENEMY AIRCRAFT ATTACKING.

Captain Updegraff, in command of the station back at Dutch, got the news at breakfast that four Jap bombers with an escort of fifteen carrier-type fighters had come through under the mists. Down below the mail plane was just taking off for Kodiak, one of the lumbering PBYs that do all the work up there where fogs and ice inhibit less sturdy machines. The Zeros dove at her; she burst into flames and her pilot, Litsey, was lucky to slide her to a crash stop on the beach and get out with his life.

Three of the Japs were not so lucky. There were three four-piper destroyers in the harbor, one of them in its second avatar as a sea-plane tender, with the Coast Guard cutter *Onondaga* and a mine-sweep, none of them armed against aircraft with anything better than the old Navy 3-inch. But the Zeros' dive brought them into range; one spiraled into the harbor, one trailed smoke and skidded into the flank of Mount Ballyhou and the land guns got a third on the getaway.

It was the first time in action for all hands; there were war whoops and mutual backslapping as the bomber sailed on past toward the army post of Fort Mears, where a stick of bombs killed twenty-five soldiers in their barracks and smashed a truck on the road. Bad enough; but less than might have been expected for an attack with no fighters to check it.

It is probable that Captain Updegraff knew little of the concentration of forces that was gathering against the Japs; even if he had, he would hardly have shared the self-congratulatory mood of his men. The Japs had come in on him with carrier planes and the size of the attack indicated something more than one of the small carriers was at work. A big carrier (or a couple of small ones) indicated a covering force of at least cruiser-and-destroyer strength; and this in turn that the "attack" was only a reconnaissance preliminary to the real movement, which would very likely be coming in with transports and guns as well as planes to cover a landing.

The American cruiser force maneuvering somewhere to the south in the fog were doing very little good if the Japs once gained possession as they were likely to do against the thoroughly insignificant defenses Dutch Harbor could then offer. His own mobile means of defense consisted of the three destroyers then in harbor with a couple of aircraft tenders now far down the island chain somewhere, carrying General Buckner on a personal inspection tour to look for likely places for aircraft strips—and of patrol squadrons 41 and 42, PBYs. The PBY, or Catalina, is the only plane in existence that can make itself at home in the borsch they use for weather in the Aleutians, but its combat efficiency is adequately described by the local nickname—Blue Coffin.

Nevertheless Updegraff's first essential was information—how many enemies and where—the PBYs out in their dispersal coves were alerted and ordered in for gas, which was centered aboard the tenders. The minesweep and destroyers got steam on all boilers; the soldiers poured out of Fort Mears and took up their emergency defensive positions while their leaders waited—and feared—the main attack.

It never arrived. The next island to Unalaska is Umnak, crowned with mountains. It seems that while the Jap commander was sending part of his air force in on Dutch Harbor he shot the rest through the sea pass west of Umnak to scout the Bering Sea flank of the islands and the coves that face north. Moving forward toward Dutch he gave them a rendezvous somewhere south of that place, so his planes came around Umnak to join him via the pass on the east side, the Unalaska side. They had found nothing on their flight out; but on this homing run they found something sensational.

Five months earlier Colonel Benjamin B. Talley of the Army Engineers had secured permission to put an airfield on Umnak and poured four thousand men into the place. Their supplies had come from Seattle, mendaciously addressed to the Blair Fish Packing Company; after they unloaded, the ships that brought them were kept jigging around in Alaskan waters so their crews would not talk in west coast bars. Just one week before the Japs came Major John Chennault sat down on the new landing strip with a squadron of P 40s; and it was these who furnished the sensation to six fat Jap bombers boring along toward their mothership with full bomb loads still aboard. The sensation was highly unpleasant since these fighters came from the west, the direction of Japan, where no American land planes had any business being. Three of the Japs went down in a flash. The others rushed off to the southeast, yelling frantically over their radios. A little later a group of homing Zeros came down the pass at about the same time as two of the PBYs of Squadron 41, running into the Umnak base for gas. There was a tangled, quick fight in which we lost a plane, the Japs two, both patrol jobs were damaged and some of the escaping enemy got close enough for a look at the runway and the rows of tents at Umnak. Then the tumult whirled off toward the Jap ships.

Chennault's planes had to give up and come back for more fuel before they finished the Japs, but in a strategic sense that was probably a good thing, since some of their planes reached the ships to give their admiral the bad news. He advanced under a weather front, a big one and it was now all along the Aleutian chain with gales on the surface and fast-moving clouds that only now and then left a clear space on the surface a hundred yards across. Widespread scouting was impossible. He had to make up his mind on a program and stick to it.

The original plan was undoubtedly to knock off Dutch Harbor and while the morning's armed reconnaissance would have warned the Americans, he considered that the information gained in the process would do him more good than the slender amount of warning we got would do us. The appearance of P 40s and an army air base in that wilderness had reversed the roles. The Americans now had sure knowledge of what they were up against while he was left in the dark with a very limited amount of time to work out a solution. How many more hidden fields did our forces have and how many planes were on them?

Apparently he decided to put up combat patrols and wait till a slight break in the weather brought more light on the situation. It would be around noon when these combat patrols shot down a PBY (it was Lieutenant Cusick's), and a couple of hours later another PBY came through the cloud, hung over the Jap armada for long enough to get a good count and then escaped despite being hit by one of the fighters. Now (the Jap knew) they had his strength and approximate position while he was still ignorant of what he was up against and there was a strong possibility that Dutch Harbor was a trap. He turned slowly back toward Japan.

As a matter of fact the American command was still under the fog of war late that night. The radio reports of the successful PBY had been garbled. The plane itself had had its rudder shot away and lost its last gasoline through holes in the tank. It came down on the water, and the crew was picked off by a Coast Guard cutter whose skipper quite reasonably refused to open up his radio with so many enemy surface units in the neighborhood.

With the dawn both Squadron 41 and 42 were out and Lieutenant M. C. Freerks, on his way in from patrol, spotted the enemy 210 miles southwest of Umnak—two cruisers (there later turned out to be a third), a big carrier, a small one and numerous destroyers. He stayed with them twenty minutes and got a clearer report through. Wind, fog and snowstorms were so thick that the Jap had not flown off that morning; if there had been a strong American striking force available a carbon copy of the big smashup of the day at Midway might have been produced but the only striking force consisted of six Army B 26s at Cold Bay, another secret airstrip built at the same time as Umnak. These went out with torpedoes which they had never flown before.

They found the Japs all right, in the early afternoon, and went in on their ships. Only one of the planes got close enough to make a good drop and that one got too close, for he dumped his torpedo squarely on the deck of a Jap carrier and it didn't go off. Later in the afternoon the weather where the Japs were moderated a trifle. They flew planes and came back to Dutch on a revenge raid. In the process they shot down two more PBYs, hit a wooden oil tank, and set fire to the old barrack ship *Northwestern*, which they could not sink because her bottom had been filled with concrete to keep her from drifting.

The Umnak fighters chiseled in on this racket and knocked down several of the enemy; just how many, uncertain. Later still a couple of newly-arrived B 17s came out from Kodiak and dropped bombs through a low overcast, bringing back word of a couple of probable hits. The hits are dubious, but it was apparently the presence of these monster bombers that made the Jap fleet change course, as it did during the day. Toward evening our radio operators back at Dutch began to pick up Jap planes calling frantically from the murk to learn where their ships were. In the most kindhearted way our radiomen gave them quite wrong directions and the fight was over.

Count up: we lost four PBYs, a fighter and one of the B 26s

besides the army men killed at Mears. They lost all or very nearly all the planes from two carriers, forty at least. Considering the potentialities and intentions of the force that had come along the Aleutian chain, an American victory. But while we were still counting it as such a radio message came from the little weather station at Kiska— "Unidentified ships entering harbor" and then silence. The battle had been won; the campaign was only beginning.

IV

It is singularly difficult to get any kind of grip on the operations that followed. To begin with, it was colonial warfare, a type not seen in America since General Crook chased Geronimo—a war of incidents whose effect is cumulative, in which the death of ten men constitutes a victory or a catastrophe. The detailed narration would be about as interesting—or useful—as the Anglo-Saxon chronicle.

It was also a war in a double dark, of fog and outrageous censorship, complicated by the fact that the command arrangement on our side was one of the most singular known to history. As soon as the Cold Bay and Umnak establishments got to operating smoothly they were erected into the Eleventh Army Air Force. This was a part of the Alaska Defense Command under General Buckner and he, as before, fell under the orders of General Dewitt back in Frisco. But for tactical purposes, the Eleventh fell under navy command and its operations were described in navy communiqués.

At the beginning indeed, the Eleventh had no operations. The Japs had put the horizon between themselves and the B 26s of Umnak and Cold Bay. The B 17s, we are told, had "operational trouble," which can mean anything. In this case it meant they could not fly to the three outer islands—Kiska, Agattu, Attu—after the weather stations went dead. Neither could most of the planes of 41 and 42. They were down on the water, down under it or worn out, man and machine. Squadron 43 was rushing up to meet the emergency of the Japanese attack with 12 new PBYs but it did not begin to fly from the tender *Casco* in a bay off Atka Island till June 10. That same day Lieutenant J. E. Bowers of 41, with his plane only fifty feet above the water, found the Japs at Kiska—ships in the anchorage, a tent city on shore.

He got off the news. That day two other PBYs made Kiska, dropping bombs with what results they never knew because they were in and out of streaming mist. When their accounts were added up they amounted to one Jap heavy cruiser, two lights and a destroyer at anchor, with at least six transports. At the normal Japanese loadings this would make about ten thousand monkeys ashore and the figure was so announced by the Navy. A lot of people took this as an understatement to excuse defeat when the excitable Alaskan delegate in Congress, annoyed by previous censorship troubles, said the real number of invaders was twenty-five thousand.

Even ten thousand was a lot of Japs. Rear Admiral R. A. Theobald, in command of the area for the Navy, realized at once that if they got themselves dug in they would be making trouble; also that since their Midway defeat, the logical Japanese line would be to divert whatever free force they had to expand this foothold in the north.

Submarines were on the way for the defense; also many more army planes and another PBY squadron, 51, but all were tantalizingly distant with the campaign being fought. The admiral had the very limited support five cruisers could give in a sea the size of the Mediterranean and little prospect of getting troops; the campaigns that were to be those of Guadalcanal and North Africa were being mounted. The first phase of the campaign was therefore pure air against the Jap beachheads with the PBYs doing all the work. They took off from the tender at Atka, which is four hundred odd miles from Dutch and the same distance from Kiska and for four days conducted a fantastic bomb siege.

There is a volcano on Kiska. Our pilots went up through the perpetual overcast till they could see its pillar of smoke, turned next to it, and putting the elephantine PBYs into crash-angle dives, came thundering down through. They never knew quite what they would find underneath except that one thing would be heavy and extraordinarily accurate flak. The Japs discovered that the cloud layer hung always at just a thousand feet off the water and adjusted their guns accordingly. Not a plane of all engaged was unhit; and at the bottom of the dive, both pilot and co-pilot had to stand up, heaving full strength on their yokes to bring their damaged monster out of her dive with her wings flapping madly. Remarkably, only one plane was lost. In return our pilots got at least three of a groupment of seven four-motored Kawanishis as they lay on the surface and dumped at least one big bomb each into a transport, a cruiser and a destroyer.

The destroyer at least would be a pretty sick citizen after that with bases so far away, but the same day she was hit a Jap scout plane burst through the mist of Atka to find our tender and since she was already down to the last of her gas and bombs, she pulled out. The presence of both the Kawanishis and the destroyer told something to Admiral Theobald. The latter was a new job; the former are the opposite number of our PBY and must have been flown in in a hurry up the long route of the Kuriles after the original landing. The Japs were reinforcing and preparing to stay; and for the moment countermeasures were up to Army Air.

This wasn't good enough. The B 17s were still having their mysterious operational trouble and the six-hundred-mile run out from Umnak was just a little too long for machines of their type. A squadron of six B 24 Liberators (dubbed the "pink elephants" because of their African painting) had arrived during the PBY attacks, but as they came in under the low-hung clouds on their very first mission the leading plane got a direct hit that blew it all to pieces with such violence that two of the others were nearly wrecked. After this the Liberators stayed up at 18,000, dropping through the clouds. So did the B 17s when they came in, and no one knows for sure what they did hit. Float Zeros began to come up and bother them and the Kawanishis to poke all along the island chain. Through breaks in the mist it was visible that the Jap was building a fighter strip on Kiska.

He was gaining, and this in spite of the terrible setback he got on the Fourth of July, when the submarine *Growler* worked through the entrance of Kiska Harbor in water so shallow and boulder-strewn that the Japs apparently never thought of giving it special attention. Inside the periscope showed three Jap destroyers nested near shore. The sub hit one amidships with her first shot; readjusted and hit the second. The wave of the double explosion where they went to pieces threw her about, which gave the third destroyer time to heave short and fire two torpedoes of her own, which swished over our sub as she took aim for a third shot. It hit the destroyer square; she was broken into two parts that were burning feverishly and the other two Japs had disappeared as our boat submerged to work out of harbor with Jap seaplanes overhead.

Within three weeks five more Japanese destroyers were sent down off Kiska by our submarines. After that things seemed to have tapered off; they began to use nets and other protective devices and they got gun shy about employing destroyers in those foggy waters.

They were gaining. A couple of P 38 Lightnings (there were some at Umnak now) laid an air ambush for the Kawanishis and shot down two of them, but this was small stuff. Theobald's five cruisers on August 7 gave Kiska a surface bombardment, but most of these ships were on loan from other areas and under a strict prohibition against becoming seriously engaged. The bombardment consisted only of a couple of salvos flung into the fog at speed from ten miles out and was not repeated. It hardly could have been; August 7 was the date of the landing on Guadalcanal and one day later the Battle of Savo Island made cruisers the number one shortage item in the United States Fleet. It is quite likely that the knowledge that all our available surface force would be pinned in the South Pacific led the Japs at this juncture to change policy in the north.

Up to this time there had been numerous Japanese subs reported in the area and some of them were bombed, but they had made no attacks. The explanation worked out by our fliers at the time was that these subs were being used to reinforce Kiska—no other ships could be seen going in but the installations there continued to grow. Now in mid-August the Jap U-boats began to take the offensive against our ships. Simultaneously work at Kiska was speeded up; seaplane ramps and a couple of hangars were noted, road construction began, telephone poles went up along the roads, there was a submarine base and tailings to show where Japs were tunneling into the rock. The enemy's grand strategy had been thrown out of gear at Midway; but he was now in the position of a chess player offering his adversary pawns in both the South Pacific and the Aleutians. When we concentrated the major forces necessary to capture one the other would push through to queen.

The American reply was to check the advancing Aleutian pawn with light forces, which meant air. To handle this air campaign an air admiral was brought up—Rear Admiral J. W. Reeves, "Black

Jack" Reeves of the *Wasp*, the small, tough, unconventional man who had taken the Spitfires to relieve Malta, new to his stars.

Japanese attention had been fixed on Atka by not infrequent contacts with our seaplanes and their tenders there. On August 30 they even got a torpedo into the tender *Casco* off the island. The submarine that fired it was knocked off by an admirable piece of co-ordination between a PBY which bombed the undersea craft so it could not submerge and the destroyer *Reed* that was whistled up to sink her by gunfire.

But the important thing is the Japs were watching Atka. There is another island some hundred miles further out the chain—Adak, rising precipitous from the sea into three giant peaks with a bay and a brief foreshore nestling among them, exactly fighter-plane distance from Kiska. The bombers bound for the Jap base had photographed Adak from every angle on their way out and in whenever there was a break in the fogs till every inch of the place was mapped. On August 26 scouts of the Alaska Defense Command (they called themselves Castner's Cutthroats and claimed to eat Commandos for breakfast) were thrown on that foreshore from rubber boats in the dark. They had no food but dried salmon and no sleep; they found no Japs.

The report they sent back brought out one of the most singular caravans of ships that ever flew the American flag—old freighters, a couple of fishing scows, a paddle-wheel river boat, a couple of yachts, a schooner towed by tugs. On August 30 while the Jap sub was being sunk at Atka they pulled in under a fog you could walk on and began to get their gear ashore, army engineers and Seabees together. Rain came in on them along the flat projectory and froze where it struck. Icy seas rushed across the foreshore and drenched everybody to the skin.

When the boxes were opened it was discovered that the Seabees had little construction equipment (possibly some of it got smashed in the surf) and the Army almost no guns. It is characteristic of Admiral Reeves that he could swap navy artillery for army crackers and leave Washington to straighten out the paper work after the war, while in seventy-two hours his mixed force got a landing strip up long enough to take the first fighter flown in from Umnak.

V

It has been said that the Japanese Aleutian operation was a success because with limited means they succeeded in forcing us to a great expenditure of effort and material. This would be true if it could be demonstrated that in some more essential field we lost ground for lack of the forces used in the north; or if Admiral Reeves's expenditures were higher in proportion to his resources than those of the enemy. Neither proposition can be made to stand up. The Aleutians remained a low priority theater for both sides, but lower on ours than on that of the Japs. They had more men there; they got construction gangs started before we did and they were early and lavish in the theater with what they esteemed as the proper type of military tools—Kawanishis, Float Zeros, submarines and destroyers. Where they missed out was in failing to realize that colonial warfare is always an engineering problem. Build Fort Duquesne and you hold the Northwest Territory; Build Adak and—

On September 14 the new runway was fully ready. A powerful force of Libs and B 17s took off for Kiska, for the first time with full fighter escort. They had a clear day for Alaska, only one that would cause all planes at La Guardia Field to be grounded, and so our fliers had themselves a time. The runway begun so long before the one on Adak was still incomplete, but they dug up what there was of it. They popped three big cargo ships in the harbor, sank a couple of small minesweeps and bombed the daylights out of three seaplane tenders. P 39s went down to stitch rows of holes across the decks of three submarines with their 37 millimeter cannon and five planes were shot down. Most of the Japanese camp burned and the docks in their submarine base were blown apart while our losses were two planes and an accidental crash.

There were no more days like that. First Japanese reaction was apparently to think that the big raid was a softener-upper for a major attack. They pulled in their detachments from Attu and Agattu and prepared to get some blood for the Emperor before dying. When we only sent more planes over they grew calmer, sent the Attu party back and continued the laborious task of digging a fighter strip out of Kiska by hand labor while a bomber strip began to grow on the other island.

Admiral Reeves now sent his bombers over quite regularly, but "results were not observed" became a more and more frequent line in the communiqués and it was only rarely that, as on September 25, they could catch a ship in the harbor. That day seven Jap planes were knocked down and a week later three more, but the Jap fighters were going more and more shy. The Float Zero was no match for our land-based planes and after awhile they admitted it by not sending any more up from the Kuriles.

On the other hand as winter clamped down on that stormiest of all seas, they developed a system of blockade running by night and storm that was sufficiently effective for its purpose of keeping the garrisons alive and helping their strength to grow by a little. Some of it was probably done by submarines; some was certainly done by small surface ships.

The weather and other Aleutian conditions continued to bring down more of our planes than the Japs—a whole formation of five Libs in December, for instance, two of them vanishing from the earth, the other three making crash landings at fogged-in fields. It was during this winter that Lieutenant C. E. Rodebaugh got himself a DFC when four Zeros attacked his PBY. He flew round and round the small island, one wing so close to the cliffs that they could not dive on him without spilling, till their gas gave out and they went home. It was also during this winter that we lost a big minesweeper, the *Wasmuth*, when pounding seas tore depth charges loose from her stern and blew her up on them.

Incidents: by March 15, "the only good bombing day so far this year," pilots returning from Attu and Kiska described both places as stronger than ever, with several new flak batteries in position and a whole series of revetments. On both islands the strips had crawled forward (though still incomplete) and the only gain we had to show for the winter was that a new small strip had been set up on the forwardly island of Amchitka, which had been passed up by the Japs as an unpalatable ice-water swamp. The whole Aleutian campaign had reached a stagnation of locked pawns. Among men who got their mail three months after it was written, their pay six months after it was due and reading matter only after it had been barbered by the censor's shears, morale was definitely low.

VI

Far in the south Guadalcanal flew the Stars and Stripes; the new carriers and battleships were roaming the Pacific, the African invasion was so much a success that Army and Navy could contemplate a serious campaign in the Aleutians without shuddering at the cost. Through late February and windy March ships began to run along the chain bringing men and equipment for an offensive. Fleet Air Wing 4, that had flown the PBYs till they fell apart, got some new Venturas and used them from Amchitka and Adak.

Rear Admiral Thomas Kinkaid, who had led the fleet through the Battle of the Eastern Solomons moved in with his staff; rumor said there were battleships coming, and the correspondents (who had been, not hyperbolically but actually restricted to writing about how Alaskan mountains were named for colleges) speculated that the attack would be made during the short belt of good weather between mid-April and the end of May.

The Japs made the same speculation. It was thought they might; and that they might reinforce to meet the new thrust. Far out to the west of Adak to intercept any effort at such reinforcement Admiral Kinkaid had sent a patrol force under Rear Admiral Charles H. McMorris, another man new to his stars, who in the *San Francisco* had led the line on the night of October 11 when all those Jap ships were sunk off Cape Esperance.

Give him a glance as he stands on his bridge, a tall man with a red face, an Alabaman without an accent. He was in the destroyer *Shaw* during the last war, the ship that had her bows blown off and got home anyway; now described as a man who could go flaming sarcastic when crossed, swearing at anyone within sound of his voice, but just as quick to award a "well done." Both characteristics traced to an extraordinary speed of thought process which found it difficult to comprehend slower minds—an officer on his staff once said McMorris would gently pick up a sheaf of papers and leaf through them, memorizing everyone and carrying on a conversation at the same time, like Thomas Babington Macaulay. He had his flag in the light cruiser *Richmond*, one of the old *Omaha* class, designed in 1914, built at the close of the last war, with more than

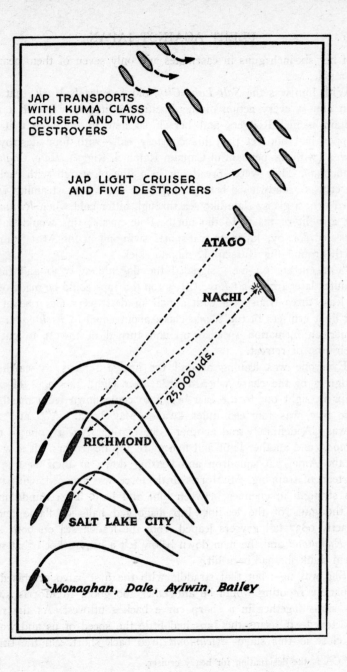

JAP TRANSPORTS
WITH KUMA CLASS
CRUISER AND TWO
DESTROYERS

JAP LIGHT CRUISER
AND FIVE DESTROYERS

ATAGO

NACHI

25,000 yds.

RICHMOND

SALT LAKE CITY

Monaghan, Dale, Aylwin, Bailey

half her six-inch guns in casemates and only seven of them bearing on a side.

With him was the *Salt Lake City*, old *Swayback Maru*, that had seen almost every action of the Pacific fighting, now under a new captain named Rodgers and herself so new to the area that the skipper had not yet paid his courtesy call—with four destroyers, *Bailey* (with the pennant of Captain Ralph S. Riggs), *Dale*, *Coghlan*, *Monaghan*. They were spread out in a line of search with each of the cruisers sandwiched between a pair of destroyers, steaming westward over a glassy slate-like sea through bitter cold when *Richmond* got a sight of masts to the north. Pole masts; this would be the expected convoy, Japanese transports swinging in for Attu from far north around the Russian Komandorskies.

"Concentrate on me," signaled the flagship at 0730 and fifteen minutes later from *Salt Lake City*'s top the Japs could be made out—at least three transports with a pair of destroyers and one of the old light cruisers of the *Kuma* class, about equal to *Richmond*. The American formation speeded up and turned northwest to cut off their line of retreat.

Everyone was leaning around the bridge screens to watch the progress of the chase when a little after eight, messages of more ships in sight out to the east began to come down from masthead. The first was fourteen miles away—"May be a CA"* and then it was CA definitely and another—one of their *Nachis*, one of their *Atagos*, and another light and five more Jap destroyers, all now east of the American squadron and bearing down at their best speed. Instead of trapping, McMorris' little force was trapped, with twice his strength in enemies between him and base. To remind him of it the guns of the leading Jap disgorged balls of flame and at exactly 0837 tall geysers leaped from the leaden sea on both sides of *Richmond* and the men down below felt a heavy shock that made them think she had been hit.

She was not; but that straddle with the first salvo promised the Japanese shooting would be altogether too good. McMorris swung his ships together in a sharp curve back southwest. As the range shortened—it seems the Japs had little the speed of us and wanted to close at this stage—*Richmond* fired back short. On the turn it

* CA is the designation for heavy cruiser.

seems the enemy recognized that we had a heavy cruiser. They
shifted targets and dumped a couple of salvos short of this main
antagonist. By 0842 she was shooting back, fast. The second salvo
was a beautiful straddle and at the third the American squadron
drew an enormous dividend from a combination of good gunnery
and good luck.

It went right in on the *Nachi* at the base of the bridge, the ship that
had been flying signals which marked her as the flag. A huge flame

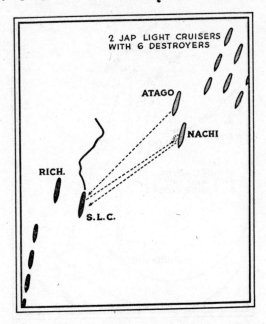

swept up and spread till it engulfed the whole towering pagoda. Beneath it the hull spat smoke; her salvos missed a beat and she dropped
back.

Salt Lake shifted to the *Atago*; got a couple of straddles on her
and maybe a hit. But the Jap damage control was all right; eight
minutes later they were coming along again in pursuit, firing as
before. Their two light cruisers were off to port, east of the heavies
with the destroyers around them, covering the transports. The range
was still 25,000 yards—too long for anything but the eight-inch guns
of the heavies.

Now as the *Salt Lake* worked southwest, carrying the load of the whole fleet, she could fire only the five guns of her two after turrets. The Japs had all twenty of their big guns bearing and were dumping shells into the sea all round the American heavy. "Left ten degrees rudder," Captain Rodgers would say, and then to his exec, "Well, which way shall we turn next?" as he strove to figure out how the Japs would correct their fire. It was remarked that while the *Atago's* salvos were falling in close bunches still, those from the *Nachi* were

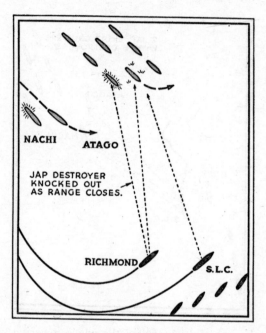

spread wide and sometimes did not contain the right number of shells. Something wrong with that ship, possibly her main fire control station knocked out by that first punishing hit; but at 0910 *Salt Lake City* herself took a hit aft, fortunately not a damaging blow.

At 0920 the *Nachi* was hit again, a beauty on the superstructure aft, with a long stream of smoke which this time did not die down. She slowed; the *Atago* shot past her, and quick as thought McMorris swung his whole squadron to the northeast and contact with the Japanese lights. *Richmond's* guns opened up as the range closed, the first Jap light was surrounded by splashes and maybe hit as he turned away. One of their destroyers was definitely punched and dropped out, with another standing by. Their whole squadron spread in movements of wild disco-ordination with no signals from the flag. Suddenly the fight was turning northwest.

At little after 1000 the *Nachi* got herself under control and straightened out with the *Atago*. They came along again and about this time it seems to have occurred to the Japanese light cruiser men that they

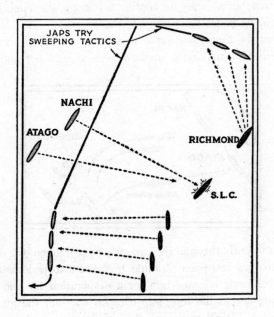

could practice the sweeping tactics Harwood had used on the *Graf Spee* off the River Plate. They swung out to side and side for a torpedo attack, each with a tail of two destroyers. But the *Richmond* opened up on one flank, our four destroyers on the other; one Jap group sheered off nervously and the other remained at long range.

It was clearly our battle to nearly 1100 but now whatever gods of luck there be straightened things out for the favors they had awarded us earlier. *Salt Lake* was hit three times in quick succession, one of the shells through a fuel tank down into the engine spaces. Bering Sea ice water rushed in and was only checked by damage-control parties

working chest deep. Worse still, some of it got into the fuel oil. Sea
water will not burn; the *Salt Lake*'s speed dropped off, an enemy
salvo landed so close aboard that it jarred the whole ship, the steering gear went sour so she could not dodge. Her destroyers rushed
out to cover her with smoke.

Back at the Adak base army bombers were feverishly unloading
the fragmentation missiles with which they had filled up for a go at
Kiska, and taking in armor piercers. Another cruiser was raising
steam for sea; ships were in motion all along the Aleutian chain.
But it would be hours before any of them got there and hours were
too much as the *Salt Lake* came to a stop with all her fires extin-
guished with *Dale* making a smoke screen around her and the Japs

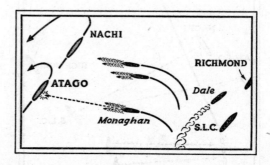

firing intermittently through the gaps where it thinned. Captain Riggs
of the destroyers had been pleading to make a torpedo attack. Now
Admiral McMorris released him for a desperation try and the three
went rushing across the long gap of open sea into the guns of two
heavy cruisers. "We'll never see those fellows again," said someone
on *Salt Lake*'s bridge.

Bailey was hit; hit again. Her speed dropped off to 15 knots; she
swirled around and let her torpedoes go at long range, 9,000 yards
from the enemy, lest she should not have a chance to let them go at
all. The others raced past her a half step, firing their own torpedoes
in their guns. They noted how the *Nachi* was shooting only from a
single turret and as they watched, saw a salvo from the *Coghlan*'s
5-inch go right into the face of one of the *Atago*'s gunhouses. As the
three coasted around their curve, the *Salt Lake* away behind them

suddenly burst through the smoke screen at full speed and opened up
with all her guns.

That was the battle. The Japs turned west and south to get away
from the run of the torpedoes and kept right on going. With a badly
crippled destroyer and a cruiser that could not go very far, McMorris
was in no condition to pursue forces double his own, no matter how
badly damaged or poorly co-ordinated.

VII

And that, as it turned out, was essentially the campaign. In the
south, American troopships were beginning to come around the cape
of New Guinea into Bismarck Sea; MacArthur's planes were bombarding Wewak and our warships operating in Kula Gulf. The Japs
needed every ship they could get for the swift night attacks with gun
and torpedo they were planning, to stop our crawl up the Solomon
chain, and their military investment in that area was larger than in
the Aleutians. They decided to cut the loss in that unsatisfactory
northern campaign and when the American bombers rode daily over
Attu and Kiska in their preliminary softening up, Tokyo did nothing
but announce that the fighting in the islands had "become a series of
tragic and heroic incidents for the Japanese soldier."

On May 7 the blow was due to fall. The biggest invasion force
since Guadalcanal steamed along the island chain, headed by the old
battleships *Nevada, Idaho* and *Pennsylvania* with the escort carrier
Nassau in support and transports bearing a full division of army
troops to land on Attu—too big a force to miss overwhelming its
objective. But the blundering mischance native to that land of storms
rode with them as with everyone else who had penetrated there. Off
Adak they ran into a fog remarkable even for the Aleutians; for
three days the fleet groped blindly around Bering Sea, using radar
all the time, hoping the enemy had not been warned.

On May 11 in the morning they made in on Attu and while the
battleships raked with gunfire the trenches that our air scouts had
photographed along the beach, landing craft put the infantry men
ashore in bays north and south of the peninsula that is just westward from Attu's central mass.

There were no Japs to meet them. The trenches were merely lines of spading across the black soil, put there to fool photographers. But when the advance across the saddle of hills to hook up the two detachments began, it was discovered that the enemy were in presence all right, dug into caves and cliffs where it was almost impossible to get at them, even to locate them so artillery fire could be laid down. Then came the second discovery; the troops were of the Seventh Division, desert trained. Though they had been given warm clothing their foot gear was the ordinary military low shoe, which allowed the feet to get beautifully wet on that boggy beach during the short Aleutian day and to freeze during the zero Aleutian night. (Why the experienced Arctic fighters of the Alaska Defense Command were not used for this job no one has ever explained.) There were soon as many frozen feet casualties as there were from Jap bullets, the divisional commander had to be removed, the whole battle for Attu went badly and blunderingly and ended on a note of horror with a Jap suicide charge in the course of which they burst into a field hospital, killed the doctors and the wounded.

Well, they were wiped out—2100 dead (or more—that many were buried) and just 11 prisoners from the island. That promised extremely rough going at Kiska where there were so many more Japs, and preparations for this bigger attack were made with extreme care. Everyone knows what happened when it was made in August. Nothing happened; there was not a Jap left on the island, though there had been AA fire from it only two days before.

Thus the Aleutian campaign ended as it began, a campaign of uncertainty, brilliance and blunders, distant from glory. The men fought well; as many decorations were earned there as in any theater of the war (though not always awarded), some of the officers thought, well. It has seemed futile and unsatisfactory to many observers on our side; but if so for us, how much more for the enemy—for theirs was the heavier loss, their's the high hopes and deep disappointments; and not we but they had to bear the weight of the final postscript:

"Washington. A Pacific Fleet Announcement: Paramushiru and Shimushu in the Kurile Islands were bombed by Ventura search planes of Fleet Air Wing Four before dawn today. All our aircraft returned."

The Turkey-Shoot of Saipan

IT HELPS comprehension of naval battles to regard them as belonging to three general types. In one both parties approach the contact willingly; confident, even when their forces are inferior, that they have some tactical or technical means of bringing off a victory. Examples: Midway, Jutland. In the second type, one of the fleets has been caught in a situation from which there is no outlet but battle; forced to fight, not for the attainment of some strategic mission, but for its life. Examples: Santiago, Tsushima. Somewhere in between lies the battle in which one side is trying to do something by means of ships but without fighting a naval battle, and in which the tactics revolve around the raider's efforts to get away, like Dogger Bank in the last war.

After the great three-day fight off Guadalcanal in November, 1942, the contest of mutual confidence was no longer for the Japanese. They made violent air and destroyer attacks all through the remainder of the campaign for the Solomons, culminating in the cruiser battle of Empress Augusta Bay, a year after the night Admiral Lee ran up the Slot. But there was no more fire in their bellies. They struck at airfields, supply dumps, convoys when they thought they could find them unprotected. They were constantly trying to avoid battle and to break it off when it was forced upon them, and they did not risk their major units even for raiding purposes. After the Battle of Santa Cruz in October, 1942, their carriers were no more seen save by prowling submarines. After Guadalcanal in November, there were no more of their battleships, and this endured for a year and a half.

It was not altogether unexpected. The details of prewar anticipations differed among themselves and from the actual working out of the movements of conflict, but through all ran the major line so clearly expressed in that best of all imaginary histories, Hector Bywater's *Great Pacific War*. The United States would have to work through the maze of Japanese islands below the equator, during which process the Japanese, inferior on the battle line, would wage a campaign of attrition. When the island screen had been penetrated there would be a campaign for Guam in the Marianas, and since the lodgment of an American Fleet there would threaten Japan with blockade, the enemy would come out and strike with all his strength in a tremendous sea battle which would decide every real military issue of the war. The Japs would approach that battle with confidence, for they could choose their own hour and would have had the opportunity to prepare something in the line of tactical or technical surprise.

It is easy to see where the actual event differed from the predictions. The Japs had more South Pacific islands than any anticipation called for and they used them primarily as air bases, which no one had anticipated. Their temporary superiority on the battle line as the result of Pearl Harbor and the self-confidence that brought them too late to Midway to take advantage of that superiority were unforeseen; and so was the possibility that sea-borne air power would enable us to bypass such enormous bases as Truk and Rabaul. But by the spring of 1944 the war was well along the main highroad of predicted strategy. The American Fleet had twice hit Truk with great force; it was no longer a factor. With the capture of the Green and Admiralty islands and the landing at Cape Gloucester, Rabaul was out of the picture. At Kwajalein and Eniwetok we had gained intermediate bases that made possible the solution of the supply problem during the great swing forward toward Guam, key island of the war; and the moment envisioned by Bywater and many another had come.

Guam is not an isolated island but a member of a group, the Marianas, rocky and volcanic, nearly five hundred miles long. The northern islands are mostly uninhabited and are all unimportant. Everything that matters is concentrated on Guam, Rota, Tinian, and Saipan (with the exception of one small staging airstrip on Pagan). These are at the southern end of the chain, heavily populated by a cheerful people of singularly mixed origin and dietary habits, the Chamorros. It rains among these islands practically every day; the temperature is seldom below eighty; and since Magellan came there in 1521 they have normally been under the domination of an exterior military power which wanted them for reasons of strategy. The Japs took the Chamorro girls for their Yoshiwara houses and set the men to growing sugar and working on fortifications under a ferocious corvée in order to preserve the Asiatic Co-Prosperity Sphere against the encroachments of the white races.

Of all the islands Saipan is the best provided with the requisites of a place of arms—an excellent natural harbor on the western side, near the local metropolis of Garapan; and a good and wide anchorage inside the southeastern tip, called Magicienne Bay after a wandering

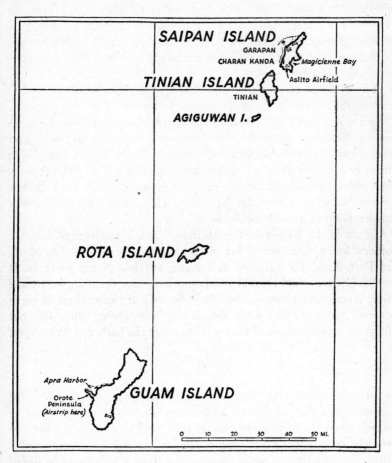

British frigate. The island is one of cliffs and caves. When the Japs got the place from the spoils of Germany in 1919 they set up artillery among the natural features in places where it could not be got at by bombs. Later they built a good airfield at Aslito in the south, and also smaller strips at Garapan and toward the northern tip.

The most practical beaches were on the eastern side where Magicienne Bay gives shelter that is often necessary in this region, which is the mother of Pacific storms as Greenland of those in the Atlantic. There were underwater obstructions offshore at all these beaches and presumably mines. When our fleet, sweeping north past Truk on February 22, 1944, gave the place a good going-over by means of carrier planes, they found the AA fire was hearty and fairly accurate, indicating that the garrison was composed of good troops in considerable numbers.

Tinian lies south of Saipan, so near that medium artillery can fire across the strait. It is more rugged and rocky than its neighbor. There was a small airfield and a smallish harbor where search planes in the February air strike found assorted sampans, and here also there was plenty of AA artillery. South of Tinian again, and visible from it, is the small island of Agiguwan with no military installations but with a radio station. Some sixty miles farther on is Rota, flattest of the Marianas, where the Japs had a considerable air station with dispersal areas in outlying fields.

Guam is the largest of the Marianas, rough and rugged like the others, but with a central flat plateau. It has the best harbor of all, at Port Apra, for situation and room, but full of the coral heads which Congress had refused an appropriation for dredging before the war. There was room on the island for military operations of some extent; and there was a big airfield on Orote Point, which juts out from the western flank of the island to cover the harbor at Port Apra.

II

In spite of the familiarity of many American officers with the ground on Guam, Admiral Nimitz picked Saipan as the point of attack when the matter came up in staff conference. There would be trouble enough with Jap planes anyway, staged down the Bonins from the homeland; if we hit Saipan first these planes could be forced to fight at the end of their maximum run, whereas if Guam were the target they might slip into fields on the other islands and so be in position to attack.

The place was thoroughly surveyed by photo planes during the February strike and again later. From the pictures the interpreters estimated that the Japs could not have many more than twenty-five thousand troops on the island, even allowing for their usual crowding and concealments. But as these were fanatics who would fight till their ears fell off, it was necessary to provide the attack with numbers as well as the fire superiority they would get from sea and air. Therefore three divisions were placed under command of General Holland Smith—"Howling Mad Smith"; two of them were Marines (the Second and Fourth) and the third was the 27th Division of the Army, a National Guard outfit which had performed creditably in the amphibious operation at Makin.

The tactical problem of getting them ashore with minimum losses differed in degree but not in kind from that which had been so brilliantly solved at Kwajalein and Eniwetok. To the crushing artillery cover that had been given in those attacks could be added support from a new type of weapon—the rocket, here employed on a large scale for the first time. That ought to take care of the Japs ashore.

But to consider the shore problem only was oversimplification. The Japs had been saving up the major units of their surface fleet and all their naval air service during eighteen months in which none of them had seen action. Eighteen months—in that time they would have replaced plane, carrier, and pilot losses; their fliers could be expected to be the same type we had met at Midway, as good as ours. They could choose their own moment for attack during the operations, and no admiral asks a more favorable opportunity to strike a blow than when his opponent is encumbered by a fleet of slow transports, which exert upon tactics the effect of an iron band, constricting them within a narrow circle.

This is to say that the enemy was expected to approach that decisive battle with confidence and a new bag of tricks.

To meet them, Nimitz chose Raymond Spruance, the "thinking machine" who had won Midway, his most trusted officer for those immense combinations that involve fleets and oceans, a leader capable of abnegating even his chances for the long-desired sea victory if the process would gain him the essential objective of Saipan. For Spruance was organized a new Fifth Fleet. The new fast battleships were under Rear Admiral Willis Augustus Lee, who had led the charge up the Slot the night the Jap battleships went down; they would have to bear the brunt of any gun fighting that was done. A bombardment group was organized from the old battleships—*Maryland, Tennessee, California*—the fat boys, built out with bulges as protection against the excellent Jap torpedoes till they looked pregnant. These furnished punch; a handful of cruisers were added to give rapidity of fire; and the command of the whole was given to Rear Admiral Jesse Oldendorf, careful and precise, who had had the anti-submarine command at Trinidad when the going was tough. The transports and their guard of more old battleships were under Vice Admiral R. K. Turner, the amphibious expert.

The fleet that would have to carry the shock of any Japanese counteraction was Task Force 58, the carrier force, commanded by Vice Admiral Mark A. Mitscher, small and wizened, active as a monkey, Voltairean in face and speech, always wearing a baseball cap with a long peak. He had flown the NC-1 in the first attempt to cross the Atlantic and had commanded the *Hornet* when she carried Doolittle and his bombers on their way to Tokyo.

His force was New Navy; of that whole carrier group only one ship had been in the water when the war broke out and that one was *Enterprise*, which had been in everything. At Midway Spruance had had the tactical inspiration of keeping his carriers widely separated and thus only one of them suffered injury, while the Japs bunched theirs and lost them all. Mitscher's organization was a logical extrapolation from this; his carriers were divided into groups, each under a separate admiral, with each group about evenly divided* among the big new carriers of the *Essex* type and those light carriers built on cruiser hulls and loaded largely with fighter squadrons. To each group were attached the antiaircraft cruisers which have become such a nightmare to the Japanese bomber squadrons, other cruisers for surface work, and destroyers for everything. For tactical purposes Lee's battleships were added to the whole force.

Behind Mitscher came the escort carrier groups of Rear Admirals Ragsdale and Connolly, an aero-naval innovation. Up to this time in the Pacific it had been possible to support each forward step from some air base on land. But the Marianas were right out in the blue, beyond the range of anything we had except the long-legged search planes. This time the air support would all have to come from carrier

*As listed in Jensen's *Carrier War,* which shows an ideal rather than an actual organization.

decks and there would have to be a lot of it, for Saipan was no coral island that could be shot over by the guns of a destroyer. But the Jap fleet was expected to show up and put in a demand for every carrier plane we could get in the air; and it would be sure to come just at the moment when some crisis in the land operations had developed and support there was most needed. There were available a number of those escort carriers on merchant hulls, which the Kaiser yards had been emitting as rapidly as a drunk emits burps; and since the Jap attempts to use their submarines had been so flat a failure, these ships were not needed for their designed purpose. They had been employed in carrying planes forward during the drive for the central Pacific; now they were given composite fighter-bomber squadrons and sent out to lie just beyond gun range from the shore, furnishing air support for the land operations. Some of the fighters mounted rockets (for the first time) which were regarded with suspicion by the pilots.

It was the largest fleet in history on any basis of comparison. Late-comers had trouble finding anchorage space in the lagoon where it assembled, a place larger than Manhattan Island.

III

"If we can land on Saipan," said one of the admirals to a press conference at Pearl Harbor, "we can land anywhere there are Japa-nese." The whole operation had to be one of the most exquisite co-ordination, reaching all the way from Washington to Chungking. In early June they were ready to try it and the fleet steamed west, Task Force 58 well in the lead with its planes out beyond the horizon.

Far in the north a cruiser squadron was pushing through the fogs, bound for Paramushiru; behind it, army bombers were being readied on the strips at Adak and Kiska to attack in co-ordination. Far in the south the bombers of the MacArthur command were waiting for the word to strike at Yap, Palau, and even Mindanao. The Seventh Army Air Force among the islands was going for Truk, Ponape, and Nauru. Far in the west, in China, coolies were carrying tins of gaso-line to load the B29s which would bring true the old Japanese night-mare of being bombed in their own homes.

Mitscher's operational plan was to give all the airfields in the Marianas a close fighter sweep at dawn on June 12 to knock down whatever Jap planes were airborne and to beat up those on the ground, thus eliminating the local air defense. The dive bombers would follow later in the day, going for defense installations but letting the big airfield at Aslito severely alone, for the landing operations were aimed at winning it for our own use at the earliest possible moment. Lee with his fast battleships would follow Mitscher in the afternoon, combing over the barracks areas as he had at Nauru, then swinging out into the offing to join Mitscher.

From the air strikes all around the circle of their empire, the Japs would be sure something was in the wind; it was our usual way of announcing a major move. All of these air attacks except the one on the Marianas were timed for late on the tenth or early on the eleventh. What with the bombing of the Japanese homeland, it was hoped that some confusion in the oriental mind might result, until the news of the fighter sweep followed by dive bomber and battleship attack on Saipan came in. At this point the Japs could deduce where the real attack was being made. But they would hardly be able to rally planes from the islands of the empire. They might send out their fleet and Spruance hoped they would, for by the time it could arrive Mitscher would long since have turned over the job of supporting the Marines to Oldendorf, Ragsdale and Connolly. In the meanwhile the first Jap reaction would certainly be to send numbers of planes from Japan itself, staging down the chain of the Bonins.

Therefore when Turner and company arrived off Saipan and some of Mitscher's force could be spared, two of the latter's task groups were to remain with the fast battleships, while the groups of Admirals Harrill and Clark, with *Essex, Hornet, Yorktown*, and four of the light carriers, ran north at their best speed and hit the airfields in the Jimas some time during the morning of the sixteenth. This would be just about right to catch the Japanese reserves of planes coming down from Japan and to catch most of them on the ground; for the Jap planes would want to make the long hop from Iwo to Saipan during the day, so as to arrive at dusk.

Admiral Clark was to have charge of this force, his first independent command—"Jocko" Clark, a big light-haired man with the full lips, jowled cheeks, and high nose bridge of an Indian (and in fact he had a strong infusion of Cherokee blood, so that he was always caricatured in the fleet as a bonneted brave and often saluted with war whoops). His energy was uproarious, undampered by the fact that digestive troubles forced him to live on tenderized chicken, creamed vegetables, and milk; he had been known to shout instructions across nearly half a mile of water to another carrier and to make them heard. Halsey-type temperament.

This was the plan and these the men. But war never goes exactly to plan; its effects are those of mutually antagonistic plans encountering each other. Before dawn on June 10 the Liberators hit every island in the Truk atoll. Ponape and Palau were also struck during the day and fast Mitchell light bombers gave Ocean Island and Nauru a thorough going-over. Marine fighter-bombers went after the outposts still held by the Japs in the Marshalls. The cruisers at Paramushiru were on time. All this was according to schedule. But the B29s were delayed; and more important still, in spite of the heavy combat patrols Mitscher had up, a couple of Jap snoopers got through and sighted his ships a full day early.

The Tokyo radio was pleased with the news. That night it declared: "It has been announced here that the Japanese Navy in the near future will win a great naval victory in the central Pacific. We are all waiting for the news." Apparently they too had a plan.

IV

The fact that Mitscher's ships had been discovered too soon knocked on the head any chance of getting a complete tactical surprise at Saipan. But Mitscher felt after a staff conference that he could still gain enough surprise to make it worth while speeding up and arriving a whole day early. He was all fast ships, but weather built up ahead so that it was afternoon of the eleventh, Sunday, when his planes flew off for the first attack that had originally been scheduled for the morning of the twelfth. There were "some two hundred" Grumman Hellcats. They hit all four of the southern Marianas at once—a pure fighter sweep.

As expected, the Japs were on the alert, but they apparently had not counted on our fighters coming so strong or quite so soon. Their air groups were well scattered, teamed badly, and broke up under the more precise attack of the American fighters, which came in tight knots, one after another like the units of a well-directed cavalry charge. Fighting Two, already one of our hottest squadrons in the Pacific, was high gun with twenty-four certified kills, but one brand-new unit in combat for the first time did almost as well. Search planes from the *Essex* spotted a Jap convoy just outside Saipan Harbor (it had apparently delayed long enough to unload even after our ships were sighted the previous night) and the dive bombers were sent after them during the evening. They hit everything there was and 11 of the convoy went down—a big oiler, 5 assorted cargo carriers, 3 corvettes, and a destroyer. When the ACI officers had finished their questions and totted up the reports, we had the loss of 11 fighters to regret (three of the pilots were picked up); but the convoy had been knocked off and 123 Jap planes had been downed. They could not have many more left in the Marianas.

Sketch maps made at the time show Mitscher's force with the battleships penetrating the wide gap between Tinian and Rota to run up the west side of the islands for its dawn attack of the twelfth, while the Clark detachment ran along the eastern flank of the chain. This seems a logical disposition of the forces from which the islands were hit that next morning, with the dive bombers and torpedo carriers now attacking under cover of the fighters.

During the night of the eleventh-twelfth there had been an air alert and a few Jap planes had come around dropping flares, but only out of curiosity, for they made no attempt to attack; and in the morning only sixteen came up to challenge ours. They were rapidly dispatched and the bombers went ahead with their business, which was a ground strike aimed at the fixed artillery positions of Saipan. The fliers reported that heavy and pretty accurate flak came up at them, and located the batteries for the task battleships to shell during the afternoon. One of the torpedo pilots, Bill Martin, did more than that. His was one of four planes shot down; he parachuted to a reef off the sugar-mill town of Charan Kanoa, and when a rescue plane found him he had buoyed the whole reef with cloth on bits of stick—a set of impromptu navigational markings that was extremely useful later.

That day a small tanker and a couple of cargo ships which had not been able to get out of Saipan Harbor were sunk there; and our search planes, looking for the remains of the convoy that had been hit the day before, missed it but picked up instead another six-ship

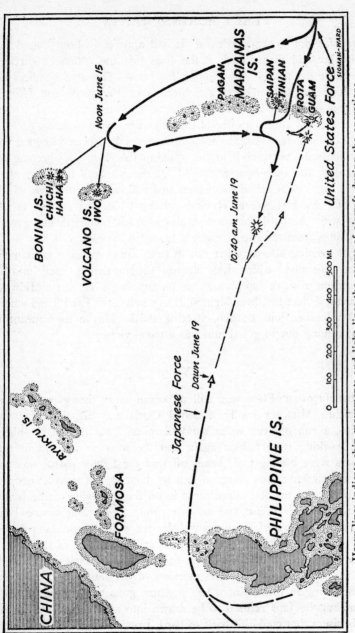

Heavy lines indicate ship movements and light lines the course of aircraft during the operations
which ended in the Saipan turkey-shoot on June 19, 1944

convoy far out to the northwest. It had apparently been bound for
Saipan but had turned back at the news that the American carriers
were loose again and was running for home. The dive bombers all
had things to do, but twenty fighters from *Yorktown* and *Hornet*
went out—a seven-hundred-mile round trip—and managed to set
two destroyers afire with one of the ships they were protecting.

The notable fact is that these proceedings had been intended for
the thirteenth, but owing to the speedup that had now become an
extra day, the time was employed by the bombers in going after
targets that had revealed themselves and making sure of those which
they had attacked before. Toward evening Oldendorf arrived in the
offing with the battleships and cruisers of his bombardment group,
and planes from the escort carriers began to appear.

That evening also a report ran in that caused genuine excitement
in the flag plot, which was already congratulating itself on the
destruction of more Jap planes than on any single day since Midway.
A Japanese fleet had been sighted, heavy units, off Tawi Tawi where
the Philippines join Borneo, steering north. Maybe they meant it
about coming out to get themselves a naval victory.

V

That Japanese Fleet was still an ocean away, however. On the
fourteenth Mitscher coolly detached Clark and his ships for the
Bonins, a run of over seven hundred miles. That day the bombers
were working over Saipan again and the men on the antiaircraft
cruisers were beefing their heads off that the fighter patrol was too
damned efficient; there were no Japs to shoot at, not even a snooper.
Oldendorf and his battleships went in on the west side of the island
toward Agingan Point, and another group along Magicienne Bay,
with the objective of forcing any batteries which might later prove
troublesome to show themselves and covering the work of the underwater demolition squads who were to get rid of obstacles and mines.

They started at 0540 in the morning of the fourteenth, well out,
corkscrewing in to a point where machine guns would have reached
them; but the Japs refused to be drawn into any contest with those
big bruisers that could hit back so hard. From the deck of *Tennessee*
could be seen only a town that looked like a minor Honolulu, white

houses among vegetation along a narrow littoral at the foot of hills—
the town of Charan Kanoa, silent completely, with an occasional light
plume of dust going up when something was hit. When the *Tennessee*
moved out into the layoff area for the night there was comment from

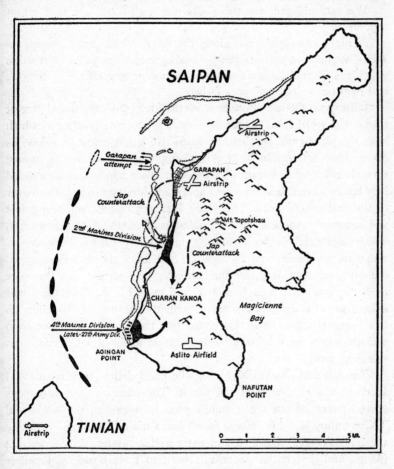

the young officers in the wardroom to the point that they were
ashamed to be fighting the war in such comfort, sitting down to a
good dinner after a good shower after a day's work that was noisy
but not dangerous.

"Just you wait," said one of the seniors. "When the pinch comes those carriers and fast battleships will be off chasing will-o'-the-wisps somewhere while we're doing the fighting."

"Well, if the Japs are good enough to break through the fast battleships we won't stand much of a chance."

"We can still put out the shells and we've still got that armor around us."

All night destroyers ran along the coast of Saipan, throwing in shells, as much to produce that psychological and physical exhaustion which makes real resistance impossible as for any effect on targets; and next day—June 15—was D-Day.

Halfway up the island on its western side is the capital and largest town—Garapan. Near it there are some practicable beaches to which both the planes and bombarding ships had given attention. Now, as dawn of the fifteenth broke, the battleship *Colorado* moved in toward these beaches with a train of transports from which men descended into landing craft, which formed and made for the beach under cover of the battleship's guns. The shore batteries opened up, firing fast and accurately; there were white splashes all among the landing craft, which zigzagged, broke formation, and finally turned back out of range to reassemble and try again. Once more the batteries rapped out—not quite so many, for the battleship was getting hits. But once more the boats lost their formation and turned back. Then there was a long pause and a third attempt, with the landing craft coming in from several angles; but this ended like the others and about 0930 the transports were hoisting their boats in again and *Colorado* was steaming away.

Vice Admiral Chuichi Nagumo, who had led the Jap fleet to Pearl Harbor, was in charge of the island. The fake was an outrageous success; now he put out a vainglorious broadcast to the world and Tokyo telling how his defense forces had sunk a battleship, "probably the *New Jersey*," damaged two more and a carrier, shot down 124 planes, and driven the Americans back to their boats by Japanese valor. Tokyo Rose had the story that evening.

If the movement at the north could have been carried farther, it might have yielded some extremely useful results in locating the guns around Garapan, which were to prove troublesome later. But a bad situation had developed down at the landing point on both sides of

Charan Kanoa, which made it necessary for the battleship and her attendant transports to leave.

The arrangement there was for the battleships to lie pretty well out on the flanks of the operation, using their big guns, with the cruisers and destroyers in close support at the center; the Fourth Marines making their landing at Agingan Point while the Second Marines went in north of the town.

The thing had been planned to the last inch and ounce of shell fire; but here the Japs had rocks and caves screened by vegetation from eyes in the air, and sense enough not to fire the guns that were in them till they could get something by shooting. There had been a sample of this the night before at Nafutan Point, where *California* had been working over the shore positions with a cruiser and a division of destroyers. The battleship pulled out first; when she was beyond range the Japs suddenly opened rapid fire from a well-hidden battery in a cliff against the lighter vessels whose armor they could penetrate. These vessels had to pull out under a smoke screen and this delayed the whole landing of the fifteenth for some twenty minutes while the big ships blasted down the cliff to get rid of that battery.

At Agingan there was no such luck now in persuading the enemy to announce his presence. When the amphibian tanks went in at a little before 0900 under clouds of smoke and a blaze of rockets they met a perfectly murderous fire. At the most southerly of the three Agingan beaches it was an enfilade so bad that the Marines were driven out of position to a landing five hundred yards north of where they should have been. This firing was from small stuff, but at the same time some medium guns farther back in the ravine behind Charan Kanoa were firing on the line of the reef (which had been perfectly calibrated) with such effect that only a few of the LVTs were able to get in and disbark their crews; a good many were hit and the casualties were high. The cruisers did not seem to be able to get this fire down; the battleships were heavily engaged with some big guns on steep Mount Tapotshau behind the town; and in *Tennessee* at least they had discovered there was nothing to be ashamed of, for the ship had been hit and had dead men aboard.

Half an hour after the first men reached the beach there were some ten thousand Marines on Agingan; but no artillery carriers had got through to help them, several LCMs with tanks aboard had capsized trying to get through Charan Kanoa channel, and the ten thousand were pinned down by machine-gun fire beside a narrow strip of beach, where they were being pounded by mortar shells which came arching over the reverse slopes of hills to lay explosions along the line with an accuracy that was mathematical and frightening. One marine officer at least thought the situation critical. There was a hasty reorganization of the forces afloat which sent *Maryland* to help out the cruisers against the medium guns, brought *Colorado* down to take over *Maryland's* spot against the Second Division beach, and brought into action earlier than planned both the dive bombers from the CVEs and the fighters with their rockets. The LCMs were ordered to disbark their tanks directly on the reef and let them go in under their own power.

If the Japs had achieved something of a surprise by the strength of their dispersed artillery, they now got one in return. The big guns of the battleships were too much for the Jap medium artillery. One battleship hit an ammunition dump back of Charan Kanoa; another set a fuel dump burning with so much smoke that it hampered the Jap fire control. The rocket-armed fighters were beyond all expectation effective against the mortar positions. "You just drive right in on them and they haven't got a thing they can send back," exclaimed an enthusiastic pilot; "I'll never carry anything else on my plane as long as I live." A number of tanks broke down on the coral of the reef, but those that did get ashore released the Marines from their predicament; and by two in the afternoon it was possible to get two battalions of artillery ashore, organized and firing, while a few patrols began to work up the hills around Charan Kanoa and pick off the Jap observation posts.

At about the same time the airmen found indisputable evidence that the Japs were organizing a heavy counterattack around Aslito airfield with a group of tanks. Our own tanks could not reach the area because the narrow strip between was crowded with Marines and landing craft; Mitscher's dive bombers came over and broke up the organization of the counterattack.

Toward evening of the fifteenth it became apparent that the objective line for the day would not quite be reached; but the Japs seemed too fought out to take any advantage of this. So everything was dug in, the command posts went ashore (that of the Fourth Marines was only fifty yards from the water's edge), and communication wire was strung.

At twilight the destroyers came in, and all night they fired into Charan Kanoa and the valley behind. It was as well they did; with the day the Japs made a counterattack designed to split the tenuous connection between the Second and Fourth divisions. A good deal of the sting had been taken out of it by that all-night shooting; now the Marines expertly cut the attacking column to pieces from both flanks, pinched out the burning town as an incident, and went on with the plan of the day, which was for the Second to attack north along the coast toward Garapan, the Fourth to work south and west around Agingan Point toward Aslito field.

There was hard fighting all day among the rocks and draws, mostly platoon operations, with the planes from the CVEs working hard on targets of call. The beaches were still congested, with wounded going out and supplies coming in, and it was still not possible to get the army men ashore. It would seem to have been this night that the heavy ships moved out of the immediate area (they shelled Guam at dawn on the seventeenth); and the Japs tried to use the occasion for another counterattack.

Some twenty-five tanks—all they had left—were put into an effort down the Charan Kanoa Valley while a good-sized force of Jap infantry, in those heavy barges they use, slipped down the shore from Garapan under cover of the last dark before dawn and tried a counterlanding behind the position of the Second Marines. The barge attack was broken up by the guns of our landing craft before it got a man ashore. As for the inland effort, General Harry Schmidt of the Fourth Marines had expected it to be made in exactly that way; and having secured some crests of the central mountain chain, he had executed a half-wheel, bringing the bulk of his forces facing north. Between his own fire and that of the ships the attack was badly beaten up, all the tanks being destroyed. At daybreak and with good airplane observation the big guns of the old battleships demolished the Japanese infantry concentrations.

During that day, the seventeenth, the army division was landed; it pushed through the rear of the Fourth Marines and began to close round Aslito Field. General Smith now had a good idea of the enemy positions and a count of their strength. There were about two divisions north of him (minus their casualties, which had been heavy) and about a regiment around Aslito. He had also gained a beachhead sufficiently large so that parts of it were no longer within range of Japanese artillery—which meant that he was able to maintain himself without the help of guns on the sea. The enemy had been hit so hard as apparently to be in need of reorganization, and was for the moment quiescent.

This success was not twenty-four hours too early. For the seventeenth also brought news that Mitscher and Spruance would have to leave the Marines to their own devices for the time being. *The whole Japanese southern fleet, with battleships, cruisers, destroyers, tankers and a parade of new carriers, had been sighted rounding Luzon and steaming northeastward!*

VI

As Jocko Clark's force ran north it began to hit weather, and by morning of the fifteenth it was bucking a half gale, with an overcast many hundreds of feet high, low clouds scudding along the surface, and rain squalls sometimes hiding half the ships. By noon the force was in range of the Bonins but the carriers were pitching so violently that some of the air officers doubted whether Clark would order them to fly.

He did so order them, however—sending off strikes against all the known airfields at Chichi Jima and Haha Jima in the Bonins proper and Iwo Jima in the Kazan Islands, which are a prolongation of the chain, the nearest our ships had ever come to Japan. The Japs were caught napping by such boldness and such weather; at Iwo they had only two planes off the ground out of sixteen, and at Chichi, where they had about forty aloft, they were neither high up nor well formed when our fighters hit them. Thirty-three were shot down with hardly a return.

The bombing did not go quite so well; one section discovered and lamed a big cargo ship, but it had to be finished off by a destroyer from the screen. Again and again fliers had to hunt for a full hour over their targets to find holes in the cloud cover; some brought back full loads and all had navigation trouble returning to the carriers.

In the afternoon a second strike was flown off, but as the sun went down the sea rose instead of flattening, and it was a wild business getting the planes in at night with lights flashing on and off across the heaving decks. At least one plane did not quite make it on the light carrier *Belleau Wood*; the gas tank went and a huge puff of windblown flame leaped up, so high that everyone in the force thought the ship was gone. But our damage control had advanced since the day the first *Lexington* went down; they had the fire out so quickly that the flight operations of the next day were not in the least interfered with.

That night Clark received information that the Japs (as Mitscher and Spruance had foreseen) were sending a lot of planes down from Japan itself to help the defense of Saipan. Fortunately the weather moderated to some extent and the next morning our pilots could see what they were hitting. The Jap relief planes were coming through all right, the big majority of them bombers; so there was no effective opposition for our forces, who disposed of forty-seven more on the ground and in the sky, meanwhile hitting the runways too.

The Marianas were now fairly well isolated by air and sea, and aboard Clark's ships they formed the "Jocko Jima Real Estate Development Corporation," with printed certificates of membership. Men who were with him say he wanted to stay in the area and conduct an aerial blockade of the Bonins, the first in history; but that was impossible. The news was in from the Philippines, and on the seventeenth Clark's detached group was running down to rejoin Mitscher, with his combat patrols knocking down long-range Jap snoopers at the rate of three a day.

VII

It is time now to look at the situation from the Japanese point of view, so far as this can be deduced. That peculiar race observes a rule of etiquette not unknown to other Orientals, of never telling an interlocutor anything he does not wish to hear. But Japan carries it to far greater lengths. When the Empress was at her lying-in in the days before the war, for instance, the first announcement from the imperial bedchamber was that she had given birth to the son for which everyone was hoping. It was blandly explained to foreigners who knew the announcement to be untrue that the mistake could be corrected in print at some later date, but it was simply impolite to disappoint all those people.

Now add to this the normal quota of Japanese Emperor-worship; it becomes clear that Vice Admiral Chuichi Nagumo, entrusted with the defense of Saipan by the Son of Ten Thousand Years, would be violating the most ordinary rules of politeness and reverence if he reported anything less than a smashing victory when the Americans came to call. Any errors could be wiped out later, if necessary in blood—his blood.

The politely mendacious information furnished by Nagumo as to his alleged victory was all that Shigataro Shimada (Admiral King's opposite number) had on which to base a plan of campaign. There was no compulsion on him to believe all of it, but at the very least reasonable estimate he could assume that we had some crippled ships and quite heavy plane losses sustained in battle, with still more air loss taken operationally during that rough weather in the Bonins; that one of our attacks on Saipan had been beaten off, and that the successful beachhead was so weakly held that the Marines in it needed the constant gunnery and air support of the fleet; and furthermore that the Jap airstrips in the Marianas were virtually intact.

The last item was the only one that was even approximately true. It was the effect of that extra day which had slipped in when Mitscher speeded up after being sighted by the Jap scouts; and is a good illustration of how small events in war can turn into big ones. The small strip at Garapan had been cut up and the Tinian strip, such as it was. But Aslito was still in Jap hands and in good shape; a few hours would fix up Rota; and the big field at Orote Point on Guam had hardly been touched. Mitscher's early arrival had caused him to use a whole day's extra bombs on Saipan, and though we were not short (for no American commander lets himself get below the strength necessary to fight a major battle) it was necessary to save bombs for targets that were actively hostile, and the idea of shooting up Orote had been quietly dropped.

The Japanese admiral had available at least five carriers of the very largest size, with four of the type we call CVLs, which for a single emergency operation could probably carry more planes than their American cognates. This gave him a floating air force larger than those that came up to Pearl Harbor or Midway, and no poor comparison for Mitscher's own. And Mitscher had lost so many planes (Shimada estimated) that the American force would be far inferior. The scale would be still further tipped by a strong formation of land-based planes staged down through the Bonins.

The experience of carrier battles—the eastern Solomons, Santa Cruz, Coral Sea—showed that the damage inflicted by the two sides was about proportionate to the number of planes engaged. Shimada could therefore count on hitting us hard. He had an ingenious plan by which his own fleet, coming from the direction of the Philippines, was to escape any damage whatever. *His planes would fly off at exactly double the normal range, from a point northeast of the Philippines. Somewhere along a straight line between that point and the Marianas the American Fleet would be found and attacked, with the land-based planes helping. Then all would land at the Marianas fields, presumably to gas up and strike again.* We do not know whether there was a Japanese plan for their heavy-gunnery ship to run in and kill off our cripples, but it would be logical.

One of the best characteristics a military man can have is that of refusing to be shaken from a good plan by loss and damage, which must always be expected in war. By the seventeenth at least, the Jap admiral in direct charge of the expedition must have received news that the force coming down through the Bonins had been heavily hit by Clark; that the runways of the Jimas had been pitted; and that not until the twenty-third, at the earliest, could they be repaired and new air groups be flown down from Japan. He came on.

Then as he rounded the Philippines and headed out into the Pacific, the American submarine *Cavalla* slipped through his screens and torpedoed *Shokaku*, the big veteran carrier that had seen so many of the Pacific battles. He still came on. His planes were flown off in the half-light just before dawn of the nineteenth, with the crews of the carriers lined up along their decks, lifting their arms three times in salute and shouting "Banzai!" as they had before Pearl Harbor.

VIII

It was from *Cavalla* that Admiral Spruance received word the Jap fleet was at sea, their planes in the air, and the damaged carrier a drag on their fleet speed. Back at Pearl Harbor Admiral Nimitz had the news too, and as always when nervous, went out to shoot on his private pistol range behind his headquarters. The men who saw him that day describe him as cheerful and confident. Confidence was never more justified; for the Fifth Fleet battle plan, which cannot have been fully confected before the Jap planes were actually on the way, found a place for every element in an intensely complex situation.

On Saipan the Fourth Marines sliced through to Magicienne Bay around the foot of the central mountain and the whole Twenty-seventh Division attacked a single Jap regiment at Aslito Field, capturing it shortly after daybreak with the help of planes from the CVEs. One less airfield for those Jap planes to land on. Oldendorf's old battleships formed line and steamed out into the offing to meet anything that broke through Task Force 58. Clark had joined Mitscher with time to spare; the latter, with the fast battleships, ran out along the easily discoverable line by which the Japanese planes would have to come from their fleet toward the Marianas, pushing his own scouts still farther ahead.

The battleships were at the tail of the formation, which caused some of the junior tacticians in the ready rooms to growl over a mixed-up mess of distribution; but they changed their minds when, a good hour after daybreak, with light perfect and sea smooth, the whole fleet turned in succession to face the east wind and began to send off planes. The battleships with all those guns were still at the tail, but now between the carriers and the enemy.

At 1007 came the first alarm—"Unidentified planes picked up bearing 333," followed sharply by "Scramble all ready rooms," with the news that the enemy planes were at altitudes between twenty-two and twenty-four thousand feet, which is high up enough to mean big squadrons of dive bombers. From every field that the Japs still possessed in the Marianas, every plane in operating condition was coming out to join the battle. Our own fighters went up at once; our bombers, fully loaded to get as many explosives off the carriers as possible, took the air after them and swung in an easy circle twenty miles on the disengaged side toward Guam.

At 1040 vapor trails high in air and the sound of guns faintly heard told that the battle had been engaged, and within the next ten minutes no less than seven Jap air groups were spotted coming in, the least of them 40 planes strong and others ranging up to 75 planes strong—some 400 all told. There are no accounts of the battle from those air groups, nor ever will be; but we know they must have received one of the most dreadful surprises in military history. They expected to find our fleet close to the island and entangled in shore operations, with most of the fighters still on their decks or just rising; they met our air groups far at sea while they themselves were still in cruising formation, and they met our fighters at their own level of sky where they could not be avoided. Worst of all, they expected to find a fleet with damaged ships and decimated fighter groups; they met one whose fighter squadrons alone outnumbered their whole force.

These were the aviators Japan had spent a year and a half in training to replace the losses of Midway: their first team, their best. Under the circumstances they reverted to the usual behavior of the Oriental when faced with an inexplicable situation—a mechanical performance of duty. Of the first group of Japs between 10 and 15 splashed in less than five minutes. Our older pilots noted how those that were left closed up their formations and came straight along, very much as they had done in the early days of the Solomons campaign.

Then a flier from *Lexington* noticed something else and broadcast it. The Jap fighters, like their bombers, were sticking to formation, making no effort to peel off and attack ours unless they just happened to be between the Americans and the Jap bombers that were their targets. Were they, perhaps, short of fuel, unwilling to engage seriously before they had gassed up in the islands? It does not seem likely; when one of these formations was hit directly it burst like a tomato can struck by a bullet, all the Jap pilots going off into a series of intricate wingovers, Immelmanns, and climbing turns, highly wasteful of fuel.

Our planes were individually tactically better, mechanically better also; but the morale question, the surprise, seems to have been the determining factor with pilots who were well enough trained but lacking in combat experience. When ours got the news from the *Lexington* man, they abandoned the usual tactic of a quick pass at the bomber groups followed by an equally quick pullout; instead, they hung on the tails of those doomed Jap formations, pouring in bullets as long as they had any. A *Cabot* fighter counted 15 going down in flames at one time. Fighting 15 from *Essex* set a record by shooting down 68 planes. Lieutenant Alec Vraciu got 6 alone, and along the gunwalks of the carriers they stared aloft in astonishment with nothing to do. Of all that huge armada of Jap planes, only 18 broke through our fighter groups to the ships and 12 of these were shot down in the screen. One got a near miss that caused a few splinter casualties aboard one carrier, one dropped a single bomb that fell harmlessly in the middle of the formation, and there was exactly one bomb hit out of it all—on the heavy armor of a battleship. Our own losses were utterly insignificant.

But not all the Japanese, faced with such opposition, attempted to come through. After forty-five minutes of fighting, some groups began to sheer off around the fleet and make for the Marianas airfields. They must have received by radio news that Aslito was lost, that Orote Point (on Guam) alone was open. They must have counted on being able to land there.

The final element of Spruance's plan was designed to take care of this expectation of theirs. Commander Shively of Air Group 8 was ordered to take command of all the bomber and torpedo squadrons (which, it will be remembered, were flying around near Guam, loaded with bombs but not in the fight)—to take them all in and dig Orote Point Field to rubble.

As Shively called the air groups to assembly, high in air above Orote Point, he could see planes suddenly begin to thicken over the field below, Japs and our own fighters all mingled. There was no time to waste; he led the bombers in without staying for a perfect formation. The flak was terrific, but he had enough planes to have destroyed a fleet and they had no fighter opposition. As Shively swung back into the clouds he could bear witness that the runway on which the Jap planes had expected to land was now nothing but crater merging into crater.

At this point the battle turned into a massacre. For the Japanese had very literally no place to go. Most of them flew around till they were knocked down by our fighters; a few attempted to land on the pitted runway and tipped over into burning wreckage; a few went into the water and never came up. When it was all over and the bugles sounded secure from general quarters at a little after one

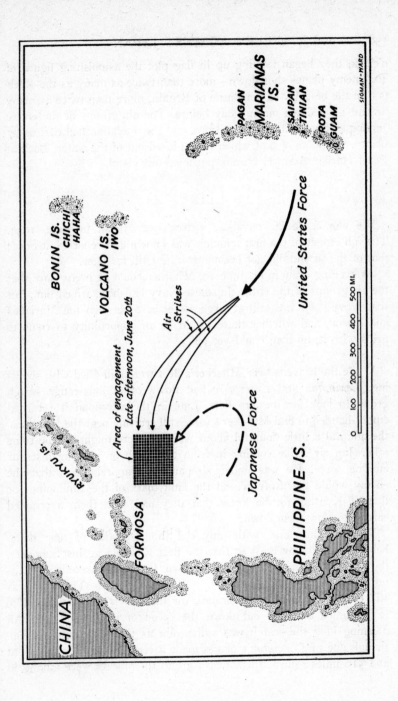

CHINA

FORMOSA

RYUKYU IS.

PHILIPPINE IS.

Area of engagement
Late afternoon, June 20th

Air
Strikes

Japanese Force

United States Force

BONIN IS.
CHICHI
HAHA

VOLCANO IS.
IWO

PAGAN

MARIANAS
IS.

SAIPAN
TINIAN

ROTA
GUAM

SIGMAN · WARD

0   100   200   300   400   500 MI.

o'clock, they began totaling up in flag plot the astonishing figure of 404 enemy planes shot down—more than twice as many as the RAF got on the best day of the Battle of Britain, more than twice as many as had gone down on any day before. The air groups of the entire Japanese Navy had been wiped out, and the operation had cost us 27 planes, the pilots of 9 of which were picked out of the water. Back at Pearl Harbor Admiral Nimitz put away his pistol.

IX

We won a double naval-air victory over Japan in June, 1944. The full extent of the first triumph was known and reported at once; that of the second did not become manifest till far later.

As evening drew in on June 19, Mitscher could be pretty sure that the air groups of the entire Japanese Navy had been wiped out. But that Navy itself was still at large somewhere between the Marianas and Luzon, and whether there would be an opportunity to come to grips with it, no man could yet tell.

While the heavens over Mitscher's fleet were still filled with shouting, *Lexington* and *Enterprise* had flown off a long-range search group to look for the Jap fleet. Late in the afternoon it returned empty-handed to find Mitscher's force still cruising near the Marianas, the admiral a little doubtful about whether there might not be some other Jap air strike coming in from the north or west against our landing force. He was under no particular apprehension that the enemy would get away behind the land mass of the Philippines or that of Kyushu, for he knew that they had with them a crippled carrier to slow them down.

When night came, with only the thinnest slice of new moon behind the light overcast so that the fleet was safe against snoopers, the admiral turned prows west; dawn found him running north-northwest with search groups far out around the fan. The wind was still easterly, a grievous hindrance, for the carriers had to turn into it to launch and this cut down the speed of the whole fleet. All morning long the search was vain; vain as the clock turned noon, though one of *Lexington*'s planes made a record flight 500 miles out and 510 miles return. In that task group the officers were talking in low voices; Admiral "Black Jack" Reeves was in the grim mood he usually had when opportunities were missed, and here was daylight slipping by—daylight which should offer the precious opportunity to catch the whole Japanese Fleet denuded of its air strength.

Noon went and the men had chow; one o'clock, two, three, and in our fleet they were beginning to despair, for the Japs had obviously

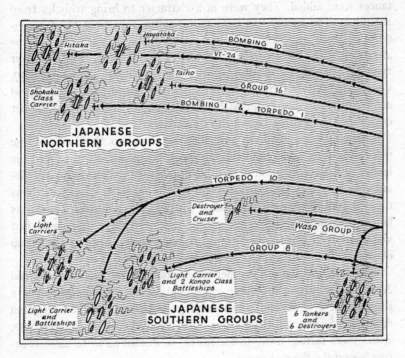

been running away westward since they learned they would not get their planes back, some time in the previous afternoon. Another night would surely put them beyond the reach of pursuit, crippled carrier and all.

At 1540 came a radio message: "This is my first report; here they are, a task force stretching beyond the horizon"—with the signature of Lieutenant Robert Nelson of *Enterprise* Air Group 10. His position was nearly due west; a few minutes later came two more reports from north of west, then one from south of that. Admiral Mitscher had calculated his interception course exactly, and as more data accumulated it was clear that the scouts had caught the Japs pulled up to refuel from a big group of tankers accompanying their fleet.

Since dawn the ready room blackboards had borne the doubly underlined legend: "Get the carriers"; now—as our ships turned into the wind and began to launch planes—latitudes, longitudes and distances were added. They were of a character to bring whistles from the pilots. The enemy had been found at the very limit of plane endurance from our fleet, and it was already well after four in the afternoon when the air groups assembled in the skies, with two-hour runs to make and the sunset of a moonless night coming at 1839. One leader in Air Group 8 remembers how a fruity Alabama drawl came over the voice radio with, "Well suh, we all have just 50 per cent chance of getting back to those carriers."

"Shut up," he snapped and they flew on—to the limit of the theoretical range. No Jap fleet, but down below and a little ahead the leader spied a formation of six big lumbering tankers with six destroyers on their flanks which went into a series of wild S turns as they heard the buzz of our planes. He was about to attack them as better than nothing when out ahead some thirty-five miles, and just visible in light already beginning to grow tricky, appeared a group of ships. The leader gave orders to push on.

"Now we all have a 25 per cent chance of getting back," said Alabama; they flew over the ships and found them nothing but a single light cruiser and accompanying destroyer; but beyond them again, southwestward twenty-five miles, there the whole Jap fleet was, with others farther away to the north, so distant as to be mere cockroaches on the floor of ocean.

Group 8 turned toward the southern ships, which themselves were divided into three subgroups—one of them with a light carrier, a pair of battleships clearly identifiable as those useful *Kongos*, and some destroyers; one with another light carrier, three battleships, and four destroyers; and the farthermost with two more light carriers and an escort that could not be made out for distance. There were a few Jap fighters, high up, but they made no effort, apparently not liking the look of the Grummans that were giving our planes cover as they rode down on the carrier that was with the *Kongos*.

X

The first AA burst from the Jap ships below was a big one, apparently from a main battery gun, right in front of Leader Shively's plane; he noted that it had a singularly beautiful burgundy color; then he was in his dive on the twisting carrier, while the other planes of his group came down behind him and a few split off to amuse the Jap battleships, whose fire was both accurate and fierce. As Shively pulled up and away he noted that the carrier had been hit at least twice; there were holes in her deck and there was smoke coming up through them, while intermittent puffs of flame were emerging from the gunwalk level. One of the *Kongos* had been hit also and was burning.

Just then the torpedo planes from one of our light carriers came in low down. Shively saw their fish splash and at least one tall column of water go up along the Jap flattop's side. It was apparent that something was wrong with her deck, which seemed to be sagging amidships from a broken back, and then big rolling clouds of smoke hid the ship in the distance and Shively was rallying his group to lead them on the long run home, noting almost automatically as he did so that the time was 1830.

He did not pass over either the tanker force or the isolated cruiser and destroyer on his way in, but some of his men did; they reported that one of the tankers was gone and another just rolling under as they passed, and that two more were burning like fireworks. The lone destroyer was sinking too, having suffered one of those singular mischances of war when a single American fighter came down to give her a few bursts of strafer fire and set off the depth charges on the stern, blowing her all apart. (All this must have been the work of the *Wasp's* air group, which had come later and longer than the others, and lacking fuel to reach the enemy warship groups, had fallen on the tankers as the best available target.)

North of this action—which was one of the strangest of the war because of the lack of enemy air opposition (one, but only one of the Jap fighters had made a pass at Shively himself)—the planes from our other carriers were coming in on the ships that Group 8 had seen as points in the distance. Group 16 flew straight for them. These turned out to be the big Jap carriers, three new ones that had never been in action before—*Hitaka*, *Hayataka*, and *Taiho*, the last being biggest of all—with one of the *Shokaku* class. They were distributed according to the plan which Spruance had used at Midway, but which had now been discarded in our service since we had carriers enough for a better tactic: each flattop was by herself with a circle of attendant cruisers and destroyers.

As our planes came over, the Jap ships went into their circling dance, a dance without rhyme or reason—each ship dodging in a separate area of water so that although the flak they sent up in red, green, yellow and purple bursts looked ominous, it was loose and unco-ordinated, really dangerous only as our planes came very near a target. Far worse were the Jap Zeke fighters, of which the big carriers still had some left—about forty, say some accounts; as few as eighteen, say others. Another American carrier had sent Grumman fighters into the attack, carrying bombs this day; half of them were forced to jettison their bombs and go into dogfights with the Zekes, and though the others bombed, two that did not jettison were shot down.

It may have been the shouts of this fight going on above the level of broken clouds that attracted the attention of Fighting Sixteen. At the warning that there were Zeros present, they went upstairs, to find nothing but some Grummans doing stunts; and when they went down again, could not find the bombers they were supposed to cover. But this did not discourage the men of Bombing Sixteen, who were veterans and very good. At least eight of them planted thousand-pounders in a row down the flight deck of a Jap carrier which they took to be *Hitaka*, but which was probably the very similar *Taiho*. And they were followed by the torpedo squadron, which did at least as well with its complement of 500-pounders. A couple were shot down and one of them, Lieutenant McClellan, lay in the water and had a fish's eye view of the rest of the battle.

He was too far away to see what happened around *Hayataka*, which one section of Bombing Ten hit with a pair of big bombs; or what happened round the Jap light carriers, where Torpedo Ten got at least eight bomb hits while its accompanying fighters knocked off seven Zeros. He was too far away to see what happened when Bombing and Torpedo One went in on the *Shokaku*-class carrier and ripped her all up. But he did see, far on the fading horizon, the windup of the most spectacular and heroic attack of the whole battle.

This attack was delivered by VT-24, four torpedo planes under Lieutenant Brown, carrying the heavy torpedoes and taking their chances on getting back. Being from a light carrier, they had followed in the big group from the accompanying heavy. Brown noted how the bombers swooped toward a carrier in the Jap northernmost group to the neglect of a big *Hayataka*-class flattop behind, and whistled his three torpedo planes down into a long diving turn against the latter. One pilot missed his way in the clouds; that left two to ride with Brown into the most intense antiaircraft fire of all, for there were no other planes to distract it and all the ships of the Jap escort were firing at VT-24. Just as they spread to come in from different angles, Brown's plane was hit and its fuselage began to fill with flame.

"Bail out," his crewman heard him say thickly, and obediently jumped—two men, Babcock and Platz.

They struck the water and floated safe just as all three of our planes launched their torpedoes almost simultaneously. They saw the carrier pivot sharp on her heel and remarked how narrow her immense length made her look; saw a couple of planes on her after flight deck jump and smoke, as the turret gun of one of our planes strafed them in the pullout over her stern. Then the tight turn that the carrier had entered brought her around to port, at right angles to her former course, to take all three American torpedoes amidships at practically the same place.

There was a triple explosion so violent that the men in the water thought their chests were caved in; and Lieutenant McClellan, miles distant, heard the *berroom* over all other sounds and saw the mushroom of smoke go up. Fires burst from the side of the carrier and, as the two men in the water watched, they spread along her length, brighter and brighter in the gathering gloom, throwing up smoke that engulfed the carrier's whole island. Her escort ships were cruising helplessly around her in circles; a battleship almost ran Babcock down. But the battleship could do nothing; none of them could; they steamed away, leaving only a single destroyer, which presently began to play a searchlight on the floundering giant, now listing steeply and down by the head. There were more explosions as the current began to drift Babcock and Platz away; then the glow of the fires was quenched; the destroyer searchlight swung full circle and found nothing to interrupt it.

It was the end of the *Hitaka*.

XI

Now it was night. Somewhere to the southeast Lieutenant McClellan was lying in no great discomfort on his rubber raft in the warm water and watching the other Jap carrier similarly dissolve, torn by explosions which from time to time ripped whole chunks from her side and sent debris into the air like balls tossed by a juggler, till she too slipped under. He did not know that an American submarine, *Albacore*, had persistently dogged the Jap fleet and caught up with it here, in time to finish the damaged *Taiho*. Somewhere to the east, one of Brown's squadron mates had spotted the leader's injured plane far below, all blackened by fire and showing a tendency to weave. The squadron leader was incoherent over the radio, badly wounded and bleeding, but his companion was trying to coach him in. For a time the two planes flew along together; then a level of cloud slipped between them and Brown was no more seen. The coach himself ran out of gas, and piled into a rubber boat with his crew.

All over that part of the ocean American planes were nursing their last drops of fuel in the effort to get back to the American Fleet from which they had come too far. And the fleet? It had been running full speed to close the gap since the planes were launched. At seven that evening the men aboard our carriers received the first bit of news: a long-range dispatch to say two enemy carriers were smoking. It must have been after eight—with darkness already closing around the circle of upper sky—when they began to pick up the voices of pilots on short-range radio. These voices carried the accent of men who had been under intense nervous strain for hours; had gone through a hell of antiaircraft fire with Zeros after them; had seen comrades go down; were in some cases wounded and with damaged planes. All were young and for many of them it was the first battle. "Planes down all the way back to the Jap fleet!" one would croak and be answered, "Do you think we'll ever find the carriers?" "I'm going in."

On the bridge of the flagship, Commander Gus Widhelm of the

staff (who himself had lain on the sea and watched the damaged Jap ships go by, fleeing from the last carrier battle at Santa Cruz, more than a year and a half before) turned to Admiral Mitscher and said:

"They're going to have a hell of a time getting in tonight. Most of them haven't made night landings."

"What shall we do?"

"I'd turn on the lights."

To turn on the lights would be to announce the position of our fleet to any enemy plane, ship or submarine within a hundred-mile radius. Nevertheless Admiral Mitscher swung the fleet away from the direction of the pursuit into the still steady east wind, switched on the deck and masthead lights of the carriers, and ordered the destroyers to throw searchlights on their sides.

The tired planes were already buzzing in landing circles overhead; the air was full of calls like, "*Yorktown*, where are you, please? Must land soon, have no gas left," and "Air Group Twenty-nine coming in." The admiral cut across with an order that all planes were to land on any carrier with a clear deck, regardless of where they belonged, and had it repeated at intervals as the tense business of recovering planes went on. The searchlights wavered along the flanks of the carriers, painting their fantastic camouflage to a common white glare; now and then one struck straight upward as a beacon or some ship in the screen fired a star shell to guide planes high above the clouds.

Down through the lights from time to time flashed planes that could not quite make it, throwing up columns of spray as they hit, and the water was full of aviators blowing whistles or signaling for attention with waterproof flashlights. On the carrier decks, landing crews labored frantically and young aviators at the end of endurance swore at them for not working faster.

Enterprise landed two planes at once, a fighter who took his cut but came in fairly well up the deck, and a desperate bomber with only a few precious drops left who managed to make the stern of the deck without signal as the other plane rolled in ahead. Another fighter pilot was just coming in when he noticed just below him an SB2C he had not seen before and, cutting sharp down to avoid it, drove one wheel into the water, which flipped his plane over on its back and carried him down forty feet before he could get free. As he swam up through the black water he grabbed a piece of driftwood and hung on till the searchlight beam revealed that it was not driftwood but a shark's fin. Down in *Monterey's* ready room there was a violent argument between the pilots and their ACI officer, who only wanted to allow them one torpedo hit on the Japs instead of the five they claimed. On the deck of one of the big carriers there was a fire where an injured plane had crashed through the barrier and into the others spotted forward. There is even a legend that one Jap plane joined the landing circle and tried to come in, the meatballs on its wings clearly visible in the lights, but meekly accepted the landing officer's wave-off.

That legend is not true, but the fact that it is almost universally believed in the fleet tells more than any narrative about the disarray of that hour. But by 2130 it was all over, except for destroyers quartering the whole area and the blinking signal lights asking where planes and pilots were. When the ships had turned westward again and worked up to speed on the trail of the Japs, the situation became noticeably less tense. On *Lexington*, for instance, where they had recovered only one of their fighter pilots and feared that the loss would be heavy, they discovered that all the rest of their planes but one were aboard other ships. The total loss finally worked out at forty-nine planes for the whole fleet; but the pilots of more than half of these planes were picked up that night or in the morning, when a strike was flown off and passed over the area of the battle, finding nothing but a vast iridescent slick of oil that stretched for miles, dotted with dead Japs, debris, and a few fliers like McClellan, Babcock, and Platz who were picked up by float planes from our cruisers.

XII

The next day Tokyo put out a broadcast saying a hundred of our planes had been shot down and two carriers sunk, "including one of the large *Hunker Hill* [*sic*] type." Our side was bothered with considerations of accuracy, for it was difficult to obtain reports and took a long time to get them together. The first announcement was that one *Hayataka*-class carrier had been sunk and the other left burning; that one light carrier had been hit; that *Taiho* and the *Shokaku*-class ship had been badly used up; that three of the tankers had gone down, two others had been hardly used; that a destroyer had been sunk. Later another destroyer was added to the definite list and Pearl Harbor "believed" that our submarine had finished the *Shokaku*.

It would be remarkable if the *Shokaku* had not gone down; for the Jap fleet that ran so fast showed no sign of being detained by a carrier with three torpedo holes in her, and no carrier that had been hit as hard as that could possibly have held the pace. It was not until December that the sinking of this big and tough ship was announced, and very little before that when the loss of *Taiho* also became certain. Still another light carrier had been earlier added to the damaged list, late in June. The effect of these driblets of information (the way they came out was inherent in the situation rather than due to any fault of the Navy) was to convey the impression of a glancing, indecisive blow, more important for its subsidiary effects than for anything that happened in the action itself—a battle like that of the Eastern Solomons. Actually the Japanese Navy had suffered a defeat as quantitatively appalling as that of Midway and rather more important in its strategic effect.

By getting an early start, by skimping every other type of naval construction and carefully husbanding their resources, by avoiding any but a decisive battle, the Japanese had managed to assemble a carrier fleet with accompanying pilots (pilots were the bottleneck, because of training time) not far from equal to our own. It had been blown to fragments in two days. Three of the heavy carriers were gone forever, the other two in for long repairs, the light carriers hit, the flight personnel completely gone. As a result of these two days Japan no longer had a naval air service. If the next major contact occurred before she could rebuild one, it would have to be planned on lines radically different from those on which Japan had hitherto conducted her whole naval war. The repercussions were sufficient to shake Hideki Tojo from a position into which he had concentrated more offices and authority than any Japanese subject had wielded since the time of the Ashikaga Shoguns back in the fourteenth century.

XIII

The Japanese is never so dangerous as when he has been utterly defeated. As our Task Force 58 steamed back from the battle, a little surprised that it had suffered so little, not yet aware that it had damaged the enemy so much, a smallish Jap formation of twin-motored Betty bombers came crashing out of the twilight over Saipan. Most were shot down, but a couple carrying bombs laid their sticks along the beaches where floods of our equipment were still pouring ashore; a couple carrying torpedoes rushed in to drop at our old battleships where they were supporting the left flank of the Second Marines in their drive for Garapan. An old battleship swings slowly and these were in reef-strewn waters. One of them took a fish—fortunately way up in the bows where it cost her not a single casualty and only gave her a strange resemblance to a yacht.

The implications were more important than the event. Where did the bombers come from? Not from any of the Marianas fields except as they had staged through the small strip on Pagan. Not from the well-beaten Jap fleet. Therefore it must be another effort down from the north, from the Bonins. And since the Japs do not do these things by halves, this must be the vanguard of a far larger force. Our carriers all badly needed to go in for fuel and repairs to their planes, of which many had been damaged in battle and more in the rough night landings, but Admiral Spruance thought that the Jocko Jima Development Corporation had better go back and finish its real-estate project before things got any worse.

Clark and his double task group accordingly split off from the fleet again as it neared the Marianas and steered for the Bonins through weather that alternately thickened and cleared, a little dreading that they would run into another session like the last, while the center of gravity shifted to the land fighting still going on on Saipan.

The Seabees had gone to work repairing Aslito Field on the afternoon of the nineteenth while the last Jap planes trying to come down on Orote Field on Guam were still hopelessly seeking for a place to land. The Aslito runways had to be both lengthened and stiffened to take the higher powered American planes. There was a good deal of Jap shooting from hideouts, and armored bulldozers had to be used, but things got better as the army men killed half the Japanese regiment there, half pushed it back to Nafutan Point at the eastern terminus of Saipan.

That was where the trouble began to develop. Nafutan Point is a rocky place and full of caves. A good many face the sea; nearly all had two or three levels. They were interconnected by twisting passages that made flame throwers useless. The destroyers and cruisers gave accurate fire support from the water, but what the hell use was that when the Japs simply retired around the corner or down a level? At least one such cave had concrete partitions and a gun protected by automatic armored doors. "In nine out of ten cases it was necessary to supplement the standard procedure with new and experimental methods." The men of the Twenty-seventh Division, A.U.S., wanted to take their time, study out these methods and do a clean job.

This was diametrically opposed to the attack procedure of the Marines, whose system was to break up organized resistance by slamming in hard and fast, then mop up the stragglers later, their own tight discipline and careful guard mounts keeping these stragglers from achieving anything but an occasional assassination. It is also necessary to remark that the Marines were far more skillful in every operation of war than the army division, which had been a long time in garrison, and were consequently not a little impatient of the latter's slowness and fumbling. Schmidt's Second Marines were having heavy going against the defenses of Garapan, which had been well organized. On the east side of the island the Japs had expected our assault from the sea and had elaborately prepared against it. The Fourth Marines along the shores of Magicienne Bay were taking these defenses in flank and rear, but they were still defenses which occupied all the division's time and effort. There was a gap at the center where the island's central core rose to the steep, rugged caves of Mount Tapotshau.

The Twenty-seventh Division was needed to plug this gap—to capture Tapotshau in a slam-bang marine-type operation before the Japs could reorganize their shattered forces round it, even if enclaves of the enemy were left along the slopes. They did nothing of the kind. In fact, a week from the date of the original landing the army men were still picking at Nafutan Point, and an undercurrent of growling began to flow through the Marines and around marine headquarters as shelling from the mountains made it evident that the Japs were getting things straightened out.

That day, June 22, found Clark and his task group well north toward the Bonins. The carriers that remained with Mitscher flew off a minor strike against the staging field at Pagan to confuse the issue and did some damage there. But Clark found there were Jap snoopers flying around him all night, so he did not bother to run close in to Iwo Jima, but flew his strike from long range.

They hit that subsequently even more celebrated island just at daybreak; and there was a mutual and stunning surprise. For an immense fleet of Japanese planes—more than anyone would have believed possible—was just air-borne, forming in the skies for the long run from Iwo Jima down to Pagan in order to make the biggest attack yet on our transports. "I never saw so many meatballs in my life," said one of our fighter pilots who followed his leader in the first slash into those massed formations and the terrific dogfight that followed. On our side it had been intended as a bomber operation, the number of fighters was only sufficient for the conventional cover, and as the informative pilot continues, "We usually stuck around till the yellow bastards were all gone, but this time there were too many; they beat us off."

But as in the big fight of the nineteenth the Americans discovered that they were flying the stouter, better armed machines and that their enemies had only rudimentary and formal ideas of air tactics. If it could be called a repulse, it was certainly an expensive one for the Japs, costing them something over sixty planes while it cost our side only two. Nevertheless a good many of our bombers had to come back to the carrier decks with their racks still loaded.

Toward evening some of the Japs left from that air fight staged down through Pagan (where they had some operational loss as a result of Mitscher's bombing of the previous day) and enough of them arrived to lay a few eggs among the transports off Saipan, hitting a couple. Both army men and the Marines did some sweating that night; a big land-based air attack would cancel a good deal of their gain, the supply situation was none too good, and everyone remembered what happened at Bari when the German bombers got in.

But Clark with his force hovering around Iwo was so dangerous an entity that the Japs had to dispose of him first. Already the first big wave of their attack had been converted by his intervention into those few piddling bombs dropped in the twilight. The Japs managed to track the American Fleet during the night. In the morning they came in with a strike which was only 12 planes strong but apparently intended as a semi-suicide group to give our fleet a cripple to take care of, for the 12 pressed in with enormous resolution. Our patrols were up and well abroad; they shot down 11 of the Japs at a distance and though the last one got close enough to drop bombs, it was knocked off by the 40-millimeters of one of our light carriers, which avoided the bombs.

It was probably about noon when the next big Jap group reached Iwo from Japan. Early in the afternoon they came out against Clark's force, a 75-plane strike. This time there was no surprise and the battle turned into a repeat of the slaughter off Saipan, with our fighters catching the Japs far out and shooting down nearly all of them, while our bombers followed it up by hitting Iwo Field again.

Toward twilight the Jocko Jima Development Corporation secured from general quarters, feeling pretty proud of itself, as well it might, for it had disposed of 116 planes definitely at a cost of 5. But as it steamed away after dark, here came more Japs, a good-sized force of them, apparently late arrivals from the north. They spotted our ships all right, for it was a clear night with some moon. One of them dropped a flare with a lot of pretty stars in it and they flew around in a circle, holding a convention and obviously talking over the fact that they were so far out that not one would ever get home after spending more juice on an attack. Japanese fanaticism does not go that far. After awhile another flare was dropped and they all flew off back to the Bonins and home. That was the last attempt to relieve Saipan by air.

XIV

There remained the fighting on the island. It was June 27 before the army troops got fully into position along the Tapotshau front, and by that time the Japs were counterattacking with small infiltration parties into the Marines' flanks, costing them a good many casualties. The lines were re-formed and went forward, a couple of miles a day, till July 6. By that time our combined forces were within four miles of the north end of the island, with the army division in the center. At dawn of that morning all the Japs left made a suicide charge. They broke through the army lines and got clear into the marine artillery positions, where the latter made their defense with fuses cut so short that the shells burst fifty yards from the muzzles. Marines say that the army liaison was bad, their patrolling was bad, and they had left gaps in their line. There must have been something to it, for General

Smith of the Marines removed General Smith of the Army from his command, and several of the other officers as well, which will doubt-less be the cause of an argument lasting for generations.

But the suicide charge really was the finish. After that there were only scattered Japs who kept popping out of the caves for a couple of months. Their army commander, Lieutenant General Saito, was killed in the charge. Admiral Nagumo, not having made good on his polite lies about sinking our battleships, decorously committed suicide, and a lot of civilian Japs, encouraged by the example of this big pot, did likewise. Sherrod the correspondent, who was with the Marines, saw some of them at it—fathers beating their children's brains out on the edge of cliffs and then jumping over—and sent off a dispatch which contained a thrill of authentic horror and attracted so much attention in the United States that the impression became widespread of an entire population committing themselves to death. Actually only about one civilian Jap in ten was killed in the fighting or by suicide; the rest came in and began to live under a polity that did not require them to keep their eyes on the ground when being addressed by an officer.

With the Japanese troops, however, the proportion was reversed. When things were cleared up 23,811 bodies were counted on Saipan and there were some sealed in caves who never will be counted. The prisoners numbered 2,009, nearly all labor troops who do not carry guns except in a banzai charge. The island cost us almost exactly 15,000 casualties (the big majority wounded, of whom three-quarters would return to duty) besides the planes we had lost. Our Saipan victories had ruined the whole system of Japanese imperial defense.

The End of the Japanese Fleet

THE campaign in the Marianas, brought to a successful conclusion in August, 1944, broke the outer line of Japanese defense and set free the American Fleet. Of the two results, the latter was probably more important. Down to the night when Mitscher's planes came drifting from the sky onto carriers with their searchlight beams up-lifted, the main force of the United States Fleet had always been in a degree wedded to some defensive duty in connection with a land mass. The connection to Australia in the early days of the war; Pearl

Harbor itself and after that had been successfully defended at Midway, then Guadalcanal; the new stations in the Upper Solomons and on the heels of these, the captures of Tarawa, Kwajalein and Eniwetok.

It is true that in all these cases except the first two defensive duties were assumed as the result of offensive action. But the offensives themselves had been so limited as to point of impact that some fairly bitter things were said about "island hopping strategy" on the floor of Congress. Two factors entered into the limitation, both of them connected with Naval Air. One was that until the capture of Eniwetok we were still on the perimeter of the Japanese island empire. Our forces could raid Japanese traffic to the forward bases (and the submarines did raid it most destructively), our fleet could make occasional forays into the center of the web, like that against Truk in February. But the Japs could still stage planes in across the network of islands all the way from their homeland while we could not. As long as that condition endured our forward bases (as Munda, Tarawa, Kwajalein) required the near support of a fleet, not only for defense against air attack but to cover every supply convoy that moved in. Advances were thus limited to an area from which the fleet could keep guard over its last previous steppingstone.

The second factor was the rebirth of the Japanese carrier service after its experiences in Midway and in the Solomons. As long as there was such a service our forces could not vary greatly from the policy of supporting each advance by a base within fighter-plane range (say three hundred miles at the outside) behind. An expedition to any greater distance would require the constant wet nursing of our fleet till full conquest had been achieved; and even so would be a risky business, for with our fleet tied down, theirs was free to spearhead a counter-expedition somewhere else.

They might, for instance, have gone back to the Aleutians while we were attacking Saipan—they might even have gone to Calcutta. They possessed the necessary interior lines for either. That they attempted neither is attributable more to moral than to physical reasons. The shadow of Midway lay upon them. This moral compulsion, as obscure as the inner necessity that drove Joseph Conrad to literature, led them in the long run to attempt the impossible feat Napoleon had urged upon his admirals—that of fighting a naval

battle without risking ships. Admiral Villeneuve could have predicted the result; they lost the ships and did not win the battle.

The determining element in the great sea-air conflict that raged
across an area of ocean as wide as the continental United States in
June, 1944, was the incidence rather than the quantity of the Japanese
losses. By starving the rest of their fleet, by accepting new cruisers
in less than half the number and with less than half the gunpower
of ours, by placing upon their admirals the burden of devising tactics
to overcome a three-to-one inferiority in modern battleships, they had
managed to rebuild both their carrier strength and the land-based
wing of their naval air service to something like parity with the
American. On the morning of June 22 the Japanese land-based forces
had been cut to pieces and nearly all their carrier planes with their
pilots were gone. Of the decks from which they had flown there remained two major carriers, both damaged, one so severely that she
would not be back in action for six months; and four light carriers
in more or less disrepair, one of these also out for six months or
more.

Many more were building in both classes, and pilots were training.
The plane losses would be readily replaced. But on the restoration of
all three of these the same temporal limit lay. For six months there
would be no Japanese naval air service capable of opposing anything
but a minor task force. During the first of those six months the
Marianas fell definitely into our hands. They had been the center
of the whole spider web of outer empire. With their loss it became
impossible to stage planes out to the islands save by the immensely
roundabout route along the China coast, through the Philippines,
Halmahera and the Palaus. The United States Fleet was thus no
longer required to give its forward bases such close support. The
Japanese Fleet was prohibited from advancing beyond any point
where it could have the full support of land-based aviation.

This was not clear at once. It is never permissible for a military
commander to assume the moral disintegration of his opponent and
to base plans on that assumption, however he may suspect it. Assum-
ing that our morale had gone after Pearl Harbor as the Russians'
did after Port Arthur was precisely the error the Japs themselves had
made. As to the material damage our officers knew that most of the
Japanese Fleet aviation was at the bottom of the sea off Guam but

the extent of the damage to their carriers was still incognizable when, after the fall of the Marianas and the necessary refit to the fleet, it came time to prepare a new operation. That operation was planned with the idea that our fleet had more freedom of action than it possessed earlier, but no one at Cincpac realized the freedom was so absolute. The risk was calculated at above its actual value.

II

Every Mercator projection map shows how centrally Guam and Saipan (our bases now) are located with relation to the circle of Japanese empire. An approximately equal amount of steaming will take a fleet from the Marianas to metropolitan Japan—to the Ryukyus—Formosa—the Philippines—the outpost of the Dutch Indies at Halmahera and the Vogelkop Peninsula of New Guinea. The long belt of the Carolines lies well within that circle. An American fleet steaming out of Magicienne Bay could be bound for any objective around this circle and even if it was seen at the very moment of departure, the defender would be forced to guess correctly the point of attack in order to oppose it effectively at the moment of landing. Admiral Spruance's victory had transferred the advantage of interior lines from the Japanese to us.

This brought a change in Allied strategy and command assignments. At least since the landing in the Russells in early 1943, it had been the policy of the Pacific command not to distribute effort but to call off everything else and make an attack with its entire strength of the fleet and all its supporting forces (air, Marines) could develop. All the points that could be attacked from the central position in the Marianas were very distant from the bases; width of the Atlantic away. They were strongly held and within mutual supporting distance; that is, could not readily be isolated. The new enterprise would be roughly similar to the landing in Africa with a military campaign of continental dimensions beyond the beachhead. That meant troops.

There seemed to have been only five divisions in the Navy's private army, the Marine Corps, at that time, and two of these had been so hardly used on Saipan and Guam as to require rest. So did the Army's Twenty-seventh Division, which had been working for the Navy. The Seventh, Seventy-seventh and Ninety-sixth divisions were or had been under Nimitz' orders, but one can hardly make a war with three divisions and the navy people did not wish to see their valuable beachhead force of Marines involved in extended field operations. The Germans were breaking across France but on the most optimistic calculation it would be another year before any troops from there could fight in the Pacific.

The limiting conditions thus practically imposed a joint operation in association with the MacArthur Southwest Pacific Command, which had the troops. This in turn required that the Philippines should be the point of attack, though it is not unreasonable to believe that a good many of the navy men would have preferred to cut the tree nearer its roots at Formosa or in the Ryukyus. There is no use trying to disguise the fact that there had been some disharmony at council between the able, obstinate, self-willed general and other leaders. MacArthur had said that the Southwest Pacific Command was being starved to representatives of the press and the matter had become a point in the current political campaign—not the first time strategy has been affected by politics in American history as anyone will recall who remembers Sherman campaigning for Lincoln's re-election in the siege lines before Atlanta. This was to have an important effect during the fighting; for the present the remarkable thing is how close and smooth the co-operation of the two services turned out to be during the actual operations.

One of the reasons for this was that as Nimitz had his own army, MacArthur was now given his own fleet—the new Seventh Fleet, under command of Rear Admiral Thomas C. Kinkaid, who fought at the Eastern Solomons. It was designed to support operations primarily military. At its core were six of the old battleships, which it was no longer necessary to keep in the first line since eight of the new fast ones were available; it also had a considerable formation of escort carriers, with supporting cruisers and destroyers.

Another and potent reason for close co-operation was the return to the wars of Admiral "Bull" Halsey, now as commander of the Third Fleet, himself so very forthright and sulphuric but an expert at the business of getting along with MacArthur, whose close associate he had been in the hard drive up the ladder of the Solomons to Rabaul during 1943. After the capture of the Green and Admiralty islands had reduced that once-great Japanese base to an effective prison camp Halsey was relieved from his South Pacific Command "for a new assignment."

It is reasonable to imagine him spending part of the intervening time on leave after a year and a half in the South Pacific under the hardest conditions of war. It is also reasonable to believe that he spent part of it in close conference with MacArthur and his staff. There was no magic carpet to the Philippines, and though the Mac-Arthur forces had edged along the north coast of New Guinea till they were on Biak and the Vogelkop Peninsula, the barrier of the Carolines lay between the troops and the fleet in the Marianas. To bring them together, to neutralize the Caroline strongholds, chiefly valuable for their airfields, and to obtain the needed forward bases for the main campaign a preliminary operation was necessary.

It was decided that the MacArthur forces were to gain a foothold and set up airstrips on the island of Morotai off Halmahera while the Navy attacked the atoll of the Palaus. The two would then be in supporting distance for an attack on Yap, over which there had been so much fuss when the Japs fortified it back at the end of the last war.

At the end of March and the beginning of April the fleet under Admiral Spruance had swept down the line of these western Carolines, delivering a seven-day series of carrier raids in which 150 Jap planes were claimed destroyed and a lot of damage done to shore installations. They found not much afloat at Ulithi or Yap, but at Palau which had been called the Japanese Singapore, a considerable amount of shipping, of which sixteen cargo-carriers and five tankers were sunk, while one of our submarines got a torpedo into a Jap battleship as she fled. There was another attack in July; late in August, when the decisions on strategy had been made, MacArthur's bombers began to pound the Palaus systematically with the help of Libs from Guam and by the time September 1 was reached, our fliers reported that fighters no longer came up to meet them.

On Tuesday, September 5, the curtain of the campaign was rung up with a big carrier strike on the Palaus, while a way behind a cruiser and escort carrier force moved in against Ulithi. The latter met no opposition and investigation showed the Japs had decamped, taking with them all the grown men and most of the pretty girls (they really were pretty there—Ulithi is the paradisiacal tropic isle of legend.) The cruisers pushed on; two days later they were pounding Yap, while the fast battleships of Willis Augustus Lee were running in after forty-eight hours of carrier strikes to give the Palaus a preliminary shelling, then swinging out again to pick up Mac-Arthur's convoy for Morotai and to cover the fast carriers on a voyage west.

For a whole week the bombing and shelling of the Palau positions continued without interruption except that somewhere along the line the job was taken over by the slow battleships and escort carriers of Kinkaid while Halsey was running southwestward with his combat air patrols well out to see MacArthur into Morotai. The Japs knew that something big was stirring and radio Tokyo speculated avidly on its nature but our carrier men were shooting down even their night snoopers and they could make little of even what they did learn as the confusion of their broadcasts reveals. They did not find out till the morning of September 15 when Americans simultaneously hit the beaches both at Morotai and in the Palaus.

III

Morotai was a pushover. The landing was on the southern shore, along the straits that separate the island from Halmahera. The Japs had considerable troop concentrations on the latter island and some artillery in position, but the cruisers and destroyers shelled everything to pieces there. Apparently they had never thought of Morotai where the landing was made under cover of Rear Admiral J. S. McCain's carrier group and almost the only casualty was that the general's boat struck on a shoal and he got his feet wet going ashore. The landing parties found an airstrip which the Japs had begun there, now abandoned and partly overgrown.

The Palaus were quite a different proposition. The islands form a chain northeast to southwest 77 miles long and 20 miles wide, with a barrier reef to mark them off and numerous anchorages among the lagoons, which the Japs had greatly improved by dredging. Babeltuhap, the largest island, twice the size of Manhattan, is another such storehouse of strategic materials as New Caledonia—lignite coal, phosphates and above all the best grade of aluminum ore under the Japanese flag, which was why Spruance caught all those cargo vessels there in April. It is rough, heavily forested with ironwood and ebony.

Attacking it would be a major campaign as would an attack on the next island to the south, Koror, where the majority of the thirty thousand Japs in the Palaus were supposed to be.

Peleliu at the southern wing of the chain and Angaur just beyond it and five miles outside the barrier reef were selected as the points of attack. The former had an airstrip and there was another on Ngesebus, a small island linked to Peleliu by a causeway. If these were taken it would be easy to keep the Japs on the other islands in a state of impotent unhappiness. The First Marine Division was detailed to Peleliu, the Eighty-first Infantry (one of the MacArthur divisions) to Angaur, the whole being under command of Major General Julian Smith who had done so well with the Second Marine Division on Saipan. It was called the Third Amphibious Group.

Angaur is a formless, rather low island. The waters around it were lousy with mines, one of which knocked off a motor minesweeper during the approach, but a favoring wind carried the smoke screen in effectively to smother the shore batteries, the landing was made with little loss under cover of amphibious tanks and by night of D-Day two beachheads were solidly joined so that next morning the job of hunting the Japs from their forest hideouts could begin. There were only twenty-five hundred of them and with an entire division in they were eaten up.

Peleliu is shaped somewhat like a crooked hatchet, with the big four-strip airfield in the blade and a sharp steep ridge running the length of the half, all made of coral decayed to limestone. The landing was on beaches at the hammer end of the blade on the western side. The only estimates on the number of Japs ashore were from air scouts; they set the figure at forty-five hundred.

It was an underestimate; Peleliu turned out to be the major Jap defense post of the whole archipelago and they had learned a lot since they had fought so stupidly in the Marianas. All those cliffs and caves were honeycombed with gun positions; our ships could not get them down. The heavy cruiser *Pittsburgh* devoted half a day to a single battery whose four apertures were clearly visible through the glass. Three times or more the shells closed them with hits right on or nearby. Three times the Japs shelled them clear and opened fire again. "You can put all the steel in Pittsburgh in there and they'll still come out of their holes when you land," said someone on the

Smoke screen; destroyers cover the escort carriers off Samar by laying smoke while the splashes of Japanese shells rise around them.

The fatal salvos: *Gambier Bay* in the middle of the salvo that crippled her.

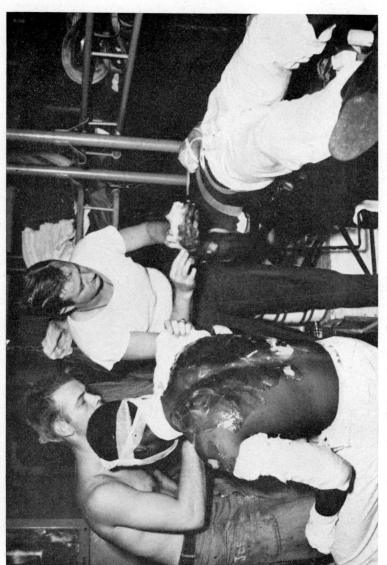

Caring for the wounded; burn cases were usually the worst in carrier war.

What the escort carriers lived through; a salvo falls close aboard an escort carrier off Samar.

Counterattack of the escort carriers; a Jap heavy cruiser in trouble and under attack from our dive-bombers and torpedo planes.

Kamikaze; the scene on the deck of one of the escort carriers as a Jap suicide bomber goes into the water just astern.

Hit by a Kamikaze; from another escort carrier men watch smoke rolling from the doomed *St. Lô* after a Jap suicider went through her deck.

End of the *St. Lô*; the third of a series of explosions which tore the American escort carrier apart after a Kamikaze plunged through her deck.

All alone; one of the Jap light carriers, already badly hurt, under attack from our carrier planes in the north. The little clouds aloft are antiaircraft fire.

Hard hit; close examination of this aviator's eye view of *Zuiho* will show that her deck is buckled amidships and has bomb holes in it; part of her antiaircraft turrets are not turning, and smoke is coming out of her from a torpedo hit aft.

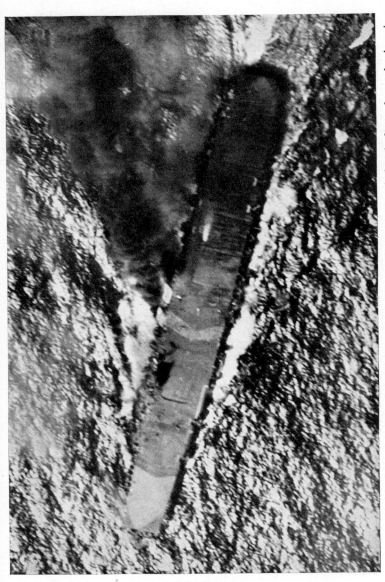

Zuikaku in bad shape; the big Japanese carrier is burning and the shape of the shadows shows she is going down by the head.

End of the *Zuikaku*; a Jap battleship maneuvers near the doomed carrier, which is already so low in the water that her hangar deck is awash.

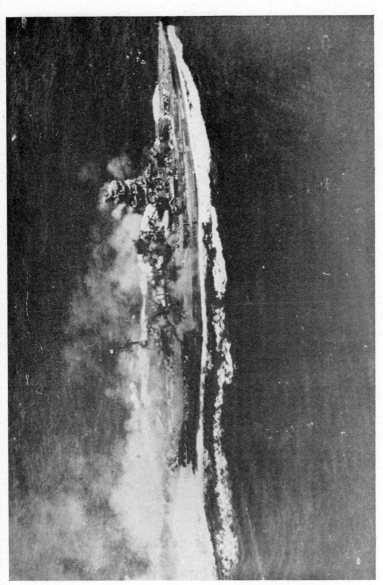

Flight-deck battleship; *Hyuga* leaving the scene of the action at her best speed, burning and with much damage.

Direct hit; a Jap heavy cruiser takes a hard one from our dive-bombers.

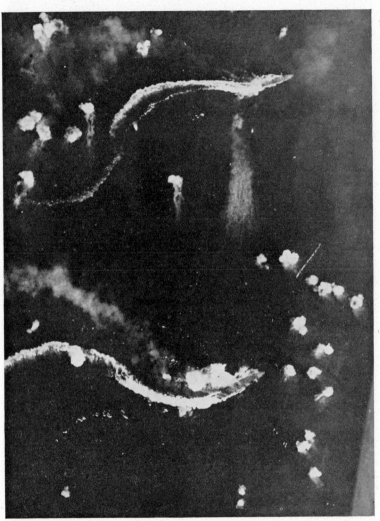

The pattern of carrier war; a Jap light carrier with an accompanying vessel, maneuvers frantically under the white plumes of flak.

Torpedo; in the background a torpedo has gone into the side of a Jap carrier; in the foreground a heavy destroyer tries to protect her.

cruiser's bridge, gazing glumly at such a scene of fury on the beach as not Guadalcanal nor Saipan had seen, for those Japs at Peleliu did not bother replying to the covering ships but saved all their fire for the landing barges.

The three marine regiments had gone in abreast, First, Fifth and Seventh from north to south, with the last intended to cut across the tip of the island, the Fifth to take the airfield and push up the east side of the ax haft, the First to go up its westward flank. All three regiments lost heavily getting to the beaches and most of the amphibian tanks were knocked out. The beaches themselves were heavily mined; in an hour and a half after the first wave, the Marines were pinned to a strip not 50 yards deep along the shore and a barrage of 155 mortar fire was walking back and forth among them with astonishing accuracy. The division was supposed to be past the airfield by evening. It had not even reached the western edge when at 1630 the Japs came on in a major counterattack, led by tanks.

It fell on the joint of the First and Fifth Marines and went right through to the beach. To men on the ships in light already failing under the clouds it looked like the wind-up and boats were ready for rescue parties but those Marines knew how to play rough. They stood their ground and knocked out every tank in the way, some with bazookas, some with grenades grimly shoved through ports by Marines who jumped on the vehicles. The supporting Japanese infantry was cut down by rifle fire of an accuracy the Japs had never before experienced and at the very center of the beachhead the few of our medium tanks that had been able to get ashore beat off a second Jap drive.

All night the enemy kept trying to infiltrate and there was constant fighting under flares while more tanks came ashore. The next day under that rain of projectiles from the hills that never ceased, the tanks led the Fifth regiment in a swift dash that led across the airfield to an area of buildings at its northern edge, but there once more the advance hung and the whole day was given to the same mad close-range fighting as the first. So was the third day and the fourth; nobody slept and one artillery regiment fought as infantry after losing all its guns to direct hits from mortar fire, while a second had to reverse pieces twice, firing both directions at ranges between three and five hundred yards. It took six days of this kind of fighting to clear the plain at the south end of the island and now the assault on the escarpment of hills began. The Marines called it Bloody Nose Ridge; the First Regiment lost two-thirds of its number there, casualties which in theory cannot be borne by any military organization.

They were borne and the regiment did not break, but part of the Eighty-first Division had to be brought over from Angaur to help out. It was lucky they were for one day after these troops got ashore the Japs came down with a big convoy of barges from Babeltuhap to reinforce and almost got all of it in. Nine of the barges were sunk but several hundred troops got ashore and the Fifth Marine Regiment had to be thrown in to help the Army against Bloody Nose. It was still not enough; The Japs had mortar positions on Ngesebus and that had to be taken by another amphibious assault on the twenty-eighth of September before the slow business of inch-by-inch fighting patrols with satchel charges and flame throwers could begin to finish off the caves. Even when a cave was cleaned it would not be finished. The whole place was honeycombed with tunnels, the Japs would get into it again next day and open fire from the mouth or booby-trap their own dead to blow burial parties to pieces.

A full month later a colonel stepping from a plane on the airfield now in thorough American occupation, was instantly killed by a sniper's bullet. No food was cooked on the island till October and in December the shock of satchel charges was still being heard among the hills. How many Japs? Over 11,000 dead were counted; there were more in the caves who never got out.

IV

The desperate fighting on Peleliu had an extremely important strategic effect. The interweaving of the movements of fast and slow battleships, fast and slow escort carriers, as intricate as the joinery of a boule cabinet has already been noted. This process had taken part of the fast carrier groups of Marc Mitscher far west on September 8 for a strike at Mindanao while other carrier groups were working on the Palaus and the slow battleships pounding Yap. It might conceivably leave the Japs in some confusion as to the actual point of the attack that was obviously building up; conceivably also it might tempt them into another air-sea battle. Our command was at this time not yet aware of how destructive the Philippine Sea battle in June had been to their carrier service and those Jap carriers would be regarded as the greatest of all dangers to a convoy moving toward the Philippines.

The Mindanao strike was a success beyond all reasonable anticipation. Its primary purpose was to deal on the ground with planes that might stage down to interfere with MacArthur at Morotai and included strikes on five fields—Delmonte and Cagayan that look out northward on to the sea of Mindanao; Valencia and Davao which face south on the gulf named for the latter; and Buayan on Sanrangani Bay at the southern tip of the island. The Japs had apparently decided we were too busy among the Carolines to care about anything else and whatever warning system they had was a complete washout. Only five of their planes took the air at Cagayan and one at Davao and these were easily shot down while "approximately sixty" others were smashed up on the ground at various places and the hangars were given a good going-over by the dive bombers.

There was a good deal of sea traffic moving off the Mindanao ports, particularly in the Gulf of Davao, and our fliers went for all of them. The total score of sinkings compiled after they got back to the carriers amounted to sixteen small cargo ships, one of larger size and a considerable number of sampans. Meanwhile the fliers bound for the sea at Mindanao field spotted in Hinatuan Bay along the east coast of the island a big convoy of thirty-two coastal cargo ships accompanied by twenty sampans. They called out the reserve air groups and as there were not many of these the cruisers and destroyers of the covering force ran in to shoot with the result that the entire convoy was sent to the bottom for the greatest single loss to the hard-pressed Japanese merchant marine in any single operation of the war.

The striking feature about this business was the total lack of preparation for anything on the part of the Japs. They had no air patrols up and the Hinatuan convoy was not really a convoy at all, merely a group of ships sailing in company without either a destroyer or a plane for anti-submarine guard. This argued that the attack of our airmen had been as much a surprise as though they were so many angels out of heaven, but Mitscher and "31 Knot Burke," his chief of staff, felt that it might also mean something else. There was a chance that in their redistribution of Japanese air forces following the June battles the plane strength in the Philippines had been whittled down to the point where it was no longer competent to make head against a first-class offensive effort.

Now McCain's group, as we have seen, went down to cover Morotai and the rest back to the Palaus. The schedule called for them to begin softening up Yap as soon as Peleliu had fallen. But that fall was unseasonably delayed with the result that Halsey and Mitscher had to continue cruising in the nameless sea between the Philippines and Carolines in order to prevent any counterstroke by the Japanese fleet from behind the screen of the Indies. This would not have absolutely prevented the attack on Yap and in fact the Twenty-fourth Army Corps (Seventh and Ninety-sixth divisions) had already sailed from Pearl Harbor for that destination by the fifteenth. But earlier that week, on the heels of the Mindanao strike, Halsey had been in touch with Nimitz. Now on September 15 or 16 he flew down to see Mac-Arthur at Morotai.

Jap air strength (he said) was all we really had to worry about. The Third Fleet would care for everything else. With the help of the three disposable divisions from the Central Pacific Command (Seventh, Seventy-seventh and Ninety-sixth) would not General Mac-Arthur be prepared to take on the Philippines immediately before the Japanese could reinforce? It would be while they were still conferring that the reports from Peleliu began to come in with their obvious message that the conquest of that island would not be made on schedule, the Japs had made a super-Saipan of it. Its lagoon would be of no use as an advanced base while overlooked by Japanese who had radio sets to tell their friends what was going on and artillery to shoot up the ships. Yap was likely to be even worse, delaying indefinitely the grand project against the Philippines.

The general thought that with those three extra divisions he could take on the Philippines immediately. Advancing the date would have the disadvantage of setting him in the islands at the rainy season, when the eastern Philippines are among the wettest spots on earth; but the advantage that if he got his beachhead firmly established during that unfavorable weather when large and rapid movements were impossible, there would be a long dry season for campaigning. This involved a complete change in the whole method of the attack, which had been planned to begin in a dry season; but if it succeeded, would advance the total process of the reconquest of the islands by something like a year. MacArthur was flexible-minded enough to put his fortune to that touch.

As a substitute for the advanced base in the Palaus the train was directed to Ulithi, arriving with its repair ships, tankers and those boxlike craft housing assorted workshops which are known in the Navy as "floating whore houses" on September 21. The thing was kept secret for some time and there is reason to believe that the Jap did not know where we were hiding damaged ships to give them temporary repairs before sending them back across the ocean.

V

In its military sense, "immediately" is a longer word than it looks. Not only must all supply and troop movements for the Philippines be speeded up by a matter of months, but it was also necessary to get the Morotai airfields in operative shape, since both provide air support during the early phases of the operation and a staging area later. It would be late October before the army of the Southwest Pacific could hit the beaches in the Philippines.

This determined the general plan of the fleet movements. The Japs had no air strength to speak of on Mindanao but our underground in the islands, which was exceeding good, reported a considerable amount of planes in Luzon and the supporting installations there would require attention with special reference to the repair shops and fuel tanks that become so important when continuous action is engaged. It would be essential to put a strike of three or four days' duration on Formosa and the Ryukyus just before the actual invasion. These were both the reserve areas from which planes would be sent to the Philippines in an emergency and the staging points through which they would come down from the central depots in Japan. Somewhere between these operations most of the Third Fleet, particularly the carriers and destroyers, would need some time in port. They had been cruising for a month and when the drive to the Philippines started could anticipate a month more of it, probably including fighting of the most violent character. All sorts of small things were out of order, like burned boiler tubes in some of the destroyers, an elevator that was scoring its shaft on one of the light carriers and a catapult that needed repair on one of the big ones.

This refit period would have to be slipped in between the Luzon strike and that against the islands to the north, with the unavoidable danger that during the interval the Japs would stage replacement planes down to Luzon. There could be a second Luzon strike after the Formosa operation but of course by that time the Japs would presumably have things under cover on the Luzon fields. This was why special attention was to be given to fuel depots and shops; also why a detachment of Halsey's gunnery ships was told off to run up to Marcus Island during the refit interval and give it a shelling. A Japanese contemplating the successive points of attack—Mindanao, Luzon, Marcus, Formosa—might conclude that we were working up to a landing in the Bonins or elsewhere in the north.

After the Mindanao strike then, the fleet cruised back east, both planes and ships making a brief appearance in support of the Marines at Bloody Nose Hill, where Halsey picked them up and then ran back toward Luzon. At least four groups of carriers were in it, which according to the published "ideal" plan of organization would have amounted to eight of the big *Essex* class carriers and as many lights, but we know that eleven big carriers were in commission at that time, so probably the air strength was greater than the ideal organization plan called for it to be. The air groups hit at the fields around Manila on September 20 at dawn.

There was strategic surprise all right, for Manila Bay, Olongapo and Subic were all filled with shipping, which got very roughly used. The score as compiled after all the accounts and photos were collated was a flotilla leader sunk along with five tankers and five assorted cargo ships. Tactical surprise seems to have been lacking; the carrier boys came back reporting that the Japs had at last managed to set up a system of antiaircraft radar which spotted them coming in over the mountains that line Luzon beach and shore. The result was that most of the ships were under way and the Jap planes air-borne.

That produced a violent air fight, especially over Clark and Nichols fields, but our formations were altogether too strong for the Japs, who seemed to have been merely the local defense forces as those over Mindanao had been. One hundred and eleven of them were shot down in the air, but that did not discourage the rest who trailed some of our bomber groups home to the ships. As twilight came in they began a long series of racking night attacks in the usual Japanese manner, mostly with torpedoes. Our night patrols had improved since the Japanese tried this back in the Marshalls and the enemy seems to have been fairly disorganized by the loss of a good many key personnel during the day fighting. They were beaten off with loss and no damage to our side.

Next morning, September 21, as there was less Jap air opposition the bombers had more time to get at both the ground installations and the shipping. Most of the latter was now trying to get out of the area but those small Jap vessels cannot go far in a night's steaming and the general effect was merely to draw them out of concealment to where they could be seen and attacked. A box score issued at the close of the operation upped the number of planes shot down by 58; claimed 188 destroyed on the ground (this figure can be taken with salt) and made up a total of 40 "ships that could be classified as ships" sunk with six small craft and "extensive damage to buildings, warehouses, railroad equipment, storage tanks, harbor installations, hangars, shops."

"The operations of the Third Fleet," the Pearl Harbor communiqué went on, "had forced the enemy to withdraw his naval forces from their former anchorages in the Philippines and to seek new refuges in the same general area, have disrupted inter-island communications, and have broken his air force in the Philippines as operations of the Fifth Fleet broke the enemy's carrier-based air force in the Battle of the Philippine Sea." That night the carriers were steaming away with a record of only eleven planes of their own shot down (there were a good many more that crash landed) and a job well done. On the light carrier *Princeton*, a notably happy ship, young Lieutenant Leigh passed out the news in his famous imitation of a famous voice, beginning "My-y-y friends—" and all the men were delighted. He added at the end that a Black Cat scouting the area to the south during the night had caught two Jap destroyer escorts fueling alongside a tanker and bombed all three together so that the destroyer escorts rolled in opposite directions to sink while the tanker went straight down in the center. Everybody took it for a burlesque and laughed like anything, but it was perfectly true and a good pendant to a good day.

VI

There was a certain element of wishful thinking in the Pearl Harbor roundup, as was to appear later, but for the moment the hi-jinks aboard the carrier were justified. They had achieved significant results at insignificant cost and had demonstrated that the Japanese method of a lightly held outpost line with strong reserves in the main resistance area (copied from German land strategy) was not very applicable to aero-naval war. The attacking carriers moved too fast, breaking up the perimeter defenses before the counterattack groups could be mobilized.

But the operation had in essence been a tip and run raid in great force. The Formosa strike was a thrust into the Japanese reserve area and it was regarded with considerable apprehension in the fleet. Aero-naval war is too new to have many such maxims as land fighting possesses, but at least one would seem to require no particular demonstration—that it is a bad idea to take carriers into an area where they can be attacked by land planes from three different directions. The counterattacker can use the shuttle principle and arrive at the point of contact with no worries about fuel supply. He can from his variety of fields run constant attacks till the defense of the carriers breaks down from sheer physical exhaustion like that of the British ships in the evacuation of Norway.

Admiral Mitscher expected to cancel this through speed, good tactics and hitting the Jap airdromes hard enough to render their counterattacks impotent. After the layover at Ulithi he steamed north then, picked up the detachment that had shelled Marcus and on the morning after that attack his planes charged suddenly from the skies on to Okinawa and the southern Ryukyus.

They had a field day. Jap aviation was caught grounded and only fourteen planes ever got off, all of them promptly shot down, while the claim for destruction on the ground was seventy-five. There were a couple of convoys moving among the islands, escorted by destroyers against our submarines. The dive bombers turned to on them, sending to the bottom nine assorted cargo craft with two of the escorts and a clumsy submarine tender they found in harbor. Twenty-six others were listed as damaged or probables; the proportion indicates the nature of the attack, which was a one-shot without time for a mop-up.

Instead of returning to the Ryukyus, which would be the normal procedure, the fleet took in its planes and ran fast southward all that afternoon and night of October 9. By the next morning they were in position to fly an extreme long-range strike against the Aparri Airfield and its supporting installations in northern Luzon. It was flown with the exhaust on the carrier decks showing blue in the dark before daybreak, achieved surprise and did a lot of damage* and then the ships were off to the northwest for the serious business of the occasion, the attack on Formosa.

That island is about the size of the state of Indiana but with a range of mountains equal to the Rockies near its eastern coast and only a narrow littoral there, while the mountains fall away gradually to plains looking west; its leading product is camphor. Since the Japs took it over at the close of the Chinese War in 1895 it has been for them a pioneering country and nursery of soldiers, a place continually fortified, the fetter of China. With the coming of the empire to the south and of the air age its importance had augmented; the Japs could be expected to meet us in force.

The expectation was fully justified. The planes took off to make an early strike on the morning of the eleventh, but there was no way for the loaded bombers to get over the mountain keel. They had to fly around, which gave the Japs time to take the air. There was violent fighting all around the northern end of the island and along the western slopes in which we lost twenty-two planes, which was not light considering how much we had of strategic surprise. The ground attacks that day were mostly against shipping and planes, the objects that could be moved; ninety-seven aircraft on the ground were claimed.

The evening came in with rain squalls, very dark. No sooner had it shut down than Jap snoopers began to appear, followed as they dropped flares by torpedo planes, running in small, concentrated groups, close to the water and very fast—the old technique the enemy had used with such success in the Solomons and Marshalls. This time it was not a success; our night fighters were out, new planes trained in the night tactics devised by the lamented Butch O'Hare, and they shot all the enemy down or drove them into positions where they

* Rather oddly the Navy never issued a communiqué on this attack but ployed its results into a general roundup of Halsey's operations a week later.

were smashed up by flak to a total of 11. With the 124 knocked off over Formosa, this left Halsey and Mitscher with the feeling they were gaining on the game, for not one of our ships had been touched.

After the attack was beaten off a night strike was flown, an innovation in carrier technique, and with the day another one for Formosa which this time concentrated on the immobile targets—hangars, docks, dumps, buildings. The Jap planes came up stronger than ever and though their loss was by far the heavier (87 to 23) it was considerably less both in the air and on the ground than the day before while ours had slightly mounted. There was an argument about that in flag plot which spread through all the wardrooms—were they feeding planes in from China or did they have underground hangars on Formosa? Opinion was about equally divided but for tactical purposes it did not matter. The fleet's mission was to eliminate the air forces that would oppose a Philippine invasion, draw the Japs into air fighting under whatever conditions, and since they yet showed no sign of exhaustion, there would have to be a third day of attacks. That night the twelfth, there were only snoopers around the fleet, of which a couple were done away with by the night fighters. Some of the younger men were pretty cheerful about this, thinking it meant the end of counterattacks but Halsey and Mitscher on their respective flagships were not too happy. Remaining another day was giving time to the Japs, with which, when they had it, they always made trouble. The admirals figured that whatever air strength there was in the Philippines would be drawn toward northern Luzon by this time and so split the carrier groups for the strikes of the thirteenth, half of them going for Aparri and its dispersal fields. Both there and at Formosa the opposition was light in the morning; the reports told of only eleven enemy planes shot down; few were found on the ground and the fleet turned southward toward the Luzon post. Around noon reports of bogies began to come in from the outer fighter screen, always single planes and most of them shot down. They were not the four-engine Emily the Jap uses for long-range patrols but twin-motor Bettys, land-based planes, which looked like the prelude to a real attack. At three o'clock it came; a formation of Bettys, which ran over rather than through the screen and sailed past dropping bombs from way up there. Of course they were totally ineffective against dodging ships from that altitude and the return antiaircraft fire was not much better. On most of the ships the word was to chow down for an early dinner as the Japs never do anything lightly and this move meant there was something big going up.

Twilight brought the usual squalls of rain; GQ caught many an officer with his dessert still on the table. There were shouts from our fighters all around the perimeter as the Japs charged in from every direction at once. The big battle off Guam was a picnic to this. We had a bright light there and our patrols had caught the monkeys far afield, all on one level, while here they rushed at all heights from zenith to sea level, coming out of clouds and squalls like bullets. One whole squadron of the torpedo planes got right into the middle of the carriers and dropped its fish with the ships all dodging wildly and blazing away, in intimate danger of hitting or ramming each other. No accidents; but one of the torpedo carriers came down in flames on the fantail of a big cruiser; then there was a shock that everybody could feel for miles around and we had a crippled ship.

She was the heavy cruiser *Canberra*, one of the new ones, and the fish hit her squarely amidships so that both engine rooms were flooded. While fighters and Japs still raced like comets into the darkening clouds there was a hasty conference in flag plot. The logical thing to do was sink her; our ships were less than a hundred miles from Formosa and the very intensity of the Jap attack proved that we had not been able to paralyze the Jap fields there sufficiently to prevent them from feeding planes through from the reserve. If it was bad medicine to have our whole fleet there under the constant menace of those land-based attacks, it would be still worse to have a damaged ship which could barely move at the end of a towline.

But "I'm getting pretty tired of sinking our own ships," said Admiral Halsey and decided to chance taking her in. The heavy cruiser *Boston* was assigned to take *Canberra* in tow; a seagoing tug was called from Ulithi; destroyer escort was made up with the light carrier *Cabot* for air guard and they all turned east while the fleet steamed on in southward into the darkening night with Jap snoopers still around, making minor passes from time to time.

Another major attack came about nine o'clock, apparently as the result of some assembly in the skies of Jap air groups from two directions, but by this time the fleet had its night fighters up and the reception was red hot. All round the horizon, all through the fleet, Jap planes were hitting the water and blowing up in pillars of flame 300 feet high.

"God Almighty," said Halsey, who had seen enough fighting by this time not to have been surprised at anything, "how many did we shoot down?" He was told fifty-two in that bout. The fleet pushed on into the dark with all hands standing wearily to the guns and now and again firing. There were constant alarms that this ship or that was burning but it was always only another Betty in the water. Midnight had gone before the attacks broke off and it was two or three in the morning when "Secure from GQ" was sounded, but next day at dawn all the bomber groups went out and attacked the north Luzon fields again.

VII

The bulk of the fleet seems to have been still making southward by this time, preparing to furnish cover for MacArthur's landing, but the carrier group of Admiral McCain lingered near Formosa. This was partly to interpose some sort of long-range screen between that damaged cruiser and the Jap bases; partly it was the idea of Admiral Mick Carney, Halsey's chief of staff and "dirty trick department." All our commanders have read Mahan; they understood perfectly that however the teeth of Jap land-based air may have been drawn the main danger to the invasion of the Philippines, now already moving, was the enemy fleet with its complement of carriers. Halsey wanted to get them into a battle. He had every confidence of victory, but win, lose, or draw, the Japanese Navy would be in no shape to do much with Kinkaid's covering Seventh Fleet after the kind of action he proposed to fight.

Now it had been observed all through the war that that very sly animal, the Japanese commander, would fight only on two types of occasion—when he was driven to desperation in a corner and when he had an advantage so decisive that he could wipe out his enemy at practically no cost to himself. Close on the heels of the big night air battle of the thirteenth radio Tokyo put out a broadcast in which it claimed the sinking of numerous American battleships and cruisers— and also that eleven of our carriers had burned up or blown up. The phrase was slightly unusual and when Halsey came to talk to some of his air group men who had been aloft that night, he found that they too thought some of our carriers were gone when they saw the terrific explosions and mounting columns of fire where Jap planes hit the water. The surviving Japs in the air, harried by our flak and night fighters, would have no opportunity for a checkup. Nor would this be the first time the enemy had believed their own broadcasts; we have seen in the past how that happened off Saipan.

McCain's job was accordingly one of strategic histrionics; he was to play the remanence of an American fleet trying to get away while out to the eastward the damaged cruiser and her escort furnished additional bait. The Jap fleet ought to feel tempted to come down from the empire and cut them off; Halsey would then turn back at speed, slip round them to the eastward and crack them between his hammer and the anvil of McCain. Thus even the strike on the northern Luzon fields of the fourteenth was intended to look as though made by McCain's air groups and that McCain's air groups were the only ones we had. There were light strikes.

The results of those air strikes were comparatively poor and the plan did not quite work out as intended anywhere. The Japs went for McCain all right, but it was with bombers and torpedo planes on the evening of the fourteenth. One of the latter got through the screen and slipped a torpedo into the light cruiser *Houston*, in the same place and manner *Canberra* had been hit on the previous evening. The water was very rough, the ship had no lights or power and almost turned over on them before they could cut loose enough gear on the opposite side from her hit to bring her level. Abandon ship was given and a destroyer strained herself badly trying to get alongside in the dark and pounding sea to take survivors. There was no fresh water aboard and the damage-control parties had to exist on what fruit juice they could find. They did keep her afloat though and started her back in tow to join the convoy of the other cripple; and on the fifteenth McCain moved on down to join Halsey east of Luzon, all the air groups participating in strikes on the fields around Manila Bay.

The preliminary moves of the campaign were now all done; the ideas, equipment and arrangements were all in play. The rest would be the result of the interaction of elements here present. The Jap counterattacks by air had been furious and persistent but their defense was on the whole a passive one. They knew enough about us by this time to realize that something was going to happen and they wished to fix our forces in a definite position before committing anything but their extremely mobile and quite expendable land-based planes.

These they had certainly expended without stint. A roundup made under the most careful conditions of checking showed that since the Third Fleet planes swept over Okinawa, 528 Japs had been shot out of the air, a total that compares with that of the big Battle of the Philippine Sea in June. At the time the Japs were quite satisfied that they had gotten their money's worth—11 carriers.

As a pendant to the air operations they did make a halfhearted attempt for the convoy taking the torpedoed cruisers home and Domei said, "The imperial fleet has finally made its appearance off Formosa," while Pearl Harbor let the newspapermen put it into their cables that a big battle was imminent. It did not come off; only a force of cruisers and destroyers put out from the Japanese home islands and these turned back when they sighted and were sighted by some of our carrier planes.

This did not make things any easier for the convoy, however. Land-based planes made such persistent efforts to get at the damaged ships that the *Cabot* air group had seventy-two hours of continuous action, pilot relieving pilot. It was one of the stiffest ordeals of the whole war; the Japs got another torpedo into the already wounded light cruiser and her people thought they were going to lose her for sure but they did bring her through and the *Cabot* men shot down forty-one planes while doing it, which would not have been a bad setoff even if they lost her.

VIII

From the light cruiser *Nashville*, anchored out in the gulf, a motor whaler put off and a signal came to the harassed young lieutenant who was acting as beachmaster. Would he send out a small boat, as the beach shelved so gently that the motor whaler would be aground some distance out? "Tell them to walk in like the rest of us," snapped the lieutenant.

The whaler did ground; out of it into knee-deep water jumped

General Douglas MacArthur, who waded ashore with his chin held high for the photographers. "I have returned," he remarked with effective sententiousness.

The place was the east coast of the Philippine island of Leyte, between Tacloban and Palo. The date was October 20, 1944. Inland from where the general touched dry ground the steady thump of mortars and an occasional irregular burst of rifle fire could be heard where the men of the First Cavalry Division were pushing Jap elements back into the wooded draws that lead up the side of the central mountain chain. The resistance was light and they were making good progress; in fact for the first thousand yards of it they had not had a single casualty.

This was due partly to an extremely effective preliminary bombardment from rocket ships, here used for the first time on a large scale; partly to the strategic choice of the spot where the landing was made. It is no secret now that of all guerrilla movements in occupied countries, even including the Russian, none was so effective as that in the Philippines. Our people had only to ask for any information to get it, and on Mindanao the Japanese themselves were reduced to the status of guerrillas in some districts. Before the invasion began, General MacArthur knew that the Japanese fortifications and airfields were distributed about equally between Luzon at the north end of the eight hundred-mile-long Philippine chain and Mindanao on the southern flank. But these were supported only by garrisons; the main mobile troop concentrations were on Cebu, Panay, and Negros in the central Visayas, midway between, ready to meet an attack in either direction.

From this the American commander deduced that the Japs expected him to strike one end of the line or the other to produce a war of maneuver on the larger land masses—a type of operation at which his skill was known to be considerable. As a matter of fact, he had prepared operations orders for a descent on Mindanao; but in the preliminary carrier strikes one of our pilots had been shot down there, was picked up by the guerrillas and later got out via destroyer. He brought with him convincing proofs both of the strength of the insurgent movement and of the enemy concentration. Very well; MacArthur would set up his beachhead on the narrow east coastal strip of Leyte, which could be reached from the Jap troop concentration areas on that island only by two narrow and winding roads across the mountains, one of them no better than a track. This would keep the enemy from pouring reinforcements in against him during the delicate early stages. To make his own way through the mountains he would have the support of his air force, the Fifth. This was another reason for choosing Leyte—there were airstrips at Tacloban and Dulag, small and inefficient by American standards, but capable of being rapidly developed into good operational fields.

After a violent series of attacks on Jap air bases all the way from the Ryukyus and Formosa down to Luzon and Mindanao, therefore, Halsey's fleet flung out its planes across the central Philippine islands and waters on October 16. There was little Jap aviation abroad; that day and the next three, Halsey's strikes were mostly against minor Japanese shipping, an objective of importance in the warfare of closely interlocked islands, where such vessels are a main means of military movement. By the seventeenth our gunnery ships—cruisers and destroyers—were at hand. They ran along the coasts of Samar and Northern Mindanao, bombarding whatever there were of Japanese installations and covering MacArthur's Ranger battalions as they ran in to secure the three islands of Leyte Gulf—Homonhon, Dinagat, and Suluan. There were no Japs on any of these except for some kind of small gauleiters who were quickly exterminated. The minesweeps, vanguard of the MacArthur armada, went in that night. Admiral Wilkinson was in charge of the operation and did a wonderful job; they got 180 mines out during the darker hours of the seventeenth and eighteenth without losing a ship.

Ashore, the Japs began rather tentatively to deploy troops on Leyte, mostly around the two airstrips, and a few more troop formations were brought over from Cebu to Leyte-beyond-the-mountains, while as a precautionary measure they strung a single strand of wire along the beaches. The large-scale American preparations did not impress the Japs, for they were convinced that the gestures toward Leyte were a feint, and that what MacArthur really meant to do was to pour his forces through Surigao Strait for a landing at the mouth of the Agusan River of Mindanao and a campaign up its valley behind their coastal positions; so they rushed reinforcements to the Mindanao area. The moving Japs both there and on Leyte were hit by Halsey's planes during the eighteenth and nineteenth; that night

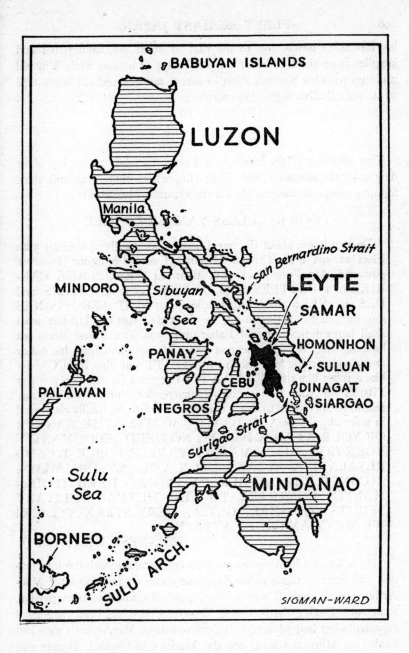

BABUYAN ISLANDS

LUZON

Manila

MINDORO

San Bernardino Strait

Sibuyan

LEYTE

Sea

SAMAR

HOMONHON

PANAY

SULUAN

CEBU

DINAGAT

PALAWAN

SIARGAO

NEGROS

Surigao Strait

Sulu
Sea

MINDANAO

BORNEO

SULU ARCH.

SIGMAN—WARD

his fast ships moved out to the east to lie at sea, taking fuel and supplies from the train after ten solid days of action, while Kinkaid came up with his Seventh Fleet of escort carriers and old battleships to support the landings next morning.

IX

That morning of the landing on Leyte—October 20—a Jap plane flew over the distant island of Peleliu, where there was still some fighting going on, and dropped a snowstorm of leaflets:

POOR RECKLESS YANKEE DOODLE

Do you know about the naval battle done by the American 58th Fleet at sea near Taiwan [Formosa] and Philippine Japanese powerful Air Force had sank their 14 AEROPLANE CARRIERS, 4 BATTLESHIPS, 10 SEVERAL CRUISERS and DESTROYERS along with sending 1201 SHIP AEROPLANES into the sea From this result, we think that you can imagine what shall happen next around Palau upen you The Fraud Roosevelt hanging the President Election under his nose and from his policy ambition working not only poor NIMITT but also MACCASIR like a robot like this WHAT A PITY it must be sacrifice you pay Thanks for your advice notes of surrender But we haven't any reason to surrender to those who are forced to be totally destroyed in a few days later ADD TO YOU, AGAINST THE MANNER OF YOUR ATTACK PAYING NO HEED TO HUMANITY YOUR GOD SHALL MAKE JAPANESE FORCE TO ADD RETALATIVE ATTACK UPON YOU, SAYING AGAIN, AGAINST THE ATTACK PAYING NO HEED TO HUMANITY CONTRARY TO THE MUTUAL MILITARY SPIRITS YOU SHALL GET AN VERY STERN ATTACK! WE MEAN AN CRUEL ATTACK!

JAPANESE MILITARY

This collector's item represents with fair accuracy both the information and state of mind in the Japanese camp on the day after MacArthur went ashore. Their defense up to this time had been passive, to be sure. During the preceding six weeks they had been challenged repeatedly but had adopted no offensive action. MacArthur's men had landed on Morotai island, and the Marines had seized Angaur and

Peleliu in the Palau group. The only Japanese resistance had been on the islands themselves—though on Peleliu it took a long and bloody engagement to subdue them. Though the Japanese savagely attacked Halsey's fleet *with land-based planes,* the Japanese fleet had not responded to this challenge.

They had no intention of avoiding battle indefinitely. Indeed, the basic principle of the Japanese military system was that the only valid defense lies in attack. Their apparent passivity up to this moment had three causes.

One was the desire to get the American forces in a position where a truly decisive blow could be struck against them; where there could be no escape for the survivors of the defeat they meant to inflict upon us. According to their way of thinking they had at least three times during the campaign for Guadalcanal (at Savo Island, the Eastern Solomons, and Santa Cruz) won battles from which they were unable to draw the full benefit because we got our cripples away and brought them back to fight on another occasion. After our attacks on Peleliu and Morotai it was obvious that a major amphibian occupation would be launched somewhere, probably against the Philippines. They wished to attack the expedition while it was astride the beach, most of its troops ashore but not all its equipment, and with our fleet still pinned to the area by the necessity of furnishing both air and artillery support. A counterattack thrown in at that precise moment would guarantee that the battle would be fought in a particular place and that all tactical arrangements could be made to Japan's best advantage. Its purpose would be to demolish the American Fleet and its transports and to leave the landing force—still without a good deal of its equipment—at the mercy of whatever Japanese ships were left from the battle. The place would now be the eastern coast of the Philippines.

In preparation for a battle in this area all the major gunnery units of the Japanese Navy had been sent down to base on Singapore. They would come up the west side of the Philippines and work through whichever of the numerous straits proved most convenient for an attack on the American forces lying east of the islands. Thus, though it was a disruption of the Japanese Army's plan for the defense of the Philippines that MacArthur should have landed on Leyte instead of on Luzon or Mindanao, it made no difference whatever in the plans of the Japanese Navy. To a certain extent it was even an advantage that he should have chosen Leyte at the bottom of its gulf; our transports would have that much less room for escape when the sky fell in on them.

The real check to their naval plan was the inroads that Halsey's fliers had made on Japanese air strength. In fact, the state of Japanese Naval Air was the second factor in the passive defense and the reason why the plan was put together as it was. The gunnery ships were to attack our fleet through the passes of the Philippines, instead of following the more obvious line of coming down from the home islands, because there simply were not enough carriers left to give them cover during so long a run and they had to depend upon land-based planes.

We had known that the battles of the preceding June had very sharply reduced the Japanese carrier strength; in fact, it was because the reduction was sharp and was in part, presumably, only temporary that MacArthur had hastened the invasion of the Philippines. Yet they were even weaker in carriers than anyone in our fleet imagined. They had their *Hayataka* operating with the gunnery ships from Singapore; but either she was not completely recovered from the wounds in the June battles or they did not care to trust her among the narrow waters of the Philippines, so she was out of it. They had their big *Zuikaku*, the veteran; three light carriers, *Chitose, Chiyoda, Zuiho*, and that was all. MacArthur's speedup of the invasion of the Philippines had caught their carrier strength at the exact bottom of the downswing. A month or two later they might have at least three more big carriers and two lights, but not now; and this was why their carrier force had not come out to challenge Halsey. But for the big battle these four carriers would run down the corridor of the latitudes at about the 126th meridian and from well out to sea strike the American forces pinned in the gulf.

This was the Japanese plan in its essentials. So far as it concerned their carriers it was a retake on the scheme that had so frightfully miscarried in June when, as you may recall, they had sent their carrier planes against our fleet off the Marianas at a range so great that only if they could land and refuel on Jap-held airfields in the Marianas could they ever get back to the carrier. Now the planes were to be shuttled across our fleet to bases ashore from a distance so great that our carriers could not strike back; and this is indicative of the third cause behind the Japanese failure to attack Halsey before he was pinned to Leyte. It may be called the "souvenir of the Nile," for the phenomenon is not new. When Napoleon Bonaparte was laying his great plan for the invasion of England in 1805, he provided for a series of fleet movements as intricate as a dream, all leading to a single purpose—to draw the British Navy from its guard over the English Channel. When it was objected that with far simpler maneuvers he could throw into the Channel forces fully adequate to crush the English in battle, the master military psychologist replied that he dared not attempt it; all his admirals "bore with them the souvenir of the Nile."

They had been present on that night when a French fleet was wiped out; and from that night on, the emphasis of their underlying ideas—not thought, but the apparatus with which they formed thoughts—was less upon inflicting damage on the enemy than upon saving their own ships. The Japanese admirals similarly were brave and devoted men. But since November, 1942, there had lain on their minds the shadow of that midnight when Willis Lee's battleships ran up the Slot and tore them all apart—that and the ominous memory of Midway.

Their whole plan was not really one for a battle but for an assassination; and it would never have been put into execution at all but for the success of a fortunate feat of deception by Halsey only a few days earlier. When Halsey's big fleet, after its strike at Formosa, had withdrawn southward, the admiral left behind in the neighborhood of Formosa a single group of carriers under Admiral McCain. This he did partly to impose a long-range screen between the Jap bases in the north and a damaged American cruiser which was limping away from the scene of the Japanese air attacks on the fleet; but he had another purpose. This was to deceive the Japanese into thinking that their air attacks had been brilliantly successful and that this single visibly remaining carrier group *was the sole remnant of American carrier strength in all the western Pacific.*

The Tokyo radio had been characteristically boasting that eleven of our carriers had burned up or blown up under their attacks from the air. In fact, when the Jap planes had been coming in on our fleet by night—and, as they were shot down, had been hitting the water and blowing up in pillars of flame three hundred feet high—many of our own airmen, seeing the explosions and mounting columns of fire, had thought that this or that American ship had been hit and was burning. The surviving Japs in the air, harried by our flak and night fighters, would have no opportunity for a checkup. Nor would this be the first time the enemy had believed their own broadcasts; we have seen in the past how that had happened off Saipan. If they believed that McCain's group was all we had left, they might venture a naval battle—whereupon Halsey, cutting back with the rest of his formidable fleet, could destroy them.

They did not venture battle then, and the American commander thought that the deception had failed; but he had merely underestimated the Japanese reaction period; it had succeeded beyond his wildest dreams. The enemy really believed that they had sunk eleven American carriers, and now they were coming out with their entire Navy for that general battle so ardently desired!

X

Yet their plan, flawed in its basic structure, was formidable enough and would have been adequate had Halsey lost as much as they thought. They themselves had lost heavily in Halsey's strikes, but by drawing planes all the way from the interior of China and from Singapore they had made good much of that loss. These planes, two hundred or more of them, were to deliver the first blow, striking out from the Luzon fields against Halsey's fleet to the east on the morning of October 24; and they would be joined by the Jap carrier planes from still further east. Both groups of planes together would fly on to Luzon after the attack and base there overnight. The orders were to press the attack home to the hilt. The Japs expected to lose a lot of planes, but they also expected that at the very least they would leave Halsey with some badly damaged ships still further to impede his mobility, and it was not an unreasonable anticipation. On the evening of the twentieth, after the landing, they had made such an attack on the covering ships off Leyte. It got a torpedo into the cruiser *Honolulu,* and HMAS *Australia* had gone staggering out of action with a bad hit on the bridge.

The double air attack, the Japs seem to have expected, would keep what carrier groups we had left from interfering with the approach march of their gunnery ships. There were two groups of these. One had at its core the battleships *Fuso* and *Yamashiro* (about equal to our *Idahos,* but even more extensively modernized); the heavy cruiser *Mogami,* completely rebuilt after her pounding at Midway and, it is said, with a flight deck aft; possibly another heavy cruiser, though this identification is very uncertain; one of the new light cruisers of the *Agano* type; and somewhere between eight and twelve destroyers. This force was to enter the Philippines south of Palawan, cross the Sulu Sea and the Mindanao Sea, and enter Leyte Gulf via Surigao Strait, arriving at dawn on the twenty-fifth. Let us call it the Surigao Strait force.

The second battle fleet was to round Palawan by the north, south of Mindoro, and crossing Sibuyan Sea reach the western Philippines via San Bernardino Strait and rounding Samar. It can be called the Sibuyan Sea force. The ships were the new battleships *Yamato* and *Musashi* (something less than our *Iowas,* something more than our *North Carolinas*); the battleship *Nagato*; the veteran battleships *Kongo* and *Haruna* that had seen so much of the Pacific war; the four heavy cruisers of the *Atago* class (the three besides the name-ship were *Takao, Chokai,* and *Maya*); one of the *Nachi* class heavy cruisers (identified by some of our airmen as *Haguro*); *Suzuyu* and *Kumano* of the *Mogami* class; *Tone* and *Chikuma,* heavy cruisers of the class named for the first ship; one new light cruiser of the *Noshiro* class; and fifteen destroyers.

The third Japanese force, sweeping down from the north, included their four carriers; a ship sometimes called a heavy cruiser but whose identification is dubious; another *Agano* class light cruiser, three of the old three-piper light cruisers, and six destroyers, in addition to the two remaining battleships, *Ise* and *Hyuga.**

* The list is particularly interesting as furnishing a back check on previous Japanese naval losses, and the close of the war with its fuller information makes the check still more accurate. They had eighteen heavy cruisers with which to start the war—four *Kakos,* four *Nachis,* four *Atagos,* four *Mogamis,* and two *Tones.* Of these eleven had been claimed as sunk by various communiqués, mainly from the air forces. But when the Jap fleet showed up for the big battle

These two ships had been rebuilt, with their after turrets replaced by a flight deck running forward to the mainmast. Such a deck would be very little use for taking in planes, but the planes from these ships and some of the land units were not expected to be taken in. They were part of the nasty technical surprise the Japs had cooked up for this occasion—the Kamikaze Special Attack Corps, of pilots vowed and trained to dive into American warships with entire plane-loads of explosives. Since January of 1943 and the action off Rennell Island the Japs had not ceased to insist that their only loss in every battle were pilots who thus immolated themselves, and the matter had become a rather puzzling commonplace of the propaganda campaign—puzzling because no Jap pilot had ever actually tried it, unless there could be counted an incident in December, 1943, when three pilots apparently attempted a suicidal attack on an LST off Cape Gloucester in New Britain. They were all shot down and the circumstances were such that it was by no means certain they had attempted suicide in any case. Thus very few people in our fleet believed in the real existence of the Kamikaze Corps, which is probably one of the things that the Japs counted on.

It has been said that one or more of their three forces was intended merely to furnish a diversion, but this is not true. The Japs knew full well the devotion of our naval leaders to the doctrines of Admiral Mahan, one of which was a radical insistence upon concentrating the

---

only the four *Kako*s, two of the *Nachi*s, and one of the *Mogami*s were missing. A postwar check shows that one of the *Kako*s was still afloat and the two missing *Nachi*s were in the region of Singapore. The Japanese built no new heavy cruisers. At the beginning of the war they had seventeen light cruisers; only three of the original seventeen came down to fight it out (the *Agano*s and *Noshiro*s were easily identifiable war-built types). Twenty-seven had been claimed sunk; the postwar check shows the number to have actually been twelve, though some of the light cruisers reported may have been *Teratzuki*s, a war-built type intermediate between a cruiser and a destroyer. The small number of destroyers, far fewer than would be considered adequate for an American force of this type, is very striking. We would want twenty-five to thirty destroyers to cover the Sibuyan Sea force alone and so would the Japs on a prewar basis. The Japs had 133 destroyers before the war and the claimed sinkings were 139, but they had built a great many destroyers during the struggle.

Incidentally, unless our official Navy release (based on Japanese records) is gravely in error, it casts an interesting light on some claims of sinkings. General MacArthur's bombers claimed to have sunk a total of thirteen cruisers; the release shows they sunk none at all.

fleet for battle. They undoubtedly expected that whatever ships we had left in good shape after the air attack of the twenty-fourth would turn against one of their battle divisions and they probably counted on losing some ships in that division. But they planned that the other battle force would then wipe out the transports and cripples in Leyte Gulf on the morning of the twenty-fifth.

In that process the gunnery ships would be aided both by land planes from Luzon and the planes of the carrier fleet which, having spent the night on the ground there, would again shuttle out across our fleet to their carrier decks at a point somewhere east of the Philippines between the twelfth and thirteenth parallels of latitude.

XI

These arrangements were of course unknown to anyone in our fleet. Halsey's first information came from the submarine *Darter*, patrolling in the South China Sea west of Palawan. She had surfaced to recharge her batteries in the dark hours before dawn of October 23 when she picked up (one may hypothesize radar) a large number of surface ships approaching, too many and too fast for a convoy. That meant a Jap battle fleet. Lieutenant Commander D. H. McClintock put their number, course, and speed on the air for Halsey's benefit; then he whistled up another submarine (*Dace*), and moved in to attack. He had struck the Sibuyan Sea force. Those two subs between them got four torpedoes apiece into *Atago*, *Maya*, and a third heavy cruiser of the same class, *Takao*. The first two went down at once; the third reeled back to Singapore with holes in her you could drive an ox cart through, and with two of the destroyers for escort. All the remaining destroyers came baying like beagles after our subs.

Darter worked close inshore with her commander preparing a counterattack—an act of astonishing boldness, for destroyers are supposed to be certain death to submarines. They did not find him; but while he was maneuvering, the boat ran aground hard on a submerged reef and nothing could be done to get her loose. McClintock abandoned his ship, blew her up, and loading his crew into rubber boats, made for the shore with them, presumably to Palawan or Balabac Island, the only land around there. Both places were in Jap possession but the guerrillas helped out and the commander was presently rescued with every man of his crew, after the most important single submarine action of the war, whether for itself or its consequences.

In the meanwhile another sub had spotted and reported the Surigao Strait force as it plowed through south of Palawan; and still another, probably alerted by radio, lay in wait for the Sibuyan Sea force and got a torpedo into one of its heavy cruisers (probably *Nachi*) off the

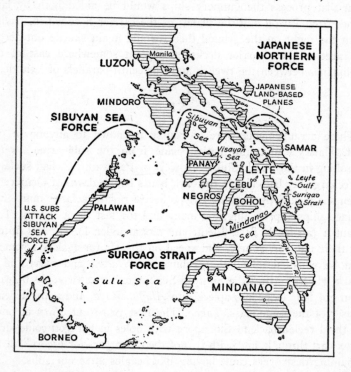

entrance to Mindoro Strait. Those Jap ships were very stoutly defended against torpedo attack but she had to be taken to Manila Bay.

With that magnificent obstinacy in pursuit of a given plan which made them such predictable opponents, the rest of the Japanese Fleet kept coming right along; and now Halsey had a count on the enemy surface forces and a fair idea of their purpose, since there are only two exits to the east from the waters they had entered.

The carrier group of Admiral McCain had run out into the ocean eastward to fill its fuel tanks and could hardly get back before the twenty-fifth. Of the other three carrier groups, F. C. Sherman's was assigned to cruise the waters east of Luzon, up in the region of the great bight formed by Legaspi Peninsula; Jerry Bogan's was south and east of this, blocking the exit of San Bernardino Strait from well to seaward; and Ralph Davison's was still farther down, bearing due east from the southern cape of Samar. Sherman and Bogan were to handle the Sibuyan Sea force; they were assigned to fly searches at dawn of the twenty-fourth. Sherman's group would search the passes north and south of Mindoro (there was just a chance that this Jap battle fleet might be bound for Manila or north around Luzon, and nothing could be neglected); Bogan's would go to Sibuyan Sea itself. Davison's planes were to spread out over the Sulu Sea and pick up the Surigao Strait force, with which touch had been lost after that one brief fleeting contact by the sub during the night.

Kinkaid's Seventh Fleet was organized into the escort carrier force under Admiral Thomas Sprague, with three groups of six ships each; and the force of six old battleships under Admiral Jesse Oldendorf. The latter had been doing a great deal of bombardment work in support of the troops. They were to continue that assignment during the twenty-fourth up to the northern end of Leyte, but when darkness fell, shift south toward the exit of Surigao Strait. The Jap force coming in this direction had by far the shortest route and should arrive first.

The escort carriers had been working close in during daylight when we had complete control of the air, and lying off at night, when we could not be sure of it. They were all badly needed to furnish troop support, for although both Dulag and Tacloban airstrips had been captured two days before, it was discovered the capacity of the former had been horribly overestimated; one end of the strip was under water and it would take nothing larger than a Piper cub. At Tacloban the strip was not only short but without sufficient parking areas.

In a pinch the planes from Sprague's carriers would help against either Jap force. Kinkaid also had some PT boats; these were shifted down to the southern end of Surigao Strait, which we could do because on the second day of the invasion—after some very hard fighting—MacArthur's men had got hold of Pintuyan Island.

It is not possible to say how these arrangements could have been improved upon. But it should be noted that the dispositions of the

two American fleets were taken, to a certain extent, without reference
to each other. Kinkaid was not under Halsey's command but under
MacArthur's, his movements subject to the latter's approval. Moreover, all the Philippines fell within the MacArthur command area,
which made him supreme officer everywhere to the west of an imaginary line stretching down the ocean somewhere just to the west of
that along which the Jap carrier force, still undetected, was advancing

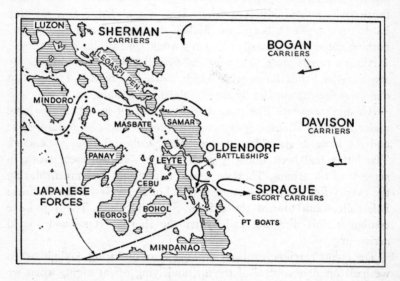

from the north. In practice MacArthur and Halsey got along very
well together and all the admiral's suggestions were accepted by the
general; but the latter liked to be consulted, which took time and
communications and cannot but have been felt as a hindrance by
blazing Halsey as the two Jap battle fleets came steaming through
smooth blue seas into the rising sun.

XII

The trail divides. To the south, in Sulu Sea, planes from *Enterprise*
(no ship ever had such a battle record as the carrier *Enterprise*)
picked up the Surigao Strait force about 0830 on October 24 near
the end of their run, south of Negros Island. Commander Frederick

Bakutis and Commander Emmanuel Riera, close friends, were leaders of the air groups from Davison's carriers. They called in the other searchers, assembling in the skies while the Japs opened long range AA fire from their big guns—something that had been once or twice seen in June and not quite believed. It was the only defense the ships had, for there was not a Jap plane around; and it must have been a considerable and fairly unpleasant surprise to the enemy to find so many carrier planes coming in on them. At about 0905 Bakutis and Riera had their men ready and tipped over into the long dive, with the fighters riding down beside them firing rockets, all concentrating on the battleships. The battle had begun.

It was a search strike designed for long range, so the bombs were only five hundred-pounders. The Japs had warning and plenty of room to move under their umbrella of flak, so the attack was not too successful. One of the battleships (accounts disagree which) got a hit aft that left her with a brightly burning fire and the other took one forward up in the eyes of the ship. The destroyers were strafed, and all our planes got off back to the carriers to prepare for the true and heavy blow, while snoopers from Sprague's escort carriers took over the task of shadowing the bunch of Japs.

The true attack was never delivered. For before the scout strikers could return to their decks, and before the other planes on them could take off, there was word of trouble in the north, with orders from Mitscher and Halsey that Davison's planes were needed in that direction at once. Sherman's scouts had, of course, missed the Jap battle force, which was not in the area east of Luzon that they were searching. Bogan's fliers found them, soon after daybreak, steaming stolidly northeastward off Tablas Island, south of Luzon. As with Davison's men in the Sulu Sea, the scouts passed the word, called in their companions, and attacked. As in the Sulu Sea action, there was an astonishing lack of trouble with Jap fighters but heavy and pretty accurate flak coming up from guns of every size carried by the ships. A few of the enemy were hit, how hard we shall never know because the damage was overlaid by what happened later. Also (this became important) the Jap movement was delayed by their jigging around under the shower of bombs. This happened around 0800. Back aboard the carriers of the two groups, the dive bombers and torpedo planes were armed for a major strike.

But before it came off Sherman's group was hit by all those two hundred land-based Jap bombers from Luzon.

It was 0801 of a murky morning with rain squalls when our combat patrols tallyhoed on the two hundred Jap planes. "Oklahoma Pete" Mitscher, the ferocious gnome, had his flag in the new *Lexington*. He came out on the bridge, waved away a helmet with "Too heavy" but advised a correspondent to get back in—those were dive bombers—as the first trails of smoke began to run down toward the sea and the high chatter of machine guns came from above. The next moment the Jap planes were coming in from all directions.

Rain squalls and overcast were on our side; so was the fact that these were planes from the enemy general reserve, not so well organized or trained as some. Commander David MacCampbell fell on a group of nearly sixty with his Fighting Fifteen, as they were circling some thirty miles from the carriers, and they fled incontinently while MacCampbell himself made a record never equaled before or since by shooting down nine.

But not all the Japs were like that and they had certain advantages lacking to those at the Philippine Sea when Spruance's groups had shot down so many, to wit; that off Luzon they were not caught in a cruising formation but had time to spread for attack, were opposed by far fewer fighters—only those of a single carrier group—and had no worries about fuel supply, so that their attacks were persistent. They lost heavily—110 was the later official account—but at 0939 a Judy came through a cloud on *Princeton* and dropped a 500-pound bomb which went through her deck on the port side amidships. A few minutes later another carrier was hit, a bomb through her deck forward.

It was a moment of comparative lull; aboard *Princeton* as aboard the other carriers of the group they had readied for the strike on the Jap battle fleet, with the TBFs lined up on the hangar deck and all armed. Captain Buracker intended to fly planes as soon as he got enough of his fighters back from the air battle and needed only one or two more when the bomb hit. There were casualties and a big fire, of course. *Princeton* dropped out of formation with the destroyers *Irwin* and *Morrison*, which often worked with her, and *Gatling* and

Cassin Young running in to pump water. The antiaircraft cruiser *Reno* circled for protection.

Before the destroyers could get their equipment working well, and before the carrier's damage-control parties could do much on their own, the fire got to those loaded torpedo planes and they went up in two violent explosions. The flight deck split right back; out of it rushed a column of flame and smoke that engulfed the whole ship to the stern. Her engines went dead, her fire mains stopped working. Admiral Sherman ordered the light cruiser *Birmingham* down to join the salvage operation; Captain Buracker, who had begun by being optimistic, gave the abandon ship order which holds for all but volunteers, and men began to drop over the side.

Even lifesaving was a fairly desperate operation under the tongues of flame jutting from the side of the ship, now rolling heavily in a swell coming all the way from across the Pacific. The jeep used by the carrier to tow planes dropped on *Morrison*'s deck and nearly brained half a dozen men. On one of the long rolls *Irwin*'s top hamper caught and was snapped off clean when *Princeton* rolled back; and the return roll was worse yet, for this time she trapped *Morrison* down against the water under her overhang and the destroyer could not swing clear. Another destroyer had to take *Morrison* in tow to jerk her out, she was swept clean at the level of her bridge—masts, funnels and director all pulled off—and ammunition from the ready boxes along the carrier gunwalk was exploding in every direction.

The Jap planes kept coming in; *Reno* was shooting at them in every direction. But Captain Inglis of *Birmingham* daringly and intelligently got his ship close along the windward side of the stricken carrier and began to pump; by 1100 he was gaining on the game. The other carrier's case, though bad enough, was not so bad. Smoke rolled up through her flight deck in a black plume, the forward end of the hangar deck where the basketball court was had a fire, and the forward elevator was shot. But she signaled she needed no help, could still take in planes, and in an emergency could get them off via catapult.

The attack and damage, however, had had the effect of disjointing Mitscher's plans for a heavy strike on the Jap battle force in Sibuyan Sea. The Japs could hardly have missed the sight of the burning ships, and where they would normally have taken all their planes

back to the field to work up another concentrated attack, they now
fed them back into the assault on Sherman's ships as rapidly as re-
armed. It was an expensive process and ran up the Jap casualties, but
Sherman's fighters could not leave the scene to escort a strike nor
could his bombers take off from carrier decks under attack. Davison's
group was accordingly called away from its job against the Jap force
in Sulu Sea and sent in on the Sibuyan strike with Bogan's men.

XIII

Bogan's fliers got there first, of course, because they started earlier;
and were no little disappointed at the failure of Sherman's planes to
rendezvous with them. They found the Japs just rounding Tablas
Island; tried to raise Sherman's planes via radio; and not succeeding,
since this was about the hour of the explosions on *Princeton*, went
in without them.

There was no Jap air opposition, only the intense flak that seems
to drift so lazily up the sky. The attackers were an entire carrier
group, which must be reckoned at not less than one hundred bomber
and torpedo planes, besides the fighters (which, having no enemies,
could devote their attention to AA positions); but the defense was
an entire battle fleet in good condition and it has been said that
modern big surface ships carry their own air cover. We had losses;
so had they, to what extent is again uncertain, save that the big new
battleships bore the brunt of this attack and both were well hit. As
Bogan's fliers soared away they noticed that one of the destroyers
was well down by the head and two more were turning back out of
the formation with a damaged cruiser under their wing, probably
Chokai.

Bogan was not at all satisfied and as soon as he could rearm his
planes sent them back. Meanwhile Davison had moved up into position and flown off his own planes, headed by an air group under
Commander Don F. Smith. The attacks of Bogan and the scout
planes had delayed the Japs so that Smith and his groups thought
them farther along their route than they actually were. The Japs had
to be found again, which made it 1430 before they were discovered
and just a little after 1600 when the attack was actually delivered
with some of Bogan's planes on their second run joining those of

Davison. The Japs were now well in to Sibuyan Sea, somewhere north of Romblon Island. The sun was westering; Smith swung his air groups around to come in on the Japs out of it, and they turned with him to face the fire and to give his bombers the shorter run.

As the enemy ships came round, Smith noted that they kept formation better than any Jap fleet he had ever seen and also that the big battleship *Musashi* must be pretty badly hurt. She did not turn with the rest but moved slowly around on an irregular course at a

speed which he estimated as eight knots. He turned loose the entire *Enterprise* air group on her—she was the big prize—and as he rode down the rising lines of flak, he estimated that she must have been fairly hard hit topside too, for her AA fire was weak and irregular.

The attack was a perfect piece of co-ordination, the first of a long stream of dive bombers reaching release point exactly as the torpedo planes made their drop on both sides of *Musashi* at once. There is no agreement as to how many times she was hit; Smith himself after he dropped his own missile estimated that at least eleven armor-piercing bombs got into her in addition to eight fish, but the ACI men tried to whittle the number of torpedoes down to six. The big ship stopped, then—as our fliers began to pull away—moved again, but in a slow circle with a huge parti-colored oil slick spreading round her.

"It was like flying into a cave," said Lieutenant Robert Cosgrove, one of the pilots who went in on the other Jap ships, but their attack on these other ships was not less concentrated or effective. *Yamato* got another bomb hit that messed up a lot of her antiaircraft positions amidships; *Kongo* and *Haruna* were both hit; *Nagato* got one on the control tower; and several of our air groups went for the heavy cruisers. *Chokai*, recognizable as the *Atago* class ship in the squadron, was laced with both bombs and torpedoes and left stopped. Two of the other heavy cruisers took lists; one of the destroyers went down. And when the fliers from the two carrier groups pulled away, the last thing they saw was the Jap fleet steaming on a reversed course back in the direction they had come, with many cripples.

An hour later, under a sun now setting, a scout found some of the Jap ships still limping westward. Halsey decided that the Sibuyan Sea fleet could be written out of the action.

XIV

Some such decision was necessary. By 1330 *Birmingham* had gotten *Princeton*'s fires so well down that there was only a small blaze burning aft and the persistent Jap attacks had been worn down to a shadow of their former intensity. "We're going to get her home," remarked Captain Buracker to Captain John M. Hoskins, who was aboard preparatory to relieving in command of the ship. But at that moment two things happened: one of the destroyers reported a submarine contact and the air patrol reported a big Jap bogey— many planes coming *from the east—from out to seaward*.

As these Japanese planes approached it was clear they were carrier-borne planes. The third Japanese fleet, their carrier force, was coming into action. The rain cloud and overcast under which Sherman's group had been working had now blown away; the ships "felt very naked." Marc Mitscher stepped out on the bridge of *Lex* with a smile crinkling his face. "Just one damn thing after another," he remarked as all fighters in the group were scrambled. Behind him Arleigh

Burke, "31-Knot" Burke, his chief of staff, ground out, "This is the time to stay and fight and beat their goddam heads off."

As it turned out, the sub contact was false; but *Birmingham* had to cut loose from *Princeton* and maneuver at large with the screen against what was likely to be the most formidable attack of all, for the Jap carrier pilots were the best they had. The attack was delivered furiously and with skill. It lasted two whole hours. But the only surprise about it was the relatively small number of planes in it

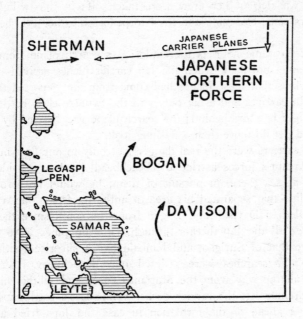

and they had come so long a distance that they had none too much juice. And they did not find our fleet badly cut up by the Luzon bombers, as they had expected to. Sherman's group was intact save for the two damaged carriers and these had lost few planes. The attack was beaten off without damage; some fifty of the Japs were splashed, the rest flew away—back to their carriers as Halsey thought.

As soon as they were gone *Birmingham* pulled alongside *Princeton* again with tow and mooring lines ready and fire mains hooked up. The blaze aft on the carrier did not seem to have gained too seriously during the interruption as the cruiser maneuvered to within fifty feet of her charge at about 1540. But at that moment there was an explosion of such intensity that it drove *Birmingham* almost on her beam ends and straight sidewise away from the carrier. Captain Hoskins found himself looking at a naked foot and realized that it was his own, no longer attached; the cruiser was enveloped in a sheet of flame, every man topside killed or wounded, blood so thick on her deck that sand had to be scattered for walking. *Princeton's* after magazine had gone and there was now no chance of saving the ship. All that was left of her crew were taken off; in the twilight the destroyers came alongside and fired torpedoes into her till she went down.

But at the same hour as the explosion a search plane from Mitscer's group—flown off when the Jap carrier planes arrived—found the Jap ships that these planes had come from and reported them— three light carriers and a big one with the two *Ise* class battleships. There might be more behind; the search plane was harried by Zeros and could get no more than a flashing look.

Those carriers were the real danger, not only to our fleet but also to MacArthur's forces astride the beachhead (Halsey considered); and out at sea there, in pursuit of them, he would be across the shadow line that separated his area of authority from MacArthur's.

He called in Davison and Bogan from the south since their job was done; all the Jap threats through the Philippines were turned back save that of Surigao, and Kinkaid had a surprise waiting for those. Night searches were ordered out, the clumsy PBYs and PB4Ys, all the way from the Marianas bases and Ulithi; his own night searchers left the carrier decks. Willis Lee's battleships were moved out ahead of the formation in case the Japs tried a night gunnery attack on our carriers. The three carrier groups were given a rendezvous and as our ships moved toward it through the night the admiral was heard to murmur that in every battle of the war so far the Japs had had the jump on us or had made us split forces. Now at long last we were going to get the jump on them—on all their carriers.

Behind him, though he did not know it, though no one on our side knew it for weeks, the battleship *Musashi*, best in the Jap navy, had gone down—the second modern battleship to be sunk by air attack, the first with fully modern antiaircraft protection. Behind him also

Irwin was pulling from the water the last of 1,440 survivors from the sunken *Princeton*. When they got him, the man was laughing his head off over the plight of a baldheaded shipmate named Salty Loftus, who as he swam had been sighted by an albatross which took his poll for an egg (or something) and made a two-point landing on it.

XV

A good deal of victory or defeat in a naval battle depends on the point of view. The British had the heavier material loss at Jutland but wrote it down as a victory because they achieved a strategic objective. The Germans likewise list it as a victory on the ground that no strategic objective was involved and the material count was in their favor. So at Coral Sea the loss of the *Lexington* was probably more serious to our Navy than that of the *Shoho* (or *Ryukaku*) was to the Japanese. They were in some position to claim and did claim a victory. The question of who really won the battle was determined by events that came at some distance both in time and space. Similarly as twilight on the night of October 24 closed over the seas that reached twelve hundred miles from Okinawa to Mindanao, the enemy had some reason to believe that although their material losses had been severe, they had played us into a position which could solve out only in a victory for themselves.

At the northern wing of that enormous battle line they had lost many planes but had seen two of our carriers burning and their snoopers detected Admiral Sherman's group making off to the north and east. It is probable, indeed it is the only way of accounting for what afterward happened, that they thought these ships, except for the cripples, were pulling altogether away from the field of action. They had made no contact yet with the other three carrier groups and would therefore have very little to contradict the primary assumption on which their whole conduct of the battle was based—that those other carriers were out of existence, sunk in the Formosa action of the thirteenth. The energy with which our carrier planes had attacked their central, Sibuyan Sea battle fleet must have been rather a surprise, but as we have seen, the attacks came seriatim and from only one carrier group at a time, which is to say that with extraordinary luck and technical skill Sherman's carriers and the escort carrier groups might just have managed the whole business.

The Japs knew about those escort carriers and knew they would be back in Leyte Gulf at dawn. Presumably they had scouted the exit of Sibuyan Sea through San Bernardino Strait during the afternoon and evening and they certainly held both the shores that look upon it. They knew we had no kind of force in there or near there. On the other hand they had the best of reasons for being aware that our submarines were lurking off Mindoro Strait along the road back and with as many damaged ships as the Japs had, submarine opposition at night was a serious problem.

The bold course, then, was for them the safe course. Some time during the night this central force in Sibuyan Sea once more reversed course and now made up of four battleships, four heavy cruisers and a light with eleven destroyers, began steaming toward San Bernardino at its best speed. All the heavy ships were hurt, and the damage to fire-control instruments around the upper works seems to have been particularly serious. But even with their guns in local control they ought to be able to butcher the armorless escort carriers, the destroyers and light cruisers which alone would be protecting MacArthur's transports.

The planes on the Luzon fields, both those originally based there and those flown in from the Jap carriers, were to make a co-ordinated attack on the same target, the carrier planes continuing back to their decks in a reversal of the previous afternoon's shuttle. The Jap carriers had steamed slowly toward the north and somewhat westward during the early part of the night in order to keep well clear of what the Japs conceived to be Halsey's fleet making eastward. Toward dawn they reversed and came back at full speed to pick up their planes.

It will be observed that the Japanese plan was essentially similar to that for the first day's battle and that it was one for a concentric attack which demanded the most exquisite timing, three fleets and two air groups arriving on the point of a pin, precise to the second. The attack on Sherman's carrier group in the bight of Luzon had failed through faulty timing, but it did not occur to the enemy that there was anything inherently wrong with their scheme, which was

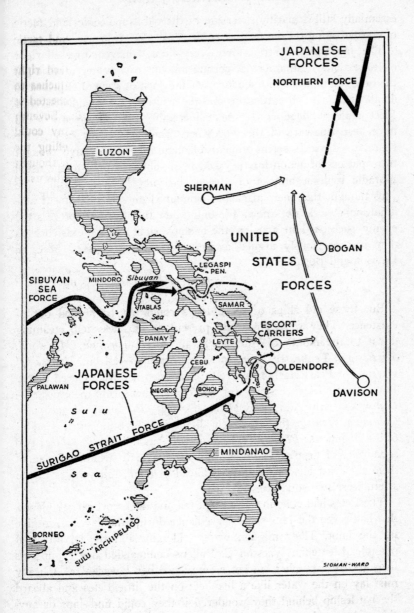

essentially still a maritime version of the old Napoleonic land tactic of concentrating on the field of battle.

The Jap Surigao Strait force, very little damaged, pressed right on toward its destination. A certain amount of mystery attaches to the question of what this squadron or the Japs in general expected to do about the six old battleships and the cruisers of Kinkaid's Seventh Fleet under Oldendorf. It seems incredible that the enemy could have been unaware of their presence. They had been shelling the shore for days. It seems implausible that they could have thought them put out of action for they had been subjected only to the usual sporadic twilight attacks of torpedo-carrying Bettys. Possibly the Japs thought that their magazines contained only bombardment ammunition—we do not know. We only know that by some process the enemy succeeded in arguing these ships right out of existence as they had previously argued away the carrier groups of McCain, Davison and Bogan.

XVI

But those old ships of Oldendorf's could not be argued out of existence. They were physically present as darkness fell, steaming down to the mouth of Surigao Strait—*West Virginia, Maryland, Mississippi, Tennessee, California, Pennsylvania*—all but *Mississippi* veterans of Pearl Harbor, where three at least had been placed by the Japs on their Index Expurgatorius. Around them were the cruisers—*Louisville* with Admiral Oldendorf's flag, *Portland, Minneapolis, Columbia, Denver*, that had seen all the hard fighting up the ladder of the Solomons; *Phoenix, Boise* and the Australian *Shropshire*; two squadrons of destroyers under Captain Kenneth McManes, one of them the Australian *Arunta*. Out ahead of them, thirty miles in the strait, were two squadrons of PTs.

The Petes had gone in when night fell and the escort carrier planes, that had given the Japs some surveillance during the day, had to give up the hunt. Their mission was to identify and report, attack if possible. Lieutenant Weston C. Pullens commanded one group; his flagship had a number but her crew named her *Lakacookie*. A heavy mist lay on the water like a blanket; on the little Petes and aboard the battleship behind they wondered if they could find Japs or anything else in that and tensions built up almost unendurably as the dark hours ticked by with no sign. Or were they really coming? On *Tennessee*'s bridge the OOD reminded his junior how he had said back at the time of Saipan that when the Jap fleet came out the fast battleships would be off chasing will-o'-the-wisps somewhere "and we'll be carrying the load."

"Yes, but they haven't come out yet and I bet the old man would just as soon not have them come out tonight when we're so short on ammo."

Short or not Oldendorf was quite prepared to go into those narrow and mine-strewn waters after the Japs if they did not come; only the Petes could tell him whether to move or stand.

At 2300 it was still murky where the battleships were, but down with Pullen's Petes the mist lifted like a cloak thrown back and he found himself looking *Fuso* right in the eye. "It was a battle wagon all right," said Lieutenant Eddins, the boat's skipper, "but I just couldn't make myself say so and in my first report I wrote her down for a heavy cruiser."

"Close for attack," ordered Pullens. *Lakacookie*'s radioman opened up with: "I have an urgent message for you," but that was all the admiral ever got, for as the motors screamed crescendo, the Jap destroyer screen out ahead, the battleships and the other ships behind them all spotted the little boat, the radio channels were jammed and a crash of gunfire came down. The range was too long for good torpedo work; Eddins swung round to get out of there with his news, one of them firing on the turn.

Lakacookie was hit forward, the bow gun knocked overboard, the whole forecastle set afire, but the splash of a near miss put out the blaze. No. 2 boat was hit, by an 8-inch that incredibly gouged out part of a torpedo to leave the detonator hanging without setting it off; No. 3 boat was hit and went down—and all that Jap armada, cruisers and destroyers, came pounding after the Petes as they raced up the shore of Pintuyan. The Japs were lighting up the whole night with their star shells and *Lakacookie*'s radioman was pounding his key like mad, trying to get the message through.

The chase lasted three-quarters of an hour and both Petes were pretty well wrecked when they got alongside their tender, which was next morning. They did not know then the two most important facts about the curtain raiser to the main show—that No. 3 boat had paid for herself with a torpedo hit on one of the Jap cruisers (it seems to have been *Abukama*) which thereupon left the formation and steamed north up Camotes Sea west of Leyte, bound God knows where under destroyer escort; and that *Lakacookie*'s message had been picked up by a PT of the other patrols and sent through.

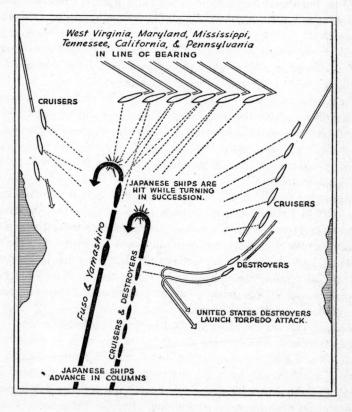

West Virginia, Maryland, Mississippi, Tennessee, California, & Pennsylvania
IN LINE OF BEARING

CRUISERS

JAPANESE SHIPS ARE HIT WHILE TURNING IN SUCCESSION.

CRUISERS

Fuso & Yamashiro

CRUISERS & DESTROYERS

DESTROYERS

UNITED STATES DESTROYERS LAUNCH TORPEDO ATTACK.

JAPANESE SHIPS ADVANCE IN COLUMNS

The Japs were coming; Oldendorf could make his dispositions. The battleships he placed across the exit to the strait in a line of bearing (see map) and set them steaming slowly to and fro. The cruisers he slid forward on either flank where the strait is only seven miles wide, himself leading *Louisville, Portland, Minneapolis* and the two lights in on the east side while Rear Admiral Berkey took the other three cruisers down the western flank. Rear Admiral Weyler had the battle line; behind each formation of cruisers was a destroyer squadron. Fire distribution patterns were worked out and we waited.

Waited till nearly dawn; then here they come, straight into the textbook position every admiral dreams of but none had ever seen till this moment, the position of the stem of a crossed T. The Japs were in line ahead, column, or rather two columns, one staggered a bit behind the other. The two battleships formed one alone; the other was led by the heavy cruiser *Mogami* with the destroyers along behind, a formation which would only occur to a Jap or a lunatic. Oldendorf released his destroyers and they rushed from both flanks, laying a cross fire of torpedoes. Nobody knows how many of those fish hit or what they hit. Two minutes before they were due to strike the Japs spotted the ride of the Valkyries and put up a star shell with the sharp crash of their secondaries following. The star shell showed our destroyers clear; it also illuminated the Jap battle line and was the signal for which Oldendorf was waiting.

"Commence firing," he said as *Louisville* did so at 0355; and before her shells had reached their target there burst upon those Jap ships such a storm as had never been seen in a naval battle before. *Mississippi* and *Tennessee* were firing on their leader, *Maryland* and *California* on the second battleship, the ships at the ends of our line shooting farther down theirs and the cruisers from the flank firing at everything. The range from the battleships was over ten sea miles; *Tennessee* at least missed with her first salvo, but the second raked right down the deck of *Yamashiro* and the third and more.

Under that concentration the Jap battleships got off exactly two salvos—one that struck raggedly in the water beyond *West Virginia*; one that fell at least five thousand yards short of *California*. Then *Yamashiro* was slewing around as though trying to turn with flames coming out all over her; from one of our destroyers they saw the door of an admiral's cabin fly open and a bright light within as the big ship hung on the turn, taking salvo after salvo, her armor crumbling like cardboard. From another destroyer they caught sight of *Fuso*'s No. 2 turret, all five hundred tons of it blasted loose and slammed back against the bridge while from the barbette beneath flame jumped up as from an oil gusher. "It was like Saturday night at a county fair, all the colors of the rainbow." Astern, the Jap destroyers were all burning, one of them blew up in a funnel of fire and whatever guns they still had were shooting wildly in all directions as though manned by crews without heads. "Cease firing," ordered the admiral and Captain Heffernan of *Tennessee* looked at his watch to find that the battle, if battle it could be called, had lasted twelve minutes and fifty seconds.

Oldendorf had called it off because amid the flash and thunder he had detected the presence of one of our destroyers, *Albert W. Grant*, lying badly hit and without power between the two lines—also because he had not wished to leave his ships quite out of ammunition and in those few minutes of action they had everyone fired more shell than any British battleship in the long evening of Jutland. *Grant* had been our only casualty; the Japs had been wiped out, for when dawn came a little later and our PTs and destroyers started quartering the area, there the hulks were still afloat and smoking, with survivors clinging to them. The wrecks mostly sank before the photo planes Admiral Oldendorf had ordered could take pictures of them. One of the survivors was Commander K. Shibayama, whose ship had been the destroyer *Asagumo*, the highest ranking officer yet captured. "My ship it sink too fast; most miserable," he wailed as he was hauled in; and that would mean that the three others which went down under Oldendorf's thunderbolts had been vessels of the same class, the new big destroyers that always worked together in divisions.

XVII

Oldendorf initiated a dispatch that he was pursuing the beaten enemy and the phrase went into the communiqué that General Mac-Arthur, as over-commander of the Seventh Fleet, issued later in the day. It is not likely that the pursuit was carried very far, since Oldendorf had to wait for dawn and the destroyers to clear the track for him against anything Japanese that might be waiting with a torpedo and when dawn came, so did news that kept him where he was. The central Jap fleet was through San Bernardino Strait.

What did they find?

Up off Samar's eastern capes a group of six escort carriers—*Fanshaw Bay, Gambier Bay, Kalinin Bay, Kitkun Bay, St. Lô* and *White Plains*, under Rear Admiral C. A. F. Sprague, "Alphabet" Sprague, "Ziggy" Sprague, a smallish man with a humorous cock to his eye, who walked with a slight list to port. These escort carriers had a considerable variety of automatic weapons, overgrown machine guns, to protect them against dive bombers, and one 5-inch gun apiece. As cover, plane guard and anti-submarine watch they had three big destroyers—*Johnston, Hoel* and *Heerman*—and four destroyer escorts—*Roberts, Raymond, Dennis* and *Butler*—of considerably less speed and gunpower. South of them, far enough to be out

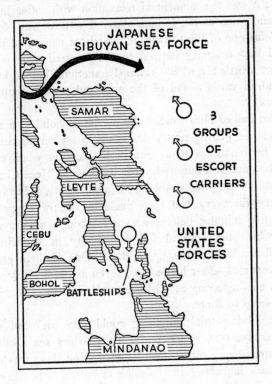

of sight, was a second group of the jeep carriers under Rear Admiral Felix V. Stump—*Kadashan Bay, Manila Bay, Marcus Island, Natoma Bay, Ommaney Bay, Savo Island*—similarly protected by three destroyers and four DEs. Farther south still at the entrance to Leyte Gulf were four more jeeps—*Petroff Bay, Sangamon, Santee, Suwannee*—with their escorts, commanded by the other Sprague, Rear Admiral Thomas L., who had general command of all the escort carriers. The last three of these were converted tankers, rather larger than the rest.

The day had come in bright behind a curtain of overcast and very hot. There were rain squalls across the ocean and the ships of Ziggy Sprague's group were steaming slowly northeastward after having launched the support missions for the troops with small fragmentation bombs in the hour just before sunup. They had secured from GQ; it was the moment of relaxation with coffee in the chiefs' quarters and cokes at the gedunk stand. The time was 0656. Aboard *White Plains* one of the torpedo pilots whose name had not been on the board that morning stepped to the forward edge of the flight deck to get a little air when—crump! something landed in the water three hundred yards ahead of the ship and a tall column of spray climbed up.

The pilot looked aloft toward the big black cloud of a rain squall. "They must be getting pretty desperate to try an air attack in the daytime" he remarked to a yeoman beside him when crump! the second salvo landed a hundred yards nearer and "Jeez Christ!" cried the yeoman pointing and grabbing his arm, "that's a Jap battleship!"

The same discovery had been made by one of Ziggy Sprague's fliers not five minutes before, who got through an urgent priority message which the admiral found difficulty in believing, but he ordered all available planes up to check. One of them got over the Japs and reported—four battleships, seven assorted cruisers and nine destroyers coming along at 30 knots and as he finished his message the guns began to shoot.

Sprague "didn't think anything could save me" but swung his ship to a course 090, which is due east, to get sea room; ordered them to launch every plane aboard (what wind there was came from 070 and made launching just possible); recalled his support strikes over Leyte (even fragmentation bombs are some help, they will smash optical glass on the upper works of a heavy ship); ordered the destroyers and destroyer escorts to make smoke astern of the squadron; called Kinkaid for all available help.

The rain squall and course change gave him a few minutes' respite; the destroyer *Johnston* provided more, zigzagging straight toward the Japs with a long ribbon of oily smoke rolling from her funnels. Nearest her was a line of four heavy cruisers, led by a *Tone* class ship clearly recognizable by the ski slide aft, with the battleships over beyond headed by *Yamato*. They all opened at the audacious midget and the water round her churned with the explosions of heavy shell that went up in pillars of red, green, yellow and purple from the dye used by the Japs for spotting. Some were so close that the officers on the open bridge were splashed to a mad likeness to clowns.

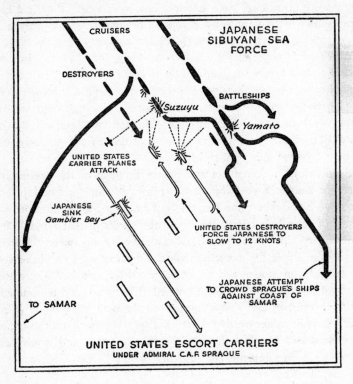

Commander Evans knew they could not continue to miss that way; at 0720 though the range was long, he laid all his torpedoes in a fan across the bows of the onrushing Japs, whipped his ship around and came back toward the tail of the US formation, still smoking. The fish ran hot and straight; as *Johnston* turned there were two dull muffled explosions from the enemy line and they saw the *Tone* class cruiser stagger. Then the destroyer got it, three 14-inch and three 6-inch simultaneously, wrecking the steering gear, killing or wounding every officer on the bridge, smashing one engine room all apart.

It was now 0730 and the jeeps were at the limit of their protecting rain cloud. Admiral Sprague ordered a course change southward, fully expecting the Japs to cut corners on him and be blown right out of the water as soon as he was in the clear, but smoke, *Johnston*'s lone attack or some peculiar oriental thought process took them the long way round and as the two fleets emerged into visibility the enemy were no nearer. Near enough, however; where they had been firing somewhat sporadically through the uncertain air they now opened up with fast, close-pattern salvos.

"My God, they're firing at us in technicolor," as the brilliant patches spread across the sea, and on *White Plains* the old chief who was talker for the fantail 5-inch watched a salvo from *Yamato* straddle the ship perfectly, three overs, three shorts. Flinging down his earphones he began to tighten his life belt. He had been on the old *Maryland* in battle practice and knew what that meant—namely, that the next salvo would come right in.

It did not. A moment before Captain Sullivan of the carrier had called for smoke. Something went wrong with the gear and just as that salvo hit, smoke came bursting out in a big black puff, not from one set of funnels but from both, and the shorts of that straddle had been so very close that their splashes only came up under the overhang of the ship's flight deck. Aboard *Yamato* they must have seen that outburst of smoke and counted only three splashes where they had fired six guns.—We have cooked that one—they undoubtedly said to themselves and shifted targets on the next salvo while *White Plains*' bridge talker testing circuits after the shock of those near misses that had wracked the whole ship's structure and would send her to dock, was murmuring into his phone, "Dear God, can you hear me? Testing, testing, dear God."

The Japs were now pestered by another torpedo attack, for as he came through the squall Sprague had ordered his "little boys" in— *Hoel* and *Heerman*, followed by the destroyer escort *Roberts* pounding along at a lesser speed and with the sorely damaged *Johnston* turning to bring up the rear at the 15 knots left to her to give whatever fire support she could. They saw five torpedoes splash from *Hoel*'s side, and then a salvo of big Jap shell hit her on the bridge and it wasn't there any more, her guns fired twice and another salvo took her amidships that sent her down right there. *Heerman* fired her fish and got away; *Roberts* fired one, was hit and blew up.

Maybe they were torpedo hits, maybe not, from this attack. The Jap admiral, apparently warned by the damage to his cruiser from the other rush, slowed suddenly to no more than 12 knots and took avoiding action, which was time borrowed from eternity for the jeeps. But as the clock turned to 0800 the enemy clearly began to gain toward the accomplishment of his purpose. Two of the covering force were gone now and one was a floating wreck; *Dennis* had been hit and none had any torpedoes left. *Fanshaw Bay* was hit and in bad shape internally. *Kalinin Bay* had been hit several times, including one from a battleship 14-inch that appears to have been an armor piercer, since it went right through her without doing anything but give her a pair of new portholes. Worst of all *Gambier Bay* had taken a hit in the engine room, lost speed and dropped back into the middle of the Jap fleet with smoke pouring out of her. From the other carriers they could see how the Jap cruisers and destroyers were all shooting at her, she was on fire, listing, and finally went down about 0850.

In spite of the delay caused by our destroyer attacks, the Japs were beginning to get level with our ships to seaward, first step in crowding them back against the coast of Samar.

XVIII

By this time the Jap admiral was also having his troubles. His ships had taken a good deal from Bogan and Davison's planes the day before, especially in the region of their sensitive fire-control instruments and range finders, which probably accounts for the fact that after nearly an hour of being shot at Ziggy Sprague could still radio cheerfully that "The Japanese shooting is very poor. We have been straddled for the last half hour." The enemy took still further damage topside from Sprague's bombers with their fragmentation missiles and his fighters that went in to strafe during the first stages of the action; and now they were beset by the planes from all the other escort carriers, which had asked permission to load with torpedoes when news of the attack on Sprague came through. At 0737 they got that difficult and heavy job done, at 0745 had launched planes.

There was an ensign named Curtwright with the *Petroff Bay*'s fighter unit in that strike, an emergency group and somewhat disorganized like all the fleet that day. The previous afternoon a formation of the new and very powerful Frances bombers had attacked the beachhead; Curtwright's and another fighter group had shot down eighteen of them without loss and came back to the carriers "laughing like New Year's Eve" and hoping that the rumors were true that the Jap fleet was coming out. Now they felt different; and more different still when not long after they were air-borne a hundred-plane bogey was reported in the very direction whither they were bound to help out the hard-pressed jeeps. There were several levels of lined cloud up there with spaces between them; down below and ahead Curtwright could see the many-colored splashes of Jap shells and occasionally catch a glimpse of one of our ships.

Just then the squadron leader sighted a big group of Zekes upstairs and tallyhoed his fighters on them. Curtwright followed in, saw the leader shoot down one Jap and another of the enemy inexplicably turn his plane over on its back and parachute out without being fired on. There was a Zeke on the tail of Curtwright's wingman; he did an Immelman, caught the Jap neatly in a burst of fire to send him down and at that moment his own plane was hit in the engine by a Zeke he never even saw. It began to smoke; he felt a violent shock which was a 20 millimeter hit in the tail of his machine, called into the mike that he was going down and wanted cover and slid for the sea below.

As he came through the overcast he could see two of our CVEs with a pair of destroyer escorts making smoke for them and a single American destroyer, which was probably *Heerman,* fighting off a file of Japs. He hit water about a thousand yards from the Jap; just as he was about to get out his rubber boat there was a tremendous explosion, the whole tail of his plane disappeared and he realized they were shooting at him. He dived out just in time to escape the shell that demolished his cockpit. The American destroyer tried to pick him up by a rope trailing over the stern, but he missed his grip as she took a hit through the stack and she could not stay.

Curtwright turned over and floated. As he moved on the swell, now all spotted and strewn with debris, he could see coming down on one side of him the line of four Jap battleships, on the other that of four heavy cruisers, now led by a *Mogami* class ship which must have been *Suzuyu*. He had fallen into a grandstand seat for the best show of the day. Now our planes began to appear aloft, there were three tremendous explosions from the *Yamato* and clear against the overcast he could see outlined the bursts of the 16-inch she had fired at the TBMs, "each burst big enough to fly a couple of squadrons through."

The torpedo carriers drove right past it and a whole squadron of them, nine in a row, flung itself at the leading cruiser. Curtwright remarked that her AA fire was late and out of line as the planes dropped their missiles. She corrected, one of the planes was hit and as the torpedoes arrived the swell was carrying him up and down so that he could see only in flashes, but through every nerve and muscle he could feel six heavy explosions. When he rose on the swell after they were done *Suzuyu* was perceptibly lower in the water and didn't seem to have either bow or stern left. She went down rapidly on a perfectly even keel, the last thing visible being her stack and upper bridge over which hung the fragment of a broken mast.

Curtwright put out his dye and waited for rescue. All above and around him now a confused series of air attacks and pseudo air attacks was going on, planes making runs till they were out of ammunition, then joining up with any formation they saw to make more, anything to distract the enemy. The mist had closed in thicker now and all through it were floating long ribbons of smoke that hung and swirled and shifted undissolving like a spiritualist ectoplasm studded with planes.

Most of the Japanese ships had damage by this time and their shooting was by no means improving, but two of their cruisers had been detached to swing around the flank of Ziggy Sprague's carriers, which were being crowded remorselessly back toward the coast, and one of the Jap battleships pushed out far enough so that she had Stump's carriers under fire from long range. "Isn't the situation getting a little tense, sir?" a young quartermaster asked the skipper of one.

Out to the south Tom Sprague's carriers were defending them-

selves desperately against the big air attack that had crossed the
one Curtwright rode with and most of these jeeps had damage so
severe that they could not for the moment land or launch planes.
The fliers got orders to land on any deck that would take them and
about 0900 began to come in on Stump's carriers and the field at
Tacloban. Stump's ships had to turn northeast toward the enemy
battleship to take them in but one of *Ommaney Bay*'s planes piloted
by a lieutenant named Clark Miller, which still had its torpedo, went
in all alone on that battleship and sent her back to join the main
formation.

A little later one of the detached Jap cruisers worked up energy
enough to try to close Ziggy Sprague's carriers and he sent his
destroyer force out to engage her with gunfire. "Destroyer force"
was *Heerman* alone. The Jap began pitching salvos still well calibrated at her, walking them one hundred yards with every fire till
one landed forward and amidships, putting the destroyer down by
the head with No. 2 gun out of action and the forward funnel uptake
draft wrecked. The thing to do was turn away fast, but that would
let the cruisers go on to the jeeps. Commander Hathaway held
course and speed, firing back, and the next salvo dropped a hundred
yards over as the Japs stuck rigidly to their system. The cruiser was
being hit too, she turned her prow north and away, and as she did
so the mist lifted from the sea in one of its uneven pulsations and far
on the horizon the men of the battered *Heerman* could see *Chikuma*
with a great mushroom of smoke coming out of her vitals.

Closer in the Jap destroyers and cruisers suddenly launched a
whole shoal of torpedoes, clearly visible as they struck water from
our ships now so close that on some the 40 millimeters were firing.
That device did not succeed either; the jeeps dodged and a fighter
pilot from *St. Lô* actually exploded two of the torpedoes in the water
with bullets from his machine guns.

Then in all that area of sea the ships of the Japanese battle fleet
one after another began turning north. The sound of firing that had
carried clear to the foxholes of Leyte died away. A signalman on
Fanshaw Bay's bridge turned to the Admiral; "Dammit sir, they're
getting away from us." It was 0937.

Where was Oldendorf? And where the *hell* was Halsey?

XIX

When he turned north and east after the Jap carrier force Halsey had sent back night searchers from *Independence* to keep track of the enemy's Sibuyan Sea expedition. A little after 2300 one of them reported—the Japs were in the region of Tablas Island, headed west. At midnight they were still approximately in the same place and it could be figured that after one extremely trying experience with our submarines in Mindoro Strait they were unanxious to try that passage again in the dark and with damaged destroyers. At 0200 another searcher reported that they had turned east and were steaming toward San Bernardino, but at only 12 knots. Conversation in flag plot was to the effect that after the battering they had received, this was probably the best fleet speed the Japs had left and the purpose of sending the damaged ships eastward at this time was probably to draw our carriers away from their true target, the enemy carrier force.

As we have seen, this overestimated Jap intelligence and under-estimated their persistence. They did not know our carrier groups were still in existence and they had by no means abandoned their San Bernardino plan. But there was no opportunity to correct this error for Halsey was making a fast run and by time the 0200 report came in was already at a range from which no other effective search could be flown. Moreover at almost the same hour one of the long-range night search planes from the Marianas found the Jap carrier force.

Radio reception that night was bad. The distance was considerable, something went wrong with the search plane's radar after it got through with the first preliminary message giving the enemy's position and the fact that his fleet consisted of battleships, carriers, cruisers and destroyers. There was nothing in this to alter the conception that here was the main and most menacing Japanese force. Halsey flung his own searchers out in the direction given, overriding the objections of some of the other officers, who said the Japs would spot our searchers and get out of there.

The enemy did in fact spot them when the search made contact an hour or so later and did turn north back toward the empire (this was a second turn north). But they were bound by invisible chains to their air groups back on the fields of Luzon, so after a short northerly run, they turned once more to a course south. One of our night fighters shot down a big four-motored Emily flying boat out there about the time of the search contact with the Japs, but it presumably had time to get off a message that the seas in the direction where they were bound were vacant.

Meanwhile, our own fleet night searchers, having made the contact, immediately lost it again when Lieutenant Steward Crapser was harried away by Zeros. The total effect of this shuffling was that as dawn drew near the two fleets were steaming on opposite courses in a way that would carry them past each other at a distance of some 50 miles, which is point-blank range in carrier war. On our ships they expected to be attacked by the full air strength of the Japanese Navy at daybreak. Not only were combat patrols flown off but also strike groups—to clear the decks and to permit that our bombers follow the Japs home and come in on them while they were landing planes. This took place before the usual hour, as soon as there was light to see by and presently the day came up with smooth sea, a northeast wind and long streaks of stratus overcast high above, across which rain squalls ran occasionally. Commander MacCampbell, who had shot down nine planes the day before was chosen by Mitscher to direct the air strike.

But no Japs. The ships moved easily through the blue sea, the planes circled in the bright air 50 miles ahead and no word came from the scouts. Our planes had been up an hour or nearly two, the scouts were on the return leg back to the carriers when word came through of seventeen Jap warships 60 miles to the north and slightly west where they had no business being. The planes of the strike group were already low on gas but the distance being so short and the opportunity so good, Mitscher sent them in anyway.

As he rode above that vast formation of bombers and torpedo planes, the heaviest carrier air strike ever yet flown in war, (there must have been not less than five hundred planes in it) MacCampbell was dumfounded to see only twenty-one Zekes come up for the defense; and probably not less dumfounded to discover that there were only four carriers below him with those flight-deck battleships. The miserable contingent of Jap fighters was dispatched in a manner almost incidental. MacCampbell put his own now unemployed fighters onto the destroyers of the Jap screen. The ships broke formation and maneuvered in a frantic individualism as Japs mostly do under air attack, forgetting everything but themselves; and now the heavy ships had no protection but their own AA fire.

There was enough of that so that as one pilot put it, "It was solid; we just slid right down in it, like you would down the slope of a roller coaster." But there were some badly upset Japs down at the end of the ride (this torrent of flames from the heavens instead of their own planes that they expected back) and no fighters to disturb the aim of our pilots. It was a picture-book attack; nineteen dive bombers and nearly as many torpedo planes on *Chitose* alone, for instance, as she wove in her pattern of maneuver. Seven of the bombers hit her along the deck and at least three torpedoes. She stopped; explosion after explosion ran through her, she was shrouded in smoke and when our pilots came on that fleet again later in the day, was no more to be found. The big *Zuikaku* appears to have got it more from the torpedo men than from the bombers in this attack. *Zuiho*'s flight deck was buckled, she had at least one torpedo in her stern and bad fires. The pictures showed *Chiyoda* with a series of bomb holes; all the other ships but one cruiser were hit with bomb or torpedo. As the planes made back for the carriers after that deadliest single strike of the war many of them were spattered with oil and some had holes you could throw a dog through, but their loss was light, they were laughing and whooping in the sky. The Japanese carrier force, what was left of the Japanese carrier force, that had been such a menace since Pearl Harbor Day, had been virtually finished at a single blow.

XX

Back on the flagships, Mitscher and Halsey's, they were neither laughing nor whooping. About the time that MacCampbell's fighters were making their first runs on the destroyers of the Jap screen a communications officer silently laid before Marc Mitscher a dispatch from Alphabet Sprague that the latter had not even bothered to encode. AM BEING ENGAGED BY ENEMY BATTLESHIPS. URGENTLY REQUEST SUPPORT.

Mitscher laid it before 31 Knot Burke; "What do you think of that?"

"I think it's bad, sir."

Both men turned to look at the fleet flagship *New Jersey*, out toward the limit of vision, already swinging her high, bottle-shaped prow. No comment was necessary. They and Halsey too knew that the jeeps could get no help from Oldendorf in time; had taken in his triumphant dispatch in the early morning hours; knew that his position in pursuit, deep in Surigao Strait, would leave him four or five hours' steaming of slow old battleships from the scene of action. Besides he had been in close support of the Army for days with precious little opportunity to fuel; his tanks were nearly dry, he was low on ammunition, though there is no record that either Halsey or Mitscher had exact information on these points at the time.

Halsey himself wasted no time in conference. He started back with his two fastest battleships *New Jersey* and *Iowa*, the behemoths at emergency flank speed. He had no objection to taking on the whole Sibuyan battle fleet with them. The other battleships were to follow at the best speed (it is said that Mitscher pleaded for two of them to be left with him to settle the hash of the Jap carrier force but Halsey would not). The carriers must wait to take in their planes and with that northeast wind, most unfortunately had to run in the wrong direction while they did it. They were to follow at their best speed, all but one group which should remain with Mitscher. (This was not the specific group of any of the rear admirals, but one specially made up for the occasion, mainly from Davison's ships.) McCain, out to the southeast, must be finished with his refueling; he was to come on and join the others off Samar, like them flying off a strike as he came, for at the speed those carriers would be traveling it would be possible to neglect the factor of wind direction in sending the strike away.

It was nearly 1100 before the carriers that had been with Halsey in the north could get their planes in and be well started on the road back. They put out their normal combat patrols at once, which ran ahead and made contact with McCain's patrols somewhere east of Leyte Gulf. By this time all the battleships were well along the road and several other things had happened.

The event of immediate importance was that the Jap planes from Luzon (land-based and carrier together) came out on their repeat of the shuttle raid that had sunk *Princeton* the day before, expecting to find their own carriers at the end of the run. Apparently this group took off before it could be advised of the disaster that had already overtaken the Jap carriers. It was one wing of this big flight that had crossed the fighters from Tom Sprague's ships and been engaged by them at the time when Ensign Curtwright went down and Sprague's ships were damaged. The Japs lost something in that encounter, it was a touch-and-carry-on affair with them, they were looking for other game.

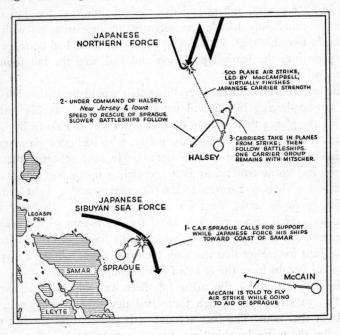

They found it all right. Beyond where those planes had expected to pick on crippled American ships, at about the point where they intended to meet their own carriers, they ran head on into the entire fighter complement of three American carrier groups. The Japs were by no means equipped for an air fight of the intensity this represented and they wanted no part of it. For the only time in the battle they panicked and ran for home. Our fighters piled all over them and came upwards of thirty shot down during the pursuit, "and the rest we hope ran out of fuel en route" back to the Luzon fields. Some of them certainly did, for they had come far.

The second event was that Tom Sprague's escort carriers counter-attacked the Jap battle fleet. A good many of the planes aloft had run out of gas and gone off to Tacloban or Dulag to land, but there were plenty still up and as soon as the Jap gunfire ceased these got orders to land on any deck that would accept them. *Kitkun Bay* at least had planes from four other jeeps but only about seven of her own. On *Kalinin Bay* a young torpedo pilot landed, famous for his volubility, who had for months talked and dreamed of attacking the Jap fleet. Now he could only babble incoherently, making motions with his hands. It took his rear seat man to explain that he had actually put a torpedo into the battleship *Kongo* and had seen the tall fountain of explosion climb.

The orders were to load everything that would fly with torpedoes and armor-piercing bombs and get after the enemy in his retreat. Among the planes that came in on that order was one flown by Lieutenant "Snuffy" Smith of *Ommaney Bay*, who had gone on a search mission west before the trouble started. He now reported that his mission had borne fruit; near Bohol, crawling up Camotes Sea, were *Abukama* with two *Teratzuki* class destroyers and a light cruiser. *Ommaney Bay*'s strike went for that lot. They hit *Abukama* with three 500-pound armor piercers, laced the destroyers with 50 caliber tracer and left them all burning, which must have been discouraging to the Japs for earlier that morning they had already taken a torpedo and some bombs from the *White Plains* group.

The attack that hit the main Jap fleet was popularly known as the "10:30 strike" as though there had never been another in the world at that hour. The best account of it comes from another pilot down on the water by this time, Lieutenant Ashcraft, a fighter man from *Savo Island* who had made a strafing run on one of the Jap heavies earlier and in the pullout felt a violent shock and saw blue beneath his feet as a 5-inch exploded right beneath his engine. He was slightly dazed at the time but unhurt, now lying in the sea watching some sharks and wondering idly which of them would eat the other as the attack went past—a pickup attack, pilots flying under unfamiliar squadron leaders, hence lacking the exquisite co-ordination that makes success.

But the Japs were now far less co-ordinated. Their defense was poor; *Haruna* fired at our fliers with only a single gun and *Chikuma* was already abandoning ship. They put her out of her misery as Ashcraft watched and it seems that at least one of the destroyers was sunk at this time while the other heavy cruisers were hit.

Now it was noon; the air above the CVE fleet was confused with clouds of smoke, our fliers returning in no sort of formation were shouting for decks to land on when into the tangle were precipitated dozens of Jap planes. Some of them were the outriders of the great air strike that had been intended to put the finishing touches on the destruction of Halsey's fleet, fleeing from that unexpected and fatal contact with his fighter squadrons.

But some, arriving just too late as everything the Jap did in this battle was too late, were the Kamikaze. They at least knew what they wanted; they wanted Ziggy Sprague's escort carriers. The bugles had just blown chow down and the lines formed; men dropped their trays and ran for the gunwalks as the enemy came in, suicide planes, fighters and normal bombers together, two or three to each of the jeeps. *White Plains* shot one down; he blew up with immense violence just off the stern, showering the whole deck with debris and fragments of Japanese meat; *Kitkun Bay* shot down three in succession. *St. Lô* was not so lucky; a Kamikaze "sailed over as though for a landing, then dove into the carrier."

She had taken in more planes than any of the other jeeps and a good many were still aboard, down in the hangar. The bomb set them off with a series of explosions whose violence was simply incredible; it seemed incredible that anyone survived them but the majority of her crew did and when they picked them up they found at least one of her officers lying on his back in the warm water, chewing a cigar and swearing gently. While the rescue work was going on there was a lull in this part of the battle.

XXI

But out to the north where Mitscher's carriers were, no lull. The scouts left behind after the early strike reported that the Japs had separated into two groups; one of cripples, which was apparently to be thrown to the wolves, one of ships still very little hurt. He passed the word to Halsey and got ordered back to concentrate on the undamaged ships. *Zuikaku* was one of the latter, not undamaged indeed, but a very big and tough ship now trying to get away; she had been three times under our bombers already and had come through. She is the one with the large island which can be seen in pictures of the battle—in one of them was smoke coming out of her sheer and a heavy list, in the next unable to turn, tilting badly and already so far down in the water that her hangar deck is level with it. She went down in the early afternoon, turning over. So did *Zuiho* that slid down, her stern the last to go.

All told there were three strikes after Halsey left, with the pilots cheerful in spite of their danger and wounds. One of them, Lieutenant Fanning, hit the barrier at 130 and flipped over on his back to fall out of the plane on his head when he let go of the safety belt; but after a cup of coffee asked to go out on the next mission.

The last strike of the day was a freak, toward twilight. Commander Hugh Winters of *Essex* who was acting as air control over the Jap fleet (MacCampbell had returned after seven hours aloft) found one of the old three-funnel cruisers still showing a good turn of speed. The admiral only reluctantly granted permission for 16 fighters to go out with 1000-pound bombs (it was so late and he remembered the night at Philippine Sea) but when he did give the permission all the pilots on the flight deck took off their caps and cheered. The first eight all put their bombs into that cruiser and down she went. Winters diverted the rest onto the flight deck battleships, which moved away into the gloom with four of those bombs in her on top of three or four torpedoes she had taken before.

But that was positively the last and the last word was the *Chiyoda* was still afloat. The cruisers formed line of battle and closed, *New Orleans* leading. As she bore down her captain was struck by a brilliant idea and radioed for permission to capture that Jap carrier and tow it home as a present for the Smithsonian Institution. He got a negative; and anyway, as the big cruiser closed in there were still some Japs aboard who opened fire rather plaintively from a 40 millimeter so she had to be sunk.

The flagship's band paraded across the flight deck playing "There'll Be a Hot Time in the Old Town Tonight" and "Stars and Stripes Forever" as the ships made south to join Halsey. However the men of the escort carriers might congratulate themselves on living on borrowed time, however the men of the sunken *Johnston* might wonder if they had not seen a defeat, aboard the carriers in the north they had no illusions. They knew that this was a great victory.

XXII

Curtwright found that his life jacket would not support him without swimming in the freshening breeze and the sea that was running, so he pulled it off, put his feet in it and began to paddle with his hands. The whole horizon was hung with smoke; far to the north he could occasionally glimpse a mast top or something similar but they presently went away and he was much alone. His allegedly waterproof watch had died on him but from the state of the sun he judged it to be about 1500 when SB2Cs began to streak over and he knew that Halsey's planes had come. Off to the north there were two heavy explosions that he could hear all those miles away; from each, smoke shot up the sky like rocket trails. One of them would mark the end of *Noshiro*, the new light cruiser that had tried to keep company with the heavyweights of the Jap Sibuyan Sea force. The other was either a destroyer or the heavy cruiser *Chikuma*. One of the heavies got it during that strike, which did as much damage as any, with three carrier groups in it, the Japs disorganized and their AA batteries in bad shape. The planes ranged on far into Sibuyan Sea; found the badly hurt *Chokai* and killed her off with dive bombs, hit the battleships again and again. Darkness put an end to it; darkness and the distance back to the carriers, which were still hurrying on.

All along the coast of Samar and into San Bernardino Strait the remains of the disordered Jap fleet were concerned only with getting away. In the last light Ashcraft saw one of our FM2s strafe a pair of their destroyers and two of the planes shot down. He swam toward them but the pilots did not get out. Under the starshine of that tropic night Halsey was ranging along the coast with his battleships; found a crippled ship which would be *Chikuma* and disposed of her with three quick salvos.

Under that same twilight of despair and glory the senior surviving officer of *Johnston* was trying to keep his men together, very bitter over the lack of rescue craft. The survivors of *Gambier Bay* were keeping together, wondering why they were still alive and why the Jap destroyer that passed them had only photographed instead of shooting as Japs usually did. All out over that sea LSTs, LCIs and anything else that would float were looking for them and others; they picked up 1,819 men before the next noon.

Far in the north our submarines had fallen on the trail of the defeated Jap carrier force; they got more torpedoes into one of the flight deck battleships and sent another of the three-funnel cruisers, *Tama*, to the bottom.

Over at the beaches of Dulag and Tacloban there was maddest confusion, with bulldozers still working on the fields and engineers laying Marston mat under flares, while every few minutes another plane would try to come in where there was no room for any more. On the command ship *Wasatch* communications were hopelessly jammed, the officer in charge again and again ordering that circuits be cleared, only to have some wildly excited young pilot break in that he was damaged, out of gas, must have space at Dulag at once. Carrier planes that could not make the fleet, escort carrier planes that could not make their decks and P38s of the Fifth Army Air Force were all screaming for space. Thirty-five of the hundred at Tacloban were crash landings though not a pilot was lost; at Dulag the figures were about the same and the field commanders were frantically trying to get things organized for they could foresee a Jap air attack on those crowded strips in the morning.

"But the most dismaying event of the day was when some Army B25s came in and reported they had sunk *Abukama* and we found out it was true. What the hell were they doing in the biggest naval battle of American history?"

XXIII

For this was Trafalgar; it was Tsushima and La Hogue and Aegospotami and Salamis and all the other utterly crushing victories, after which an entire war is changed. Seldom enough in history before had an entire navy been brought to a single battle. Never before had an entire navy lost so great a proportion of its strength as the Japs did in the fighting for Leyte Gulf.

They had come to that battle with 13 capital ships—battleships and 4 carriers. Now the latter were all gone and three of the battleships. Our submarines were still lurking off the western Philippines and they got *Kongo* when she tried to run north after the battle. Seven capital ships out of 13. They had come with 12 heavy cruisers; 6 at least had gone down and *Nachi* hit by the submarine off Mindoro Strait on the night of the twenty-third was caught by Halsey's planes in Manila Harbor on November 5 and sunk there. They had lost 4 light cruisers; they had lost 15 destroyers and 392 planes which can be taken as an estimate on the conservative side.

Not even Trafalgar had cost the losers so much materially, and as at Nelson's battle, it was not alone a material loss but the moral that counted. When the Japanese Admiralty was next heard from, months later, it was announcing that it had a new head who had "converted the entire navy into a Kamikaze corps" and proving it by sending the giant *Yamato* to her doom in an attack that had no other purpose than to furnish an afternoon's distraction for our carriers while their planes attacked the beachhead at Okinawa.

In fact the invasion of Okinawa, the invasions of Mindoro and Luzon, could hardly have been attempted without Leyte Gulf battle. If the Philippine Sea engagement set free the American Fleet to go where it wished in the Pacific, the October action liberated our transports to go where they would among the barrier of islands that stretches from metropolitan Japan to Borneo. It removed the threat of a Japanese fleet in being and especially that of a carrier fleet in being. There were to be interruptions from Japanese air in all those operations and they would be dangerous, particularly when the Kamikaze attained the proportions of the Okinawa campaign. But it was now past the power of the enemy to deal that massive, concentrated and surprising blow that is the special characteristic of carrier aviation. The staging fields for their land-based planes could be watched and were watched.

From this point of view and if one considers the Jap carrier force in the north as the number one danger to any progress we might make beyond Leyte, Halsey's action in turning from the Sibuyan Sea force (the key point of the battle and the one that will be debated as long as Jellicoe's turnaway at Jutland) was fully justified. As it turned out one or two carrier groups could have done the job there since the Jap force was smaller than expected and its planes were on the fields of Luzon. But Halsey did not know this at the time and military decisions have to be made on present information, not with reference to an abstract ideal of conduct. Whether he was so well justified in taking all the fast battleships with him on the run south is another question; Admiral Nelson once said that if he had taken eleven of the enemy's ships and allowed a twelfth to escape he would never call it well done, and it does seem as though with a couple of those ships Mitscher might have finished *Ise* and *Hyuga*, against whose 14-inch guns the cruisers hardly dared to run in. Down the long inverted telescope of history it is this that will probably keep Halsey from ranking with Nelson and set Leyte Gulf down as the Navy's battle rather than that of any individual commander.

But to make such a complaint is perhaps to set up a counsel of perfection, to overlook the true fog of war that hung over the western Pacific during those forty-eight hours of conflict. To appreciate that one has only to contemplate the action of the Japanese, how their timing missed again and again in a plan which depended on timing. There was excuse for some of these failures, for American planes were continually throwing sand in the machines. But there was very little excuse for the failure of the Luzon planes and those from the carrier fleet to co-ordinate their attack on Sherman on the morning of the twenty-fourth, when they might really have had that commander in serious trouble. There was no excuse at all for the late arrival of the Kamikaze on the twenty-fifth, when an attack coinciding with that of the battleships might have demolished Ziggy Sprague and kept Stump's carriers from helping him.

Indeed many of the Japanese actions in the battle are explicable only on the basis of some fundamental misconception, at whose origins we can only guess. Why did the Surigao Strait force run into that storm of fire from Oldendorf? They knew he was around, they had snooped him for days. Did they think he had been called north or was in no shape for battle? Either theory seems very weak.

Why did the Sibuyan Sea force turn away at 0937 of the twenty-fifth, when it had Ziggy Sprague's carriers in its grasp? All the escort carrier men insist it was because of the damage received from their planes but at the time the Japs left they were not getting very much damage any more. They must have known an hour or two before that time that the Surigao Strait fleet had been wiped out and that Halsey's carriers had not been sunk off Formosa but were up in the north pounding theirs to pieces. Perhaps they feared his return—

with good reason—or the appearance of some other course of which they were yet ignorant. For over them lay the legacy of other defeats, "the souvenir of the Nile." They entered the battle in the spirit doomed and desperate losers have always entered battle—*Ave Caesar, morituri te salutamus* and Cervera's pathetic last letter before Santiago. It was the moral breakdown that in all the other great defeats by sea from Salamis to Trafalgar has preceded the physical collapse of a naval service.

V. WHAT IT ADDS UP TO

THE battleship *Hyuga* lies in Kure Harbor with her main deck awash, in considerably worse shape than any American vessel on the morning of December 8, 1941. *Haruna*'s back has been broken; she is burned out fore and aft. Over *Nagato* flies the American flag. There are only three Japanese carriers, all in a severe state of disrepair, and it is unlikely that any of them will go to sea again. The Japanese Navy register as of the date of the surrender contained the name of only one seaworthy cruiser, and in fact no navy in history since galley days has ever been so nearly wiped out in action as that of our enemy in the Pacific.

During the naval conferences which began in the twenties it was again and again stated that Japan's allotted figure of three major warships to five for each of the Anglo-Saxon powers gave her a practical immunity from naval attack in the waters of East Asia. No one even in Japan denied it; oriental attempts to change the ratio were placed on quite other dialectical grounds. On the morning of December 10 Japan possessed 12 battleships, at least 11 carriers and 18 heavy cruisers, figures which were not sensibly altered till the Battle of Midway, six months later. As of the same December 10 England had 12 battleships, 6 carriers and 14 heavy cruisers of which she lost one carrier and three heavy cruisers during the same six months. The United States possessed 10 battleships, 7 carriers and 18 heavy cruisers and if in the six-month period we recovered two battleships that had been lost, we lost a carrier and a heavy cruiser to make up for it. Nearly all the British Fleet and a great part of the American were in the Atlantic during most of the six months to Midway.

Even after that costly engagement the Japanese possessed, if not an absolute margin of superiority in the Pacific, at least far more than the three-five ratio which was supposed to give them immunity against attack. That the attack was first delivered in the South Seas does not particularly matter in this connection. The security factor that made the three-five ratio acceptable was the extent of the Allied lines of operation, and these were not notably shortened in making the voyage to the Solomons, nor were the Japanese lines unduly lengthened while they could use the great bases and depots in the Carolines and New Britain.

Before the war and for some time during the conflict it was freely stated that the development of the airplane had rendered close block-ade impossible. Yet no blockades were ever closer than those of Italy, the Philippines and Okinawa at the time of the invasions, and both in the operations of the Third Fleet against Japan and during the invasion of southern France, sea power was able to invade the land and throttle hostile shore-based aviation in its cradle.

. . . What we have here is a series of results apparently unrelated but predictable by none of the widely held ideas of sea power and naval strategy as they stood at the beginning of the war. Indeed these results are so wholly at variance with theory as to suggest the need for an examination perhaps of the ideas of sea power in general, perhaps of their application in the conflict just closed. Such an examination will require years and volumes; but very few of the landmarks among which it must navigate are already visible.

II

One of the points which attracts attention at once is the enormous change that has taken place within the frame of naval power itself. Before the war the navies of the world were qualitatively almost identical, whatever their quantitative difference. The United States had 15 battleships, 6 carriers, 18 heavy and 19 light cruisers, 215 destroyers, 90 submarines. The Navy of France, a typical second-class sea power, had 9 battleships, 2 vessels that might be called carriers, 7 heavy and 12 light cruisers, 72 destroyers, 79 submarines. Turkey, a naval power of the third rate, could count 1 battleship, 2 light cruisers, 8 destroyers, 11 submarines. It is true that within these classes a degree of specialization had appeared between the two wars. For instance American cruisers were built large to run the great distances of the oceans and British carriers had armored decks in anticipation of attacks from planes based on the near-by shores of

Europe. This is specialization to meet the requirements of the geographical regions in which the ships are expected to operate.

But World War II has introduced quite a different type of specialization, involving entire navies and fitting them not to conduct any type of naval operation in a particular ocean, but to conduct only one kind of operation in any ocean whatever. Specialization has extended from individual ships to entire navies. During the conflict only three nations—England, the United States and Italy—built into all classes that would make up a rounded fleet. The Germans completed a few of the major ships they already had on the ways when the struggle began, but their new construction was exclusively in the submarine and destroyer classes. The Japanese built numerous destroyers, a few submarines and still fewer cruisers of a type so light that France and Italy denominated similar ships as destroyer leaders but concentrated so heavily in the direction of carriers that they were forced to abandon all the gunnery ships laid down when the war began.

Most striking of all is the case of Canada. After five years of war she became a naval power of great importance with a fleet of over two hundred vessels manned by a personnel at least as numerous as that of the Japanese Navy at a similar date. Yet this great sea force contained no ship even as large as a light cruiser, while for comparison one may note that the far smaller Australian Navy had two heavy cruisers, several light and at least one carrier. The same violent variations of type are observed elsewhere among the minor Allied navies.

No doubt this can be explained by the strain thrown on world constructional facilities by the war itself—an extension on a world scale of the case of 1917, when the American Fleet program had to be laid aside for the hurried construction of destroyers. But mingled with this influence, partly arising from it and partly in response to new concepts of international relations, there has been another development. It may be described as the specialization of fleets for function. The minor navies and perhaps some of the major ones are no longer comparable with each other in quantitative terms. They are composed of ships and planes with widely varying strategical and tactical characteristics. Another Washington Conference would have to work on the basis of those formulas with which mathematicians attempt to describe the relations of the incommensurable.

A war between Canada and Australia is not a practical possibility —but what would happen on a clash of two such fleets? The war has shown that an entire navy can specialize and unless the international organization functions better than anyone thinks it will, there are bound to be more specialized fleets and the prospects of clash between them.

III

Or will there be any such clash? To a certain extent the development was one forced upon the Allies by the nature of Axis sea operations. Those operations mark something new in the whole history of sea power. Lieutenant Commander Brodie has defined sea power as the ability to use the ocean at pleasure for the transmission of either goods or military force. The over-all strategy of the Axis was directed less toward obtaining sea power for themselves, which was the focal point of all past naval wars, than toward denying it to the Allies. (Even Napoleon's Trafalgar campaign where the effort was to avoid the British Fleet, had at its end the achievement of the kind of local and limited sea power that would enable him to cross the Channel.)

Dr. Haushofer, the muddleheaded old gentleman who was chief of the Nazi geopolitical institute, has made the point as clearly as anybody. He maintained that in the long run war boiled down to a matter of movement—of troops, supplies, equipment. Sea power had been effective in the past because the ocean presented a more rapid and less vulnerable means of travel than the land routes. A map drawn to represent traveling time rather than distance in the days of sail would place Rome nearer to London than to Paris.

It was Haushofer's contention (and that of the men who made Germany's war) that this represented the strategy of a bygone age. The coming of steam power on the whole benefited land transport more than it did that by water. The latter remained the more efficient but the advantage of speed passed from the ship to the railroad. The arrival of the internal combustion engine completed the process. It offered little improvement to sea transportation but to movement by land, in its forms of airplane and motorcar, it made accessible points beyond the reach of railroads.

Moreover and very important for war purposes, land transport was given the advantage of operating in vehicles of low unit value, so small and so capable of dispersion as hardly to constitute military objectives. Sea transportation remained at its most efficient when the unit was a large one. Land transport had thus become more efficient than transport by sea. To win her war Germany needed neither sea commerce nor sea power if she could achieve land connections with the necessary raw material producing areas; and England would inevitably be defeated in a war of attrition against the Continent because her sea communications were vulnerable while the land communications of the Nazis were not.

This was Haushofer, stating the thing in absolute and theoretical terms. As a practical matter there existed a German program for obtaining naval power and then sea power through the use of Britain's building facilities after she had been defeated, but that is not the point here, nor are the defects that caused this besotted scheme to fail. What is important here is the effect on German naval strategy and through it upon Allied sea power. The Germans were fully conscious that in the last war part of Britain's sea communications were maintained by neutrals. The new doctrine led them to a step new in naval history—an effort not to make the sea safe for themselves but to make it unsafe for everyone. They were quite content to let England distribute her warships wherever she chose as they had been in 1940, happy to let the French distribute their armies wherever they wished, the further forward the better since this made the lines of communication longer and more subject to attack.

The fact that neutrals would become involved did not matter since it was necessary to the German strategy to absorb the neutrals in the development of their land-power-land communications policy. The typical weapon of this campaign to make the seas unsafe was the magnetic mine, sown broadcast and largely by airplanes. Until absolutely convincing evidence is produced to the contrary it will always seem that the first really heartbreaking German failure of the war was the inability of this secret weapon and such successors as the series switch mine to produce any more results than they did. Nobody in Germany expected the British to find any answer to it at all any more than they could find an answer to V-2.

IV

The consistency with which the Germans overestimated the military effects of their inventions is very striking, but hardly less so than the fact that specialization of an entire navy for a single strategic purpose began with them. It is in some respects analogous to the *guerre de course* in the later days of Louis XIV, when the ships of the French Royal Navy were rented out to contractors for privateering. As Mahan has noted the British Navy was then able to disperse and hunt down the privateers. But the differences in the two cases are at least as significant as the resemblances. The Germans deliberately abandoned any effort to control the ocean; did not care whether the British dispersed or not; expected to lose numbers of their raiders and adopted the wolf-pack tactics in anticipation of these losses.

They perceived the whole problem as one in military economics, basing on the fact that a mass-produced submarine is a relatively small and cheap vessel, a target (including cargo) a large and expensive one. If one ship could be sunk for every submarine lost they would be gainers in the long run, for the destruction of a ship in the English trade included a reduction of Britain's capacity to replace that ship, while their own replacement capacity, backed by land transport, was (by their calculation) invulnerable.

They brought the element of a geographical region's total productive capacity into naval war. They made use of the fact that with the progress of science the technique of war grows continually more complex, so that it is no longer possible to speak of naval or land or even air strategy without a modifying phrase. The form as well as the total content of naval power must be considered in every calculation. In pure theory a carrier can either handle or get away from the opposition of any other class of ship and in pure theory a destroyer ought always to be able to handle submarines. But off the coast of Norway the *Scharnhorst* sank the *Glorious*; the same German battleship was eventually lost fundamentally because she lacked accompanying vessels to hold quite minor surface craft at arm's length. American submarines making radar approaches sank no less than forty-two Jap destroyers.

In their system of strategy the Germans made some errors, but in at least one important case the mistake was in underestimating their own accomplishments. During the high days of the U-boat war in 1942 they were getting four or five ships for every submarine lost instead of the one or two their theory required. Their campaign failed ultimately; but it seems to have been a failure in tactical execution rather than in theory.

The proof of this is the American submarine campaign against Japan. Naval war in several other dimensions was going on at the same time but this should not be allowed to conceal the fact that with relation to the Japanese empire we occupied the same strategic position the Germans thought they occupied with relation to England and that we conducted the same general type of campaign as they. Our arms-producing areas had efficient and invulnerable land transportation from the sources of the raw materials; their supplies had to be brought in from overseas. Our submarines attacked their lines of communication without reference to the control of the surface in the affected area by Japanese warships. The fact that none but Japanese ships moved in those waters doubtless simplified the task of our submarines, but it does not alter the other fact that as with the Nazis against England, the fundamental effort of the American submarine campaign was to make those waters unsafe for every sort of traffic. It is unnecessary to dilate on the achievements of the American submariners in that campaign except to remark that our submarines perfectly justified the German theory that it is possible to cripple the industrial potential of a nation that depends upon sea transport without obtaining control of the sea.

How far the increased effectiveness of our mine warfare contributed to this result is uncertain as yet, but it seems likely that it supplemented the work of the submarines to a very great extent indeed as the Germans expected their mines to render the approaches to all British ports unsafe. Technical answers to the "unsweepable" mines with which the German North Sea ports were closed in the last days of the war and the Japanese Fleet held in the Inland Sea for the attentions of Halsey's planes may be discovered. Such answers usually are. The new thing in mine war, the factor that makes it more dangerous than ever before, is the effectiveness of the airplane as a means of laying. There is really very little defense against single airplanes slipping in under cover of darkness to plant mines in shallow waters, and though the Germans realized this in the early days of the war they never really used the information.

The Nazi failure, then, was tactical and technical. They placed quantity before quality in the production of their submarines and this is always a mistake with a military weapon. They were so interested in getting a large number of raiders to sea that they wrongly assumed raiding craft can be operated on the principles of fleet tactics, that one able commodore to a squadron with the rest of the captains capable of no more than following the flag can accomplish as much as a dozen ships individually well led. This may be true for a battle fleet; Suffren and Tegetthof would appear to demonstrate it. But it is certainly not true for raiders and John Paul Jones' experience stands in proof of it.

V

In another very important respect the doctrines of sea power need re-examination. The fact that the Japs did control the surface of the sea within their empire, the fact that the Germans controlled the Baltic down to the very end of the war and for a time the Italians were in almost complete control of the Mediterranean, marks a change in the classic concept of sea power, a change adumbrated by Mahan himself and more clearly expressed by the Sprouts (*Toward a New Order of Seapower*). It may be expressed as the localization of sea power, coming about as an effect of the mechanical warship.

One of the points upon which Mahan was most insistent was the ubiquity of sea power. In the sailing ship days on which he based most of his calculations the ocean behaved as an almost perfect conductor of military force. A British battle fleet in the Downs could exert its strength undiminished against an enemy off Rochefort or Toulon or in the West Indies after an interval of time small in comparison with those required for other types of military movement. The only limiting condition was a very moderate amount of base facilities.

It seemed to Mahan that steam had greatly increased the importance of bases, though he was some distance from the Sprouts' remark that British sea power in Far Eastern waters hardly existed at all as of World War I, partly because of English responsibilities elsewhere, partly because the complexity of fuel and supply necessities bind a modern fleet not merely to a base, but to a base closely supported by an industrial area. This concept of localized sea power, of a navy able to challenge any other within an area of operation not limited by the proximity of its coast line, but taking in an entire ocean area, was inherent in all the documents resulting from the Washington Naval Conference and was directly stated in some of those documents. It controlled most naval thinking of the current war down to 1943 at least.

But it has now been attacked from at least three directions and so successfully that regionalized sea power was apparently a purely temporary phenomenon. The submarine, which can enter any region from any distance because of its extremely long cruising range, offers one challenge. It is a challenge that may be overcome as the Western Allies overcame the German submarines, but the failure of the Japanese to beat off our submarine attack suggests that the problem must be worked out in each individual case, that there is no inherent solution.

A far more serious challenge has been offered by the efficiency of American logistic organizations. During the Okinawa campaign Admiral Spruance was able to maintain his fleet for weeks at a distance of over 1500 miles from the nearest base, and that base a forward one which produced nothing of its own. Some ships both of his fleet and of Halsey's during the latter's attacks on the Japanese home island returned to base for such urgent matters as battle damage and burned-out boiler tubes which cannot be made good without bringing the ship to a stop in a sheltered anchorage. The margin of superiority possessed by the two leaders over their enemy during these campaigns was so great that the detachment did not seriously affect their strength. But the important point is not how many ships there were on our side during the long months of 1945 or how much pressure they brought to bear. The point is that any ships at all could thus remain at a distance of 1500 miles from the nearest advanced base over a period of months, most of the time steaming at high speeds and putting out hundreds of tons of ammunition daily.

When any fleet can do that it is obvious that with the aid of its auxiliaries it can maintain itself in any part of the world. This is to say that thanks to American methods of improving the efficiency of the train, sea power has again become ubiquitous. A battle fleet assembled at San Francisco can come to a campaign off Ceylon or Kamchatka with practically undiminished strength and remain as long as its lines of communication hold up. The limitations are no more severe than those on sailing ships. And let us not deceive ourselves; the efficiency of the American Fleet train is no exclusive possession. Others will be able to study and to employ our methods just as the Germans after the last war were able to set up assembly lines in imitation of those we used in 1917.

VI

The third and perhaps the most serious attack on the localization of sea power has come from the air. The general expectation of intelligent military opinion—and not of the Seversky-type enthusiasts alone—before the war was that the airplane would increase the phenomenon of localization. Air control of waters out to fighter plane range from the shore could be provided from fields and enemy surface ships could enter such a region only at extreme peril and for the briefest of raids. Most of the waters in which the European fighting was done fell into this category and in the early part of the war the theory certainly seemed to be borne out, the only exceptions being the immediate regions of the British Isles, where cover was given by aerial counter-concentrations, also from land bases. The closing of the Mediterranean so that relief for Malta had to run all the way round Africa was a case in point.

If this were true, then sea power was limited in its operation to regions more than 250 miles from enemy airfields; and in areas where islands provided numerous opportunities for such fields (as in the Aegean) the interdiction against sea power became absolute. Before the United States was forced into the war nobody thought of questioning this doctrine in support of which it was urged that carrier planes must always be technically inferior to land-based types.

The Japanese, in fact, based their whole bid for empire on the theory that sea power could be restrained, limited, localized by aerial operations. They also made the unjustifiable assumption that the morale as well as the equipment of the American Navy could be broken at Pearl Harbor, but they were leaving nothing to chance. All they asked was time to complete the mechanical arrangement begun as long ago as the middle twenties—to set up throughout that enormous flowing triangle from the Kuriles to Sumatra and the Solomons the chain of their island air bases.

There is less difference between the fundamental strategy of their war and that of the Germans than appears at first glance. No more than their European allies did our oriental enemies conceive of sea power in the classic sense as something to be gained and then used for whatever purpose they desired. No commander who held that classic doctrine could have steamed away from Pearl Harbor on the night of December 7. This was an act in perfect accord with the old French doctrine of crippling the enemy and then using one's fleet to achieve "ulterior objectives" against which Mahan so often inveighed. It is the action of leaders who are not trying to attain sea power but to prevent the enemy from having it.

In this fundamentally false approach to the problem may be found the reason why the Japanese never made use of the naval superiority they had in the Pacific during the first six months of the war. They used ships; in fact no warships were ever much busier than the Japanese during this period. But they were employed as transports, as escort craft and to provide floating fire support for amphibian operations. These are proper naval functions, but they are functions of a fleet which is beyond question superior to its opponents. Why the Japanese made this error is a question of considerable interest involving a number of concepts that have little bearing on the general topic of sea power. But it is germane to point out that this false strategy was at least partly the effect of the doctrine of localized sea power.

Of sea power specifically localized by the airplane. The first care of the Japanese wherever they landed was to seize the airfields or where they did not exist to set them up, and during the early part of the war their propaganda made enormous play with Hitler's phrase about unsinkable carriers. They were correctly apprehensive about the industrial resources of America, but they conceived that by skimping in other directions, they might overmatch us in the single item of airplanes, given the fact that we would have to build ships as well as planes in vast quantities before laying siege to their flowing triangle of empire.

It was possible even to calculate within limits adequate for strategic purposes just how long it would take this effete democracy to muster sufficient strength for the counterattack. In the last war American ship and plane production was just getting to the effective point at the Armistice, approximately a year and a half after the war started. The direct calculation from our industrial resources would work out to about the same point. In eighteen months the Japanese expected to have their empire so firmly established that it would be immune to attack.

It is worth noting that these calculations were accurate to a degree. It was precisely the late summer of 1943 when the new carriers *Essex, Independence* and *Princeton* appeared in the South Pacific, the first major ships of the war program. The Japanese misconception went beneath this. Its detail was that the outer rim of islands could be woven into a network of air bases, from each of which planes could support the nearest and to each of which planes from a wide area would rally in case of an attack—planes so numerous that an approaching fleet could be put out of action as readily as *Repulse* and *Prince of Wales* off Malaya or Admiral Hart's striking force in the Java Sea. Japanese gunnery ships could be put in to complete the rout as they had been against Admiral Doorman's little squadron. But the land-based planes would carry the load.

Now this amounted to maintaining that land-based planes could negate sea power, not merely locally and for a short period of time, but throughout a wide area and permanently. Like the U-boat campaign it was essentially a claim that modern technology had produced conditions under which the classic doctrines of sea power were no longer valid. Like the Germans, the Japanese apparently had a program for gaining and using sea power themselves after they had achieved their initial victory, nor does either of the Axis partners seem to have seen any inconsistency in such a program. But the essential feature under technical methods of approach widely different was the statement that classic sea power could be discounted in the modern world.

The error was the old one of looking at practices instead of principles. The Japs were so fascinated by the technical mobility of the airplane that they never seem to have thought of its inferior strategic mobility. They drew an analogy between plane and ship, whereas the true one is between plane and shell; and in due time they discovered that those unsinkable carriers were also immovable and were in fact elements of a passive defense in its least effective form, a thinly held cordon. When enlightenment came to them after the American capture of the Marshalls, they made an effort to check Navy with Navy in the Battle of the Philippine Sea. By that time the airplane had already revealed its true role in the complex of modern sea power. The effect of the plane is not to localize sea power but to overcome what localization previously existed; not to extend the influence of the land arm for 300 miles out to sea, but to enable naval power to reach 300 miles inland and almost completely to neutralize the value of fortified bases. The individual superiority of the land plane, about which so much talking was done early in the war, has proved of little consequence beside the fact that the enormous strategic mobility of the ship enables this quality to be conferred upon the planes it carries and permits a concentration of so many sea-borne aircraft at the point of attack that the defense is overwhelmed.

VII

Before considering the implications of this development it is perhaps worth while to note the inhibiting effect of false strategy upon Japanese operations during the period when they still had the superiority which the treachery at Pearl Harbor gave them. A painstaking search of the records fails to reveal a single case in which they undertook naval operations as such. Every contact between their fleet and our own down to the Battle of the Philippine Sea came about as the direct result of some operation against a land mass. At least from Midway on, the constant effort of every Jap commander was to withdraw from action as soon as our fighting ships were discovered.

During the long struggle for the Solomons this unwillingness to carry matters to a conclusion several times saved our forces from defeat (had the Japs pressed on to the last gun at Savo Island, for instance!) and when the test came at the Philippine Sea it was a system of tactics founded on this cheese-paring economy that gave us a decisive victory. The matter may be summed up by saying that they deprived their own leaders of the spirit of the offensive.

What (for us) fortunate chance caused this confusion to descend on the councils of the Navy that in the war with Russia had acted so truly on the offensive we may someday find out. We do not know now but there is something more than an outside possibility that it was the false view of air power as a competitor with sea power rather than as a form of seapower itself. It is not altogether surprising that the Japanese should have reached such a conclusion on the data available to them before the war. Air-sea power was in sharp competition with the other forms of sea power for the limited services of Japan's industrial plant and the conclusion that the two forms of military force were in competition with each other was reached by some good military thinkers in countries where the competition for industrial support did not exist.

Actually, of course, sea power has also become land power to a far greater extent than ever before. It is not impossible (for instance) for an entire division of troops to be launched unexpectedly into a land battle from carrier decks. One of the most striking technical developments of the war has been the appearance of quite new types of ships, all of them making the link between sea and land operations —attack transports, attack cargo carriers, special types of landing craft that mount rockets for the support of beachhead operations.

It is not surprising for new types of ships to appear during a war and in view of the amount of beachhead work in the conflict just closed the development of special craft for this purpose was inevitable. But note that the classes mentioned above are not merely new types of ships; they are also functionally new, occupying places in the general economy of fleets that were never filled at all before. All of them are to a certain extent at once goods-carriers and warships. The responsibility of the captain of such a vessel does not cease with the safe delivery of this cargo, it extends inland to whatever distance his guns can reach.

It is true that the new types are fighting ships only for special purposes and in a limited area—the twilight zone along the beaches where the functions formerly sharply separated between Navy and Army are now combined. But already some of the new types are expected to furnish a good deal of their own gunnery protection against aircraft on the high seas, which is an invasion of quite another combat zone. Strategic principles remain unaltered through many changes in the technical character of weapons and the effect of modern war on design is important only as evidence. But the evidence in this case points to greatly widened responsibilities being conferred on sea power by the plane, which, so far from driving navies from the seas, promises to draw them into a closer relation with armies in a single complex of winged amphibian warfare whose very principles remain to be studied.

In this complex all weapons, all techniques play a part, influencing each other as never before. The struggle of England and France during the Napoleonic period has been described as the contest of the elephant and the whale, each unable to enter the other's element. But in 1941 the Germans seized the naval base in Crete from the British by air; in 1944 the Japanese broke up an American air campaign by seizing bases in China through the movement of infantry soldiers; down to the very fall of Germany the Nazis rendered the right wing of the Russian land campaign impotent through naval control of the Baltic; and Admiral Halsey conducted what amounted to a very effective land campaign on Honshu by means of the sea-air combination. New weapons, new techniques do not simplify war nor does any one of them dominate it. They add eternally to its complication and the master strategist is increasingly called upon to be the master co-ordinator. This does not necessarily mean that all military services need to be under a single head—in fact, the complexity of modern war has become such that no force under a single head is immune to defeat at the hands of a little band of specialists. War has become an enterprise that can only be conducted by a committee.

Set In Linotype Old Style No. 1
Format by A. W. Rushmore
Manufactured by The Haddon Craftsmen
Published by HARPER & BROTHERS
New York and London